PREUS OF MISSOURI

James E. Adams

PREUS OF

MISSOURI

and the Great Lutheran Civil War

HARPER & ROW, PUBLISHERS

New York, Hagerstown, San Francisco, London

FIRST EDITION

Designed by C. Linda Dingler

Library of Congress Cataloging in Publication Data

Adams, James Edward, 1941–
   Preus of Missouri.
   Includes index.
   1. Preus, Jacob Aall Ottesen, 1920– 2. Lutheran
Church—Clergy—Biography. 3. Clergy—United States—
Biography. 4. Lutheran Church—Missouri Synod—
Doctrinal and controversial works. I. Title.
BX8080.P73A65 1977   284′.1′0924 [B]   76–62931
ISBN 0–06–060071–3

Contents

Acknowledgments

Acknowledgment is gratefully extended first for the gifts of life and love from parents: Herman and Rose Adams. Communities that inspire and shape what dreams and talents one has must also be acknowledged: the Catholic church; Subiaco Academy and Abbey, Subiaco, Arkansas; the University of Dayton Theology Department, Dayton, Ohio; McGill University Divinity School, Montreal; the *St. Louis Review* and the *St. Louis Post-Dispatch.*

Gracious Missouri Synod Lutherans of all persuasions have helped with their insights. Lutherans of all denominations who responded to inquiries are to be thanked, especially all those who bear the Preus name. Two men deserve my special thanks for their efforts in accommodating a pesky reporter: Larry Neeb of Evangelical Lutherans in Mission, and Victor Bryant of the Missouri Synod national office. The cordial staff at Concordia Historical Institute, notably Marvin Huggins, are to be thanked also in a special way, as also Russell Fridley of the Minnesota Historical Society.

Support from my wife, Patty, has been direct and indirect. She shared our home with the Muse—at times a most demanding house guest—and she offered wise editing suggestions.

Scripture quotations are from the Jerusalem Bible.

Preface

Several years ago, leaders of a band of Missouri Synod Lutherans, then coming into a period of open conflict with the conservative majority in their church, were meeting to plan strategic guidelines. Among the housekeeping items was the selection of "moderate" as a type-casting label to be promoted and used for themselves. Richard J. Neuhaus, author and philosopher in their midst, told his colleagues that their selection might be a mistake. The Missouri Synod, he said, never had an ethos of moderation, never had a "moderate" dream in all its 130-year history. "Moderate" would sound namby-pamby to Missouri Lutherans. It would sound as if a Missouri Lutheran didn't know for sure what he believed, taught, and confessed, or as if he believed, taught, and confessed those truths only halfway!

This is a story of Jacob Aall Ottesen Preus, the man who knows better than anyone else the wisdom in Neuhaus's remark. Since 1969 Preus has been president of that uncommon Lutheran denomination which seemingly neither knows nor seeks moderation. The Missouri Synod, like Preus, longs to scale the highest mountain and breath the pure but thin air that leaves others gasping. My account, above all else, is a tale that had to be told because, like the highest mountain, this "immoderate" man and his "immoderate" church are out there.

My story of Preus is not a definitive biography. That was not intended. Such a work would not have been possible while Preus remains active and while too many lips are sealed for fear of influencing the outcome of a deadly struggle in his church. Far less is this a comprehensive history of the turmoil. That history will someday have to be written. It is uncertain yet whether a definitive biography of Jack Preus will be needed to supplement the story of Lutheranism in twentieth-century America. Meanwhile, there remains this campfire-flavored tale too much for a journalist to resist telling.

My book is impressionistic reportage on Preus, a national church official who has managed, not surprisingly, to grab more than his share of headlines during this decade. It is an attempt to profile the man behind those headlines. My treatment of the life and career of Preus is not an inventory of facts, as if there were no themes, no patterns, no threads of continuity. Although my themes may not form the ultimate story line on Preus, or his opponents for that matter, themes must be discerned, even at the risk of their appearing judgmental. I would have cheated readers had I not attempted that. Readers expect a trustworthy account of basic facts, of things documentary. That account is provided here. But readers also expect a writer to present his material with a viewpoint. Readers want and deserve more than a catalog of Preus-facts.

If I have labored too hard and compacted too much in order to get the tale told before the campfire dies, it is in part explained by my instinct as a journalist to tell a story as it is happening. A journalist tells his story now, not tomorrow when as historian he might have the advantage of hindsight.

And if I have told the story too bluntly, if I have created an immoderate revelation, perhaps, in view of the subjects, I can be forgiven, and if not forgiven, then at least tolerated as one of those outsiders who gasps on the pure but thin air of that Missouri Synod mountaintop.

PREUS OF MISSOURI

1

Options at New Orleans

The elevator doors parted on the forty-first floor of the Marriott Hotel on Canal Street in New Orleans. Lutheran seminary president John Tietjen (sounds like TEE-jan) stepped out. He was dressed as usual in black clerical suit with Roman collar. He walked to the door of the presidential suite, paused for a moment, and tried to shake off the early morning grogginess. Had he dreamt the telephone call late last night that had set up this 7:30 appointment with Jack Preus? What would Preus (rhymes with choice) want so early on the fourth day of this crucial church convention which had already brought Preus a triumphant reelection and had so far indicated nothing but trouble ahead for Tietjen and his seminary colleagues?

Tietjen knocked. "Come in, John," said Lewis Niemoeller, fellow Lutheran minister and chairman of the convention committee on seminary issues. They sat, but both were to squirm in their chairs the next half-hour in unsuccessful efforts to find a comfortable position.

Standing in the background was Jacob A. O. Preus, president and chief executive officer of the Lutheran Church–Missouri Synod. He was dressed as usual in a business suit. Boyishly handsome, Preus escaped a fireplug image others might have projected with his five-foot-nine, 180-pound body. His ample, sandy blond hair, parted low to the left side, was combed firmly in place. The square set of his lower jaw was equally matched at the top of his face by a squarely framed forehead.

Preus appeared even more edgy than the others. It seemed he might not concentrate on the discussion Niemoeller was introducing. His committee, Niemoeller was saying, had arranged this meeting in a last-ditch effort to try to end the calamity surrounding Tietjen, to quell the storm Tietjen seemed intent to bring on himself and the entire church. The committee had struggled to come up with an appropriate proposal for the convention delegates, Pastor Niemoeller said.

Their proposal was a harsh one nobody wanted, he insisted, but it was necessary to deal with the serious complaints against Tietjen which had been discussed the last few days in closed hearings. Pastor Niemoeller reminded him that the talk centered on his condoning the teaching of untraditional interpretations of Holy Scripture and on his highhanded administration at Concordia Seminary in St. Louis.

The proposal the committee was reluctantly considering, Pastor Niemoeller said, would call for Tietjen's resignation before the close of the convention in four days. Resign in seventy-two hours! But if Tietjen agreed privately to resign sometime that day, this harsh indictment would never be made public. Instead, a resolution praising Tietjen's "God-pleasing" and selfless churchmanship could be submitted to the delegates. It was the only reasonable choice, Tietjen was told. It would bring peace to Concordia Seminary and would save Tietjen and his family much pain. And, of course, it was an option, not a threat.

Preus had joined the other men, more or less. At times he nodded approval of Niemoeller's points and added a few of his own; yet he wasn't concentrating fully. It seemed as if in his cosmic thoughts or drags on his Salem cigarettes he wanted somehow to transcend the unpleasantness at hand.

Tietjen asked for a copy of the resolution. He read it and asked when a response was needed. By three that afternoon at the latest, he was told, so the committee could get the proposal on the docket for the next day's business. Breathing deeply, Tietjen said he'd think about their option. He'd need a little time to consult with his wife and his friends, but they would hear from him by three. He took a final sip of coffee and left the room.

About 2:30 that afternoon, Tuesday, July 10, 1973, John Tietjen sought out Niemoeller near the massive assembly room of the New Orleans Rivergate Convention Center where some three thousand Missouri Synod faithful were convened. No, Tietjen said, he could not accept their proposal. He would not resign. He would await the will of the delegates.

A persistent Niemoeller tried again. As earlier, he hit on the theme of peaceful and private solutions. If Tietjen wouldn't resign, at least couldn't he give a commitment to modify his antagonistic defense? Could he agree to settle matters quietly back at St. Louis headquarters? Even *that* might be enough for the committee.

Did Niemoeller realize what he was asking, Tietjen responded curtly. No, he wasn't stubbornly defending himself. He was defending the integrity of his seminary and ultimately of his church. To compromise, to surrender, under these conditions—under this pretext, really—was impossible. He was not guilty of shameful tricks as seminary administrator, and he was certainly not guilty of holding and promoting heretical theories. He would not be party to any convention politicking which suggested he might be guilty of such things. Couldn't Niemoeller see that theological differences could never be resolved by convention vote? By popularity contests? Couldn't he see what power politics was doing to their beloved church?

Soon after that discussion, Jack Preus was informed. He was always well informed, particularly during conventions. Preus was mildly irritated but not surprised by Tietjen's answer. Preus must have known months ago that Tietjen wasn't going to play ball. He must have realized at that first dinner meeting the two had had in fall 1969 after they first took their leadership posts. Tietjen, like himself, was a driven man, and the two were on a collision course. But if he knew the good ship Missouri, the inevitable clash between himself and the Tietjen-led theologians would not disrupt the church for long. There would be flak for a while, but his goal—not his, really, but his church's —would soon be achieved. Concordia Seminary would soon be in safe, sure, conservative hands once again. Why, the storm might even be over by Christmas! Then the church could get on with its work of preaching the gospel. "Pure doctrine" would reign supreme once more in a large Lutheran body and could be passed on intact to future generations. Moreover, the Missouri Synod under Jack Preus would have done what no major Protestant body—or even Rome—had been able to do in the twentieth century. Missouri would have stopped "liberalism" cold. Preus and Missouri would be on their way to making history.

By the end of that 1973 governing convention, Concordia Seminary and most Missouri Synod institutions were in conservative—if not necessarily steady—hands. By a 58 percent majority, the 1050 voting delegates had declared, in effect, that Tietjen and forty-five of his fifty professors were guilty of teaching "false doctrine which cannot be tolerated in the church of God, much less excused or defended."

What was judged so false and so intolerable would not have been considered heresy by most in the Protestant, Catholic, Orthodox, and other Lutheran communities—although some Baptists, independent evangelicals, and fundamentalists might have agreed with the harsh convention judgment. Tietjen and his professors had not substituted deviant theories for the doctrine of original sin, or the doctrine of the redemptive death and resurrection of Jesus Christ, or the great Lutheran principle of justification by faith alone.

Rather they were condemned for accepting a widely used scholarly framework allowing many Bible stories to be interpreted symbolically—Adam and Eve, Jonah and the Big Fish, the Israelites crossing the Red Sea, and some New Testament accounts. These were to be analyzed in part by literary and historical criteria available to a scholar from non-Bible sources in an attempt to determine what the biblical author wanted his words to mean. Many of these Bible stories were never meant as straight historical narrative, the Concordia professors had been teaching. The life, death, and resurrection of Christ remained a matter of historical fact, but symbolic, theological interpretations could be given—and in some cases should be given—to biblical passages once considered literal narratives.

No, the conservatives said. That kind of analysis begins in blasphemy and ends in heresy. It starts with the theologian placing himself *above* the Bible and ends with all the doctrines of the Bible confused or abolished. If some Bible stories are symbolic, why not all? Where does it stop? No, such interpretation cuts too deeply into the traditional Missouri Synod doctrine of the "inspiration, inerrancy, and infallibility" of Scripture, the majority of the faithful atNew Orleans declared. Their professors were "subverting Scripture." To make sure everybody got the message, they elevated to creedal status "A Statement of Scriptural and Confessional Principles" which had been composed a year earlier by Preus. That document said the Bible spoke for itself, stood by itself, and needed no help from far-out scholars with their unbridled theologizing. The Bible needed proclamation, not explanation—at least not any explanations based on the so-called historical-critical method of biblical interpretation.

Two seemingly irreconcilable views on the nature of Scripture had been put to vote at a highly politicized church convention. The majority opted for a fundamentalistic view and damned the "liberal" view of their Concordia professors. Given the history of the Missouri Synod, the New Orleans action was not surprising, perhaps, but it was risky and more rigorous than the mainstream of evangelical Christianity in which the Missouri Synod loosely fit.

This large and polarized Lutheran denomination had demanded of its teachers and preachers much more than the representatives of the world's evangelical Christian communities were to demand a year later at the International Congress on World Evangelization in Lausanne, Switzerland. That inter-denominational assembly of three thousand conservative Christians (who would have regarded their communities every bit as faithful to the Bible as the Missouri Synod) avoided an either-or solution to this technical issue of Bible interpretation. The Lausanne delegates declared, in effect, that the Bible was "inerrant and infallible" in those parts, in those ways, and to the extent that *God* intended. They wanted it known in summer 1974 that the Bible was their final authority, but they were unprepared to speak a definitive theological word on *how* the Bible was the inspired, inerrant, and infallible Word of God.

The Missouri Synod under Preus was ready to speak that definitive word and to back it up with disciplinary measures. Many Missourians had become convinced that the "liberal" Concordia professors regarded the Bible as an onion to be peeled. In the analogy of one synod conservative, the professors were tearing off layer after layer to get to some core message of the Bible, but just as an onion has no core, so Scripture has no kernel apart from *all* its layers. "The whole Bible or a Bible full of holes."

Concordia professors and synod members who rallied to their side did not see themselves as radical or even "liberal" compromisers of Scripture. They were faithful servants using the Bible to explore the meaning of the Christian gospel for their day and time. They rejected the conservative view as a simplistic "balloon" theory of Scripture. The Bible was not like a fragile balloon that would burst if pricked in one place by the sharp tools of contemporary criticism. If there was any blasphemy afoot, it was in the conservative camp. Wasn't presuming to defend God the ultimate blasphemy?

But the faithful at New Orleans wanted none of this flexibility of biblical interpretation taught to their future pastors. John Tietjen, the archdefender of such "false doctrine," was a marked man. The resign-or-else resolution prepared by Niemoeller's committee was indeed published later that week on the convention docket. Tietjen was not deposed. Apparently there was not enough time. Moreover, Tietjen supporters warned that Missouri Synod bylaws prohibited termination of a tenured seminary president by convention vote. They hinted that abrupt removal of Tietjen at New Orleans might be challengeable later in court.

So the deed was done indirectly. An order suggesting Tietjen's ouster was passed down to the agency in charge, the Concordia Seminary board of control. Previously controlled by moderates, that board had generally backed Tietjen and had frustrated a four-year onslaught by Preus to control the seminary. Politics had changed that. The board now had enough strict-line conservative activists to assure the inevitable. It was not if, but when and how Tietjen would go. There would be some changes at Concordia Seminary, then the largest Lutheran theological school in the world.

Viewed solely as an act of church politics, what Preus and his majority did at New Orleans was put a showcase seminary on notice that it was too far out for the rank and file. That was hardly remarkable in American religion. Even so-called liberal Protestants have ways of doing that—although certainly with less drama, privately, and without unfashionable concepts like heresy.

On one level, the New Orleans judgment was a harsh act of internal communication aimed at elitist-prone theologians who hadn't communicated very well beyond their ivory towers. Or perhaps they had communicated well enough but had failed to judge the political impact of their theological views on many in the church. Either way, isolation was one luxury the Missouri Synod did not grant its theologians—as they learned the hard way.

If John Tietjen and his handful of chastised professors had been totally isolated from their denomination, they would have faded quickly from the scene, but they did not fade. To many in the Missouri Synod they were not isolated. They were not even primarily theologians. They were brothers, fellow pastors, and friends. Hundreds of graduates of Concordia, now pastors and church officials all over the country, had profound respect for their former teachers. Thousands of Missouri laity were repelled also by the harsh judgment at New Orleans. Did the Concordia community really deserve what amounted to one of the harshest corporate rebukes rendered by any denomination against its own sons in recent American church history? Missourians who were to call themselves "moderates" saw Tietjen and company as brothers wronged by an aggressive Preus-camp. Steamrolling, ward-heeling politics, the moderates claimed, had been used to incite a theological lynching when patient, evangelical measures were called for.

Still, sympathy for a handful of colleagues presumably wronged would not have been enough for moderates to keep a protest alive years after New Orleans and eventually to attempt a mass exodus from President Preus's synod. More than ecclesiastical justice and fair play was involved.

In the wake of New Orleans, Missouri moderates from every part of the United States began to believe that the Preus party and its exercise of power posed a mortal threat to the Lutheran church life, witness, and ministry they embraced. A rigid fundamentalistic approach to the Bible was only the beginning, they feared. Doors were closing also on their cherished goals for greater cooperation and identity alongside other Lutherans and Christians. They sensed that freedom to explore contemporary issues was being curtailed. Some feared that avenues to social ministries were being blocked. Some saw their hopes for less "colonialistic" approaches to foreign missions being dashed. Most saw the specter of rigid conformity to what they considered nonessentials in Lutheran faith and practice. The search for evangelical consensus was being replaced by authoritarian rule. Many felt the "freedom of the gospel," which they saw as part of their Lutheran heritage, was doomed.

Missouri moderates believed they were witnessing the end of their evangelical church and the beginning of an authoritarian sect. Many wanted no part of a sect where "pure doctrines" about the Christian gospel replaced the pure doctrine of the gospel, where concern for orthodoxy (correct Christian thinking) squeezed out orthopraxy (correct Christian practice). Such a sect would not long survive as a major force in American religion anyway, moderates argued.

For their part, many Missouri conservatives also began to believe that much more was at stake than rooting out a few entrenched professors. The Concordia professors were symptomatic of a deeply rooted disease fatal for the "confessional" church Missouri had always been. That disease was tolerance, wishy-washiness, not yes or no but an endless string of maybes. Theological tolerance produced great debating societies but not great churches. No great church, liberal or conservative, was ever created or maintained by an open-ended tolerance. Even liberal movements have to be militantly intolerant of intolerance to keep their internal consistency and vigor. When the theological gates are opened too wide for whatever motive, there is a risk of sapping the lifeblood. So thought many conservatives, and they might have amassed considerable sociological and historical data to argue their case.

Moderates were really libertines generating a "doctrinal crisis" that had to be resolved by decisive action. Missouri had to declare quickly and unequivocally what gospel it did *not* believe, teach, and hold. Later it could sort out the theological whys and wherefores. Later it could deal with the disciplinary chores. Later perhaps it could speak again of love. Now it had to speak of truth. Now it had to man the ramparts against deceivers within its own ranks.

Not all Missouri moderates felt that Preus's policies represented a fatal threat to their church, and not all conservatives felt that the moderates were a mortal threat to their conservative Lutheran identity. Indeed, speaking of "conservatives" and "moderates" as if they comprised two easily identifiable groupings does not adequetely convey the alignment of the Missouri Synod faithful. And the "conservative-moderate" split in the synod must not be equated with the "conservative-liberal" division frequently applied to mainline American churches. Most Missourians would be conservative in comparison to the divergence of theological opinion tolerated by contemporary Christians. Outside observers have remarked that the synod struggle was between less conservative Lutherans (the moderates) and more conservative Lutherans.

As the Missouri Synod doctrinal war unfolded, there were at least two categories of conservatives and two categories of moderates. At one end of the spectrum, there were a few conservatives who, in thought and action, would be considered right-wing in any contemporary Protestant environment. They believed that anything less than literal, sworn conformity by synod teachers and pastors to traditional synod doctrines was unacceptable. They were intent on organizing a political party in the church, and disrupting the church institutional life if necessary, to achieve that conformity. Some were prepared to leave the synod if that goal was not reached.

A much larger group of conservatives, perhaps 60 per cent of the church membership, believed the traditional doctrines and felt it was important to maintain them. But they were not on a crusade against moderates. They were initially unpoliticalized, considered themselves evangelical in dealing with theological disagreements, and appeared hesitant to pronounce any of their moderate colleagues guilty of heresy, even if they were convinced (and many were not) that the moderates held heretical views. Without some impetus from the right-wing, it appears unlikely that the harsh judgment at the New Orleans convention against the moderate professors would have emerged from the conservative majority. Certainly, that approach would not have been their preference.

Moderates followed a similar pattern, except in their case the left-wing provided the political impetus which seemed to take many moderates in a direction they were hesitant to go—open confrontation and eventual separation from the synod. All moderates, perhaps 40 per cent of the total membership, believed that rigid conformity to the wording of traditional synod doctrine was unnecessary. They looked forward to a gradual liberalization process that would, in their view, retain the essential Lutheran truths while discarding the "fundamentalist" accretions. Most moderates appeared not to want a synod-wide showdown to emerge from this liberalization process. They saw themselves as patient and evangelical, much like the majority of conservatives saw themselves. Moderates wanted evolution, not revolution. But when Preus and the right-wing conservative party began to shut down the ecclesiastical avenues for that evolution, the left-wing of the moderate movement took command. Moderates appeared to abandon all hope that the evolution could continue despite Preus. Moderate leaders took up the confrontational style of church politics. That was their only option, they said, against the confrontation initiated by the Preus party conservatives.

A church with a patient conservative majority and a patient moderate minority at odds would not seem destined for turmoil and schism. Yet the many cautious brothers and sisters were to have little impact in the Missouri Synod in the 1970s. Two fiercely headstrong Missourians were to call most of the shots. The issues that fractured the Missouri Synod did not emerge solely because of Jack Preus and John Tietjen, but the two men were responsible for how the issues came to be posed in such a fatalistic way for their church. They were cause as well as symbol of the theological Armageddon that the Missouri Synod became.

Apparently, neither trusted the other. Neither could give benefit of doubt to the other. Each felt the other was harmful to the church as long as he remained in a key leadership role. Preus felt Tietjen was an academic prima donna stubbornly protecting other academic darlings at the expense of peace and good theological order. "Tietjen must go," Preus had declared privately only weeks after he took office. Tietjen came to feel that Preus was a "morally bankrupt" church politician who was exploiting fear of change in order to bring an "un-Lutheran" right-wing party to absolute power in Missouri. Tietjen was to say repeatedly that the so-called doctrinal crisis supposedly created by his brand of biblical theology was a "smoke screen" diverting attention from Preus's ecclesiastical adventures.

Perhaps neither Preus nor Tietjen could have predicted how much disruption would eventually emerge from the New Orleans convention. Even if they could have foreseen, it is doubtful their Tuesday-morning meeting at the Marriott, and scores of other places before and after, would have turned out differently. They invariably emerged from such meetings more convinced than before that they had to do what they had to do. An it-was-necessary-to-destroy-the-church-to-save-it flavor seemed to prevail on both sides.

Both could doubtless philosophize that any church was a sinful human agency needing to be rattled to the foundations when it fell into evil ways. Prone by his experiences to use absolute categories, Tietjen conjured up images of runaway Machiavellian demons needing to be exorcised regardless, it seemed, of the ecclesiastical cost. Tietjen suggested it was only a matter of time before a Preus-generation Missouri would be demoniacally fragmented anyway. So why not call the demons' bluff now? It was best for the church in the long run.

During this great Lutheran civil war, Preus was often to profess his love and devotion for the Missouri Synod. No man was more loyal than he. Why then was he forcing issues which held a potential to fracture beyond healing the second largest Lutheran body in America? Consistently but less convincingly as Missouri moved closer and closer to schism, Preus insisted there would be no significant splintering. The protesters would fade, but if division came, Preus could say "so be it." He had hinted often enough when the chips were down that he was fighting a kind of second Lutheran reformation to protect the authority of the Bible. Protecting what he felt was the genuine Lutheran tradition about the nature of the Bible was for Preus a goal infinitely more important than the niceties of internal church unity and inter-Lutheran camaraderie. As a young fire-eater in a small Norwegian Lutheran sect, Jack Preus had once written that decisions about Lutheran and Christian unity were no more significant than choosing the style of one's liturgical vestments. He did not want division in Missouri, but first things still had to be put first—the truth above ecclesiastical convenience.

But, strangely, Preus rarely cast his cause in absolutist terms. He was not prone to talking about second reformations or about epochal choices in American Lutheranism. Had he projected an image of the fanatic reformer, he would have been easier to assess, less enigmatic, less a political challenge for his opponents. Instead, Preus often seemed more like a maverick at play than a fanatic at work. In his gutty idiom, he had indicated occasionally his version of the need to rattle churches. The evil he spoke of at those times was more that of numbing complacency than deadly heresy.

"What the other Lutheran churches need is a good fight to get them off dead center," he once remarked in an interview. A knockdown, dragout revealed a healthy, not a decaying, church. A good scrap among clergy would cleanse the stagnant air. Then all except the whining "liberals" with bloodied noses would return with vigor to preaching the robust, old-time Lutheran gospel.

At New Orleans, the enigmatic Jack Preus came onto the American horizon to stay. Who was this smiling, squared-jawed man tightening the creedal screws and impaling theologians? Who was this energetic, self-willed Lutheran trying so desperately to make history and seeming to have fun at the same time? He seemed miscast for the role of issuing Mafia-like ultimatums with his breakfast coffee—as his session with Tietjen in New Orleans was described by enemies. To see him laugh, to see him grin so widely his eyes shut as he moved jauntily in his hand shaking and back slapping at New Orleans was hardly to see an ecclesiastical despot.

Sure, he could be testy with real or imagined opponents in

and outside his church. He proved that when he stalked from a press conference at the New Orleans convention because of a demeaning question by one reporter and publicly dressed down another journalist for presumed biased reporting. Sure, he was an indefatigible infighter and slashing partisan for his causes against his Lutheran opponents. He proved that when he sarcastically suggested to the New Orleans assembly that the Concordia professors were interested in protecting their tenure while *he* was interested in protecting the simple faith of innocent Lutheran children now and in generations to come! True, there was a hint of the demagogue and, at times the snarl of a teamster boss.

Jack Preus seemed too sardonic, too machismo minded, too jittery, and too pre-occupied to want for one's pastor. One would have picked hundreds of other ministers at the convention for that role.

Yet an outside observer would not have been disturbed by Jack Preus in his role as a church executive. He seemed to have more going for him than against him when it came to the rough-and-tumble business of church leadership. An observer might easily have gritted his teeth at the seemingly arrogant and brittle postures of John Tietjen rather than the occasional slur, flippant rejoinder, or grandstanding tactic of Jack Preus. Preus seemed about the sort one would expect to head up a conservative Lutheran denomination. He seemed an attractive, capable, and committed churchman with a streak of cynicism and a not abnormal appetite to be wanted and respected.

Ultimately, any untutored observer who might have stumbled out of the New Orleans heat into the Missouri fire at the Rivergate Convention Center that July 1973 would have found it difficult to assess either Preus or Tietjen. An outsider would have needed to know more about that unusual church called Missouri.

2

The Missouri Waltz

Lutheran Church–Missouri Synod faithful were convening at their headquarters city of St. Louis in June 1938. Although epochal proposals on inter-Lutheran ecumenism crowded the agenda, Missourians managed time for traditional concerns. An essay was read reaffirming that women were not to vote in congregational assemblies because the Bible prohibited it. One delegate rose to object mildly to the finality of the synod's position. Conceivably women might some day be delegates at a Missouri convention, he noted.

Synod officer G. Christian Barth could not let that remark pass unchallenged. Here in awesome assembly a deviant word had been uttered. Here might be the seed of theological division. Barth requested a committee "counsel" with the brother. Before the 1938 convention ended, the wayward brother had been won over. He had retracted. The convention agreed to reaffirm the biblical reasons for never allowing women to vote. "Consensus" on doctrine and practice again reigned supreme in Missouri.

The fact that only a few decades ago the Missouri Synod interrupted a national assembly to counsel one brother for an offhand dissent reveals the synod as more state of mind than church. Missouri had tried always to be one, holy, catholic, and apostolic, but if it couldn't be all those, it could always be one.

That was its unique witness. That was the ecclesiastical waltz Missouri could always dance when other churches couldn't.

The fathers of the Missouri Synod pointed to the meaning of the Greek word for synod, a "walking together," as descriptive of their church. Outsiders inevitably saw Missouri more as marching in a lock step of tribal uniformity. But whether genuine consensus or rank conformity, their "walking together" resulted in one of the most successful immigrant churches in American religious history.

From a handful of churches at its founding, the Missouri Synod had become a colossus by the 1970s. With 2.8 million members, it was the second largest Lutheran denomination in the United States, the seventh largest of all Lutheran churches in the world, and the eighth largest religious body in America. Almost 6200 congregations held membership. As much as $325 million annually (with $26 million for annual headquarters budget) had been generated in recent years. Clergy numbered 7600, with 6150 of them active.

Missouri Synod Lutherans were among the few American religious groups to establish their own elementary schools. Second in size only to Catholic schools, that system included 1200 elementary schools with 150,000 pupils and 35 secondary schools. Missouri had 14 junior and four-year colleges, and two large seminaries.

Although the anachronistic name tied it to the single state of Missouri, the synod was international. Yet it had remained predominantly midwestern and urban, with two-thirds of all its members living within a three-hundred-mile radius of Chicago.

Missourians were never bashful in outreach. Their Concordia Publishing House produced thousands of books and manuals, becoming the third largest Protestant publishing firm in the United States. Missourians made an early commitment to radio ministry, supported chiefly by their Lutheran Laymen's League auxiliary. During the 1940s, the League's "Lutheran Radio Hour" catapulted to fame a hammer-tongued preacher named Walter Maier, a Southern Baptist-like Lutheran evangelist. Indeed, the Southern Baptist imperative to evangelize was part of the Missouri ethos. A 1968 survey of all Missouri Synod pastors in Iowa revealed Southern Baptist would be their first choice if they couldn't be Lutheran.

Then called the Evangelical Lutheran Synod of Missouri, Ohio, and Other States, the church was formed in Chicago in 1847 by German immigrants. A Saxon colony which had settled in 1839 in Perry County, Missouri, south of St. Louis, was the major founding group. Colony leader Martin Stephan, a conniving, megalomaniacal Bohemian preacher, had to be deposed within days of the arrival, but his obsession with anti-rationalism transplanted from Germany became part of the new denomination. The founding fathers, including influential C. F. W. Walther, were so concerned that the Lutheran theology of their day might be tainted with rationalism that they opted to go back two centuries to classical Lutheranism for their "pure doctrine."

The new synod became the first major Lutheran body on American soil to subscribe unconditionally to the Book of Concord (1577), the "Lutheran Confessions." Strict adherence to classical dogmas contrasted with the more ecumenically oriented Lutherans on the East Coast. Eastern Lutherans found these dogmas marginally related to preaching and church building in America, although all Lutherans in America have paid their respects to the Confessions. Amid this freer "American Lutheranism," Missouri began its role as bastion for "old Lutheranism."

Martin Stephan unwittingly left a second legacy. Laymen were so disillusioned by his behavior that they wanted an escape clause from potential clerical abuse built into any new church. They insisted that policies approved by majority vote of synod conventions could be rejected by individual congregations if the policies were considered against the Bible or simply inexpedient. The provision survived. Theoretically, the Lutheran Church-Missouri Synod (the name adopted in 1947), remains to this day the most congregationally based of all major Lutheran denominations.

What the layfolk were clutching with their right hand, however, they gave away with their left. All officers of the synod were to be ordained clergy. The president was given broad administrative powers over all teaching, preaching, and publishing. Congregations maintained the right to hire their pastors (the "divine call," in Missouri terms), but then with automatic tenure the pastors could not be fired except for outrageous theological or moral abuse. Because of its authoritarian strain and socioeconomic character, Missouri was not destined for vigorous lay leadership. Like the priest for the American Catholic church, *Herr Pastor* embodied Missouri Synod Lutheranism.

From 1830 through 1900 some five million Germans immigrated to America. Many were Lutheran, and many settled in the Midwest. Lutheran Church-Missouri Synod congregations were ready for them, conducting affairs in the German language (some places as late as 1935) and providing a new German home away from home. German cultural enclaves were built and maintained through a network of parochial schools. Missourians were homogenous because all went to the same schools, read the same publications, fought the same enemies, and, most crucially, read their Bibles the same way.

Missourians had contact with other conservative Lutherans, but insistence on "pure doctrine" for any Lutheran cooperation, much less unity, kept Missouri an arm's length from ecumenical Lutherans. Missourians regarded themselves as forming the only true visible church on earth. This awesome burden, carried enthusiastically, meant they had a sacred duty to witness against the "erring" beliefs of other Lutherans, a duty for theological boycotting.

When attending inter-Lutheran meetings, Missourians waited outside assembly rooms until the other Lutherans had concluded opening prayers. Better the faithful not go to church at all than go to an unorthodox one, cautioned Franz Pieper, whose purist views espoused while president and top theologian dominated Missouri from 1880 to 1932 and beyond. In World War I, Missouri refused to join other Lutherans in a joint chaplaincy program. Missouri has long resisted membership in the Lutheran World Federation, the cooperative agency composed of 80 percent of the world's seventy million Lutherans. This religious isolationism, after all, was a condition of membership. It was called avoiding "unionism." While hubris to outsiders, it was idealism for Missourians. Relentless contending for theological purity was a genuine gesture toward Christian unity, true ecumenism. There was more than a little Rome in Missouri. Pieper declared in 1912 that "by our doctrinal position we work not to separate but to gather and unite."

Traditional reverence for the Bible as the "inspired, inerrant, and infallible Word of God" must also be seen as a practical as well as a theological imperative. Missourians have never worshiped the Bible any more than Catholics have worshiped the pope. But Missourians have declared the Bible was the bedrock of a unified church as Catholics declared the papacy was the bedrock of a unified church.

Missouri's "inerrant and infallible" Bible was its "paper pope." Missouri had always rushed instinctively to complete its circuit of verbal authority. As one critic observed: "Pieper = Walther = Lutheran Confessions = Luther = the Bible = the Word of God." Decades earlier another Missouri theologian had cautioned Missouri against a self-appropriated "burden of infallibility." Doubtless an intellectual idealism was involved.

A kind of "Gutenberg Galaxy" syndrome prevailed. Published words took on a mysterious supercharge. There was awesome finality for the printed word in Missouri. Essays with deviant themes were "withdrawn"—as if removing the paper and ink would make the ideas disappear. Missourians have experimented with the spoken word, producing good preachers along the way. They were fastidious collectors, excellent archivists, but those who stayed in Missouri's womb were never historians, novelists, or poets. Missourians couldn't bear to play with the printed word.

The Missouri myth of an "inerrant and infallible" Bible was

anchored theologically. Some were to claim the Missouri fathers never demanded a Bible without "factual errors." The Bible was not a newspaper to be accepted or rejected for factual accuracy, according to that view. Supposedly the synod fathers recognized as crucial only the great theological truths in the Bible. The Bible was theologically accurate, theologically inerrant, and theologically infallible in the sense it errorlessly conveyed the gospel of Jesus Christ.

Yet a glance at the Walther and Pieper writings and at the traditional Missouri pronouncements reveals that such views are revisionist. Missouri tradition demanded a literal understanding of biblical passages not obviously poetic. Missouri's "Brief Statement," accepted by convention more than four decades ago, contained this initial article:

> We teach that the Holy Scriptures differ from all other books in the world in that they are the Word of God. They are the Word of God because the holy men of God who wrote the Scriptures wrote only that which the Holy Ghost communicated to them by inspiration (II Tim., 3:16; II Peter, 1:21). We teach also that the verbal inspiration of the Scriptures is not a so-called 'theological deduction,' but that it is taught by direct statements of the Scriptures (II Tim., 3:16; John 10:35; Rom., 3:2, I Cor., 2:13). Since the Holy Scriptures are the Word of God, it goes without saying that they contain no errors or contradictions, but that they are in all their parts and words the infallible truth also in those parts which treat of historical, geographical and other secular matters (John 10:35).

An anguished Missouri delegate who declared at New Orleans in 1973 that the Bible would have to be believed if it reported that Jonah swallowed the Big Fish was not a fanatic by Missouri tradition. The question whether such tradition was any longer necessary or viable should not be confused with what the tradition actually was.

Isolationist Missourians gradually relented on their strict "unionism" taboos. Barriers began to weaken as more clergy studied beyond the ghetto. Missouri inched closer to the American Lutheran mainstream, a movement that culminated in 1969 with a declaration of intercommunion with the American Lutheran Church. Limited participation in several National Council of Churches projects was approved in 1962. In 1965 Missourians adopted a set of "Missions Affirmations" which had the ring of a "declaration of interdependence" with other Christians. The Missouri Synod was "chiefly a confessional movement within the total body of Christ rather than a denomination emphasizing institutional barriers of separation," trumpeted one startling affirmation.

That June of 1965 Missouri also approved participation in the new Lutheran Council in the USA, a cooperative agency to be supported by Missouri, by the less-conservative American Lutheran Church, and by the liberal-leaning Lutheran Church in America. These big three composed about 95 percent of the country's 8.5 million Lutherans. All this represented a radically new, ecumenical self-conception for a once xenophobic midwestern church—if it held.

Signs of a backlash were flashed at the 1967 convention, among them a resolution affirming that the world was created in six twenty-four-hour days as the Bible said. Two years later Missouri rejected Oliver Harms, the soft-spoken patrician who had presided over Missouri's amazing movement of the '60s. A jocular, unpredictable conservative named Jacob Preus was elected president. He wanted "sound Lutheran doctrine" on the Bible but seemed not to want a return to isolationism. Preus seemed a political realist. He knew Missourians were different from other Lutherans only on certain issues.

Thanks to one of the most comprehensive socioreligious surveys ever conducted among any religious family, a profile is available of the typical Lutheran at the time Preus took high office in Missouri. Researchers at the Youth Research Center in Minneapolis conducted the survey (1970) and published their findings as *A Study of Generations* (Minneapolis: Augsburg Publishing House, 1972).

Lutherans are white; prefer the Republican party; are more

affluent and better educated than the general populace; grow up in cities under one hundred thousand population; attend church services more frequently than other American Protestants; and marry other Lutherans.

About half of all Lutherans see themselves as conservative ("I hold or retain the essential beliefs of the Christian faith") rather than fundamentalist ("I believe all things in Scripture are literal and historical") or liberal ("I am willing to change some aspects of the faith in the light of new understanding").

The most firmly held doctrines among Lutherans are: the virgin birth of Christ; the historical resurrection of Christ and his vicarious atonement; the real presence of Christ in the Eucharist; and the Ten Commandments as God's law. Yet only 14 percent would insist that other Lutherans and Christians conceive these doctrines in precisely the same way they do. Researchers concluded that heresy and insistence on exact agreement in theology would be an alien concept to an overwhelming majority of Lutherans in contemporary America.

Jack Preus and his party at New Orleans presumably were flying in the face of reality. But not exactly, because *A Study of Generations* data revealed that a Missourian was not a typical Lutheran on doctrinal matters. Missourians leaned toward the fundamentalist pole. For example, about 75 percent of them claimed to accept faith over science while just under half the other Lutherans made that claim.

On what presumably was the key issue at New Orleans, the authority of Scripture, *A Study of Generations* data provides clues to what Missourians were thinking. Some 82 percent said three years earlier that they believed miracles actually happened as the Bible said. Seventy-six percent stated their belief that the Bible was the verbally inspired Word of God. Thirty-nine percent of that total claimed persons who disagreed were "not true to the Christian faith." If Missourians somehow got the notion that—along with those sweeping changes of the '60s —their Bible was being undermined, some backlash seemed likely.

If the much-touted consensus on church policies was what held Missouri together, it in fact had been an ecclesiastical powder keg since at least 1945. That year forty-four "liberal" pastors and professors circulated a document denouncing the "narrow legalism" of virtually all Missouri policy. This brazen manifesto was quickly challenged by synodical authorities, but the "forty-four" were persistent, holding out almost two years before agreeing to "withdraw" their statement. A façade of consensus was put up by 1950. Nothing was conceded either to the would-be reformers or to the sizable minority who wanted them disciplined or even ousted. Missouri at midcentury was losing its innocence.

In 1959 the Missouri Synod tried to recapture the reality of consensus by law. For the first time a doctrinal pronouncement, the "Brief Statement," the airtight catalog Pieper had completed just before his death in 1931, was made binding on the conscience of all. This was a radical act, not because it called for conformity to a rigidly orthodox theology, but because Missouri at last had to resort to law for results once flowing naturally from its community.

Such a binding of individual conscience demanding an oath of loyalty was later ruled contrary to the church constitution which apparently did not allow amendments to the twin foundations of adherence to the Bible and the Lutheran Confessions. The measure was revoked in 1962. The Preus faction reenacted it in 1973, and this time there was no quick revocation.

When efforts were made to try to fit the notion of binding policies into the old constitution, the logic forced on the Preus conservatives came out something like this: When Missouri agrees by convention majority on a doctrinal statement, that statement *cannot* contradict the Bible and the Lutheran Confessions and *cannot* add anything not already implicitly contained in them. Missouri majorities couldn't be wrong if they tried! Preus-administration officials and Preus himself have softened that considerably, as well they might. The Missouri Synod has been only slightly more successful at the art of chiseling out timeless doctrines in stone than other Christian churches. Sacred words and concepts of earlier Missouri generations have had to be eaten by later generations although Missourians do that more slowly and grudgingly than other Christian communities. The Missouri faithful who were convinced in 1938 that biblical doctrine eternally prohibited women from voting, for example, gave way in 1969 to a majority of Missourians who approved the franchise for women at all levels of church life except ordination.

What Preus conservatives said on a practical level came out like this: We don't claim infallibility, but we have to govern ourselves to prevent too much disruptive diversity. A house divided cannot stand. Ambiguous teaching cannot gain respect. So we believe it is our right and duty to declare that henceforth the majority rules absolutely on matters of doctrine and practice. Hard-core dissenters should leave voluntarily or they will be expelled.

Thus Preus conservatives are leaning away from a classical notion of church toward an Americanized Protestant voluntarism. It is a form of realism, of setting limits. It is Missouri's strange, long-delayed, and enforced encounter with pluralism —mild as that pluralism was. Heresy hunting, after all, is a sociological concession to the reality of pluralism, even if a theological rejection of it.

It is not surprising that Jack Preus is presiding over this implosive Americanization of the Missouri Synod, that he is a key figure in a controversy which released into Missouri all the angels and demons of three hundred fifty years of raucous American Protestantism. He is the first Yankee-style churchman to head this German immigrant church. He is the first man to bring a secularlike, pragmatic mindset to the top elective office in Missouri. He is the first top executive that Missouri has ever experienced who is as much politician as pastor.

Preus proved an aggressive, resourceful churchman. He took hold of the Missouri presidency as active commission rather than passive platform. He turned a quasi-liturgical office into a force to be reckoned with in every corner of the Missouri Synod. St. Louis headquarters could no longer be ignored. In this he resembled the liberal Protestants who had revitalized the top offices of their denominations to move sluggish constituents leftward.

The specific content of the Preus theological platform must be clearly distinguished from the general form of the Preus revolution in Missouri. The form paralleled the tight political management Protestant liberals have practiced for decades and are practicing now to get churchwide acceptance for such changes as ordination of women. Preus may not have been as adept in his political management as his liberal Protestant counterparts (he was too earthy and too sectarian to be put in their category), but there should be no confusion. Jack Preus is squarely in the tradition of the gutsy, American Protestant church-movers. If Preus had been a liberal trying to squeeze out entrenched conservatives, he would likely have been heralded as a significant maverick by the image makers and pacesetters.

Preus, for example, is virtually a rogue without redeeming social and ecclesiastical value to the *Christian Century* magazine, which frequently reflects the prevailing opinions of the liberal Protestant establishment. On the other hand, Preus is a hero who can do no wrong to the editors of *Christianity Today,* the leading journal of evangelical Protestants. As much of the rest of the Christian world, both magazines have reacted to Preus on ideological grounds.

Ironically, if political form rather than ideological content was being used to assess Jack Preus, the two journals would have to reverse their judgments. The *Christian Century* would have to claim Preus for one of its own and praise his style. Isn't he the finest product around of the liberal Protestant tradition of mobilizing slumbering churches for specific causes, a tradition the *Christian Century* so admires? In view of the evangelical Protestant tradition of religious independence and suspicion of hierarchical church rule, *Christianity Today* would have to cast a very critical eye at how Preus is enforcing doctrine in

Missouri. Can't American church majorities in the 1970s be just as oppressive in their own way as popes were in the 1500s? Isn't Preus's Missouri running the risk of equating salvation with the works of a church? Is Preus any idol to be holding up to evangelical American Christians for emulation?

While Preus's ideology about the Bible is clearly traditional Missouriana, his push toward synodical authoritarianism is not. Of course, Missouri had always been authoritarian, but by ethnocentric instincts, not by constitution and bylaws—de facto, non de jure. Why spell out rules for how to deal with large dissenting minorities when there were none and presumably never would be? Why trouble the canon lawyers with theoretical questions about the rights of local congregations in irreconcilable clashes with majority rule since such clashes would never occur?

So the constitution had been kept simple. Missouri was a federation of Bible-believers which could create means to urge on but not coerce fellow Bible believers. That is what it is today —on paper. Obviously, Missouri had too simple a constitutional formula to expect to survive smoothly a crisis created when 60 percent of the members declared that the rest were "Bible doubters" and hence had forfeited their membership rights. Plenty could be done morally, psychologically, and economically by the majority to try to disenfranchise the 40 percent. But if the "Bible doubters" said no, they were still Bible believers as defined by the constitution, and they said they wanted to stay in Missouri and joined an autonomous congregation, very little could be done constitutionally to that Missouri congregation. Synod majorities could not force that congregation to do anything. The synod was the creature of its participating congregations; they were not its creatures.

Although founding father C. F. W. Walther was not always to practice what he preached, he had spoken eloquently in his first presidential address (1848) of minimal church government. Walther was not opposed to the politics of persuasion, but in what surely was romanticism, the politics of power was sup-

posed to be forbidden. "We have only the power of the Word
and of convincing," he said, reminding the first Missourians
there were no provisions to impose church laws on local congregations. He then posed and answered no to a question Jack
Preus posed and answered yes to some 125 years later. "Shall
we not exhaust ourselves with labors which may easily be lost
entirely because nobody is forced to submit to our resolutions?"

Preus believed the Missouri Synod was indeed wasting much
energy if the engines of church government had only the power
of persuasion as fuel. "Somebody in this church ought to have
the authority to determine how we interpret, confess our Lutheran faith and maintain it in our pulpits and classrooms," he
had declared at New Orleans. Critics were to call that one of
the most notoriously un-Lutheran utterances in recent times.

Yet Preus had not been the first Missouri executive to lean
in the direction of law and power politics. Headquarters executives were leaning toward increased centralization during the
'60s, and some of the very laws they engineered came back to
haunt their moderate friends in the next decade. But the
bureaucrats had moved quietly and slowly. Preus felt compelled
to revolutionize Missouri government overnight, it seemed.

Perhaps he realized that the theological issues of an "inerrant" Bible on which his revolution was premised would soon
be waning even in Missouri. Perhaps he realized history would
soon put its inevitable seal on Missouri. Preus once stopped
short on a simile in a *Time* magazine article comparing his
theological agenda to holding back indefinitely the parted waters of the Red Sea. Was he really a theological Don Quixote?

No, he answered by his persistence. His brand of conservative Christianity was really the wave of the future. Wasn't it the
fastest growing segment on the American religious scene? Missouri ought to capitalize on that. The problem was getting it
done with minimal government. The problem was the legacy of
limited control left by the Missouri founding fathers, those
hopeless ecclesiastical romantics. How could a church ever
amount to anything in contemporary pluralistic America if it

operated on a politics of begging compliance from its dissenting subjects, if its many hardheads couldn't be banged together and put on a single track?

There was, of course, ample territory in the Missouri Synod where Preus would not be wasting his labors. He had authority to shape and control all national synod agencies, colleges, and seminaries, but theoretically he could indulge himself endlessly in "lost labors" if there were nonconformist enclaves on the congregational level. The synod constitution declared:

> In its relation to its members, the Synod is not an ecclesiastical government exercising legislative or coercive powers, and with respect to the individual congregation's right of self-government, it is but an advisory body. Accordingly, no resolution of the Synod imposing anything on the individual congregation is of binding force if it is not in accordance with the Word of God or if it appears to be inexpedient as far as the condition of a congregation is concerned.

With the bottom line of church law running so heavily in favor of congregational autonomy, was Preus reduced ultimately to the role of a paper tiger, or, at most, a tiger on a leash which prevented him from moving in for the final kill? This is one reason even hard-line conservatives in the Preus party eventually called for a negotiated division. The Preus faction did not have a two-thirds majority required to change the constitution. So the Missouri Synod still allowed enough of a base for opposing factions to go on fighting without end. What was the sense of that? A truce should be called and the assets parceled out. The moderate war council eventually came to much the same conclusion and opted to lead an exodus. They realized that the constitution allowed them to remain indefinitely as a fighting remnant, but the cost would be too high. It was time to leave Preus's Missouri.

The Missouri provision for congregational autonomy makes the Preus juggernaut appear even more calculating than it would have been under an episcopal or strickly connectional church. Under those systems, a dominant bishop or party could follow through constitutionally till the last little mission pulpit was in line with the official ideology. The winner could take all and run with it. Not so in Missouri. To dominate Missouri ultimately one would have to intimidate rather than legislate the opposition into compliance, or he would have to make it so bad that the opposition would choose to depart. Seeking control of the Missouri Synod in the 1970s was, to say the least, a delicate challenge without clear precedent.

But Jack Preus, Lutheran infighter and conservative commando, was up for the challenge. He embarked on a mission of bringing Missouri's key "liberals" in line. Early on he seemed to believe that vague threats and sabre rattling, privately negotiated compromises, secret surrenders, and a kind of diplomacy through uncertainty would be enough to do the task, but it was not. The struggle spilled out into the wider church. The crusade had to be made public. If Preus could not privately persuade the "liberals" to submit, he would have them voted publicly into embarrassment and submission.

Given the opposing theological world views of conservatives and moderates, the Missouri Synod may well have been destined without Preus for a bitter brawl ending in division. Certainly, Preus was not as far right as some in his party. Certainly, Preus's motive was not to split Missouri but to save it. He saw the right wing as militant and the great middle as restive about the "liberal" theology. That militancy and restiveness held much more danger for the survival of Missouri than the squawks a few "liberals" might make when the Synod cracked down on them, Preus felt. One of his rules of thumb—and a good one—was that right-wing parties split from churches while centrist and liberal factions do not. Certainly, without Preus there could have been a significant splintering from the right. With a harder-line conservative or a moderate as president, there might even have been a more bitter, more bizarre, more intense religious war (if that were possible) than under Preus. The struggle, after all, involved conflicting religious principles which each side claimed to draw from the same Lutheran heritage.

Yet religious principles have been compromised before by steely eyed church partisans for the sake of peace and survival of their parent church. What keyed-up religious parties cannot do easily, if at all, is *surrender* publicly their religious principles. They can disguise, sublimate, hold in their hearts for another day and time—compromise. Rarely can they surrender all.

Whether despite or because of his good intentions, Preus created in Missouri a climate in which any compromise seemed impossible and backs were psychologically, if not constitutionally, to the wall. Tietjen also helped create that climate and shares a similiar if not equal burden. One cannot say that Preus split the Missouri Synod without also saying that Tietjen did.

But Preus must take most of the blame or the credit for what happened in Missouri because he sat in the highest office by his choice. He had sought the office. He embraced his role as church politician. Seemingly he could save Missouri and knew what was best for Missouri. He plunged ahead when advisers warned he might be taking Missouri to the brink. He ignored signs that he might be trying to do too much too quickly.

By all human calculations, though, Preus's gamble was anything but wild-eyed and irresponsible. It seemed the safest of ecclesiastical ventures. He had every reason to expect his campaign to carry without significant churchwide disruption. Assuming politics is the art of the possible, his assignment was child's play. What could be easier than getting an authoritarian-prone denomination to enforce its traditional theology? Surely Preus could be forgiven for assuming that as president of a traditionally conservative church he could operate on a seminary without laying open the bowels of the entire church. The odds were overwhelmingly favorable that he could put out a "liberal" fire at Concordia Seminary without whipping up a firestorm that would engulf all Missouri.

John Tietjen was the nemesis. Tietjen refused to play by the political rules of give and take, refused to accept a philosophy of win some-lose some. Tietjen was a zealous prophet snubbing all the king's overtures. He was literally impossible for Preus to deal with. Tietjen rejected the reality of political maneuvering which could be considered Preus's staple. The notion that Tietjen's Concordia sacrifice, say, two "liberal" biblical exegetes in exchange for a year's cease-fire from Preus's end—a concession so natural and reasonable for Preus, or many other churchmen who might have been in his position, for that matter —was utterly out of the question for Tietjen.

The terms of peace arranged by Preus, however "reasonable" on the surface, were too costly for the church to pay in Tietjen's mind. He saw his resistance as an act of responsible churchmanship as well as an act of conscience. By training and professional experience, he might have been expected to respond like a typical church bureaucrat and adjust to the incoming party the way federal functionaries adjust when a new administration takes over in Washington. He did not respond like a bureaucrat whose objective is mere survival, or like a politician who is paralyzed until he knows where the votes are.

Not that Tietjen was above sniffing the political air before he acted. He wanted to win the ecclesiastical war against Preus, and for a time he fully expected he could win, or at least not lose badly. But Tietjen did not have to "win," or even survive in, the institutional Missouri Synod in order to fulfill what he believed was his basic Christian responsibility in the face of the Preus administration. Tietjen was in many ways an old-fashioned Lutheran who valued his personal relationship to God above all else. God had called him to be president of Concordia Seminary; in that "divine call", in that structure he was to work out his salvation in fear and trembling. It was no accident that God had called him, with his vision of Lutheranism, to head Concordia Seminary at the same time Jack Preus came into the picture.

Tietjen was a deeply religious person whose ecclesiastical judgment was influenced by divine rather than human imperatives. Saying that (and it must be said) raises the image of a fanatic, which is not at all the case. If he had had a career in another Lutheran or Protestant denomination, Tietjen's radical "Lutheran" dimensions might never have come to the fore. He might never have had his time to declare: "Here I stand. I can do no other." He would have been seen as most non-Missourians see him: a mild-mannered, imminently reasonably, professional churchman. But in the context of the Missouri Synod, Tietjen was uncompromising prophet rather than professional priest. He would not, he could not, bend to accomodate Preus and the conservative majority that Preus molded. In that defiance lies his glory. Tietjen will doubtless earn a lasting place in twentieth century Christian history as a kind of Lutheran freedom fighter.

But whether Tietjen's method of resistance and the Tietjen-inspired exodus of moderates from the Missouri Synod was sound ecclesiastical strategy is another matter entirely. That Tietjen might be proved in the end to have been a more creative churchman than Preus is very doubtful. That Tietjen could have done more by cunning to blunt Preus's impact than by confrontation seems likely. That Tietjen gave Preus a greater foothold to influence American Lutheranism than Preus might otherwise have had seemed a safe conclusion by the end of 1976. From an ecclesiastical viewpoint, John Tietjen was at once Jack Preus's greatest enemy and greatest benefactor.

3

Synodical Cynicism

Several hundred Lutherans from southern Florida had gathered at Peace Lutheran Church in Fort Lauderdale. It promised to be an interesting day, that September 10, 1974. Synod president Jack Preus was in town to discuss troubles in St. Louis with the rebel Concordia Seminary professors.

Both faculty members and students had gone on strike in January 1974, basically to support their president John Tietjen. He had been suspended for fostering false doctrine. In February the professors were fired for not returning to work. About forty-five teachers and four hundred students then set up a "Concordia Seminary in Exile." Now this rump seminary, Seminex they called it, was graduating ministers with no certification from the synod. Some were getting hired by congregations in sympathy with this protest. Sure, most folks were thinking, this rebellion by the Concordia crowd couldn't be tolerated, but maybe students graduating from Seminex weren't all that bad. Only a few months before they were at the real Concordia. Maybe hiring them temporarily wasn't so risky. Wasn't certification just red tape?

Jack Preus went to work. As always there was a logical thread to his discussion, but as always the salt and pepper sprinkled generously by Preus was what carried the message—

was the message. We're all plain folks here, Preus was communicating. We can talk straight without fancy words. Yes, theological problems were causing troubles, but good folks in Florida shouldn't get the idea this was "just a bunch of theologians in St. Louis squabbling." Practical, moral problems were involved in this certification business. Because Missouri was a big denomination, folks didn't know everybody the way they once did. They had to follow rules so they didn't get any unreliables in their pulpits. We want to trust our pastor, don't we?

We want to "trust him to walk into our homes at two o'clock in the afternoon and call on our wives when we're not home with the very great likelihood that he will not seduce one of them," Preus said. That's a lot of trust, and it's a terrible thing when a pastor breaks trust, "whether it be that he had an affair with the organist or whether it be that [we] find he's sneakin' behind the garage having a nip about every fifteen minutes."

As always Jack Preus at Fort Lauderdale was communicating. He is by training and instinct a teacher and is prone to hamming. You can take Preus out of the classroom but not the classroom out of Preus. He has always been a good teacher. The fatal flaw in teaching of going over the heads of the students has never been a failing of Jack Preus. The dullest in his class won't miss the point of his analogies.

About eight months later, July 24, 1975, Jack Preus was again communicating, this time in short-sleeve session with Harvey Stegemoeller, liberal-leaning president of the synod's Concordia College in St. Paul, Minnesota. Stegemoeller had been making rumblings about challenging his governing board to head off what he suspected would soon become heresy hunting on campus. Unbending conservatives who were not necessarily taking their orders from Preus had recently assumed control of the board.

Preus wanted Stegemoeller to cool it, not to taunt this new board. He should go about his business quietly. Preus would rein in any runaway board. The main thing, Preus said, was that Stegemoeller not get on a high horse and come riding out against Preus. A "pissing contest" would only result in both of them getting wet, Preus said.

The metaphors and analogies of Jack Preus point to a basic reality about him. He demands attention. What he says and does usually makes news, if not history. He has an air of "love me or hate me, but don't ignore me" about him. Preus has always been something of a celebrity. He never tolerated long a church position or environment where he was taken for granted. He either moved on or took a key part in changing his environment. Either way he managed to be in the spotlight.

At the World Council of Churches assembly in Nairobi, Kenya, in late 1975, the name of Jacob Preus was placed in nomination for a fiscal office. Preus wasn't there, and the Missouri Synod has never been affiliated with the council. He had been mistaken for David Preus, a cousin, president of the American Lutheran Church, and the mistake was quickly corrected, but the incident stands as an impressive backhand tribute. In the eyes and ears of many in the world Christian community, the name *Preus* automatically meant Jack Preus.

There is some truth to claims made recently by Preus enthusiasts at Concordia Seminary in Springfield, Illinois, (relocated at Fort Wayne, Indiana in 1976) that "the Preus name is becoming synonymous with Lutheranism in America." And as soon becomes obvious, Jack Preus is no cornfed, Bible-thumping fundamentalist with a mail-order degree and a large set of tonsils. He is a smiling, erratic but formidable polemicist whose influence has been felt for good or ill throughout Lutheranism in America.

Son of a former midwestern governor, Preus is well educated, witty, independently wealthy, and professionally ambitious. He has boyish enthusiasm and boundless energy and displays considerable persuasive powers. Doubtless, he would have risen in any profession.

But for all his talents, Preus assumed a demanding role when he became president of the severely divided Missouri Synod. His role was shaped largely by the political elements which elected him. Having joined Missouri only eleven years previously from a purist Lutheran sect, Preus had been handpicked by strict-line conservatives to return Missouri to "pure doctrine" and practice whatever the cost. He had been anointed to bring not peace but the sword. He had been selected not to build but to tear down. Jack Preus was to be avenging angel.

At times he played the part well, other times not so well. Every prophet resists and wants to be king instead. Preus wanted to keep Missouri intact whatever the cost. He began to long for peace and prosperity as much as for purity of doctrine. Sure, Preus could huff and puff to try to scare the "liberals" into submission. He could expose them. He could scheme against them. He could bargin with them. But in the end could he wield the sword of destruction that might drive them out and perhaps bring schism? Was Preus such a good avenging angel after all?

In many ways, Jack Preus was as tough and resilient a clerical infighter as could be found for this formidable job, but he had some characteristics that ill-equipped him to meet smoothly the challenges ahead. He seemed to have as many personal as corporate ego needs. He shot from the hip. He had a sharp temper when crossed. He displayed an eggshell-thin sensitivity to criticism that he had to expect day and night, from right and left. He was conservative, of course, but hardly the purist some of his political allies were. Preus was an ecclesiastical outsider who would not be swayed by cronyism when Missouri "liberals" had to be manhandled. But he was an uneasy outsider trying so hard to become genuine insider that he became far more attached to the institution than many ultra conservative friends expected. There were hints he became more attached to the earthly Missouri than even his wife, Delpha, and his brother and adviser Robert Preus had anticipated.

The fact that Jack Preus was a newcomer in the Missouri establishment meant at once assets and liabilities. As a Lutheran cleric, trained and experienced elsewhere in his young adult ministry, Preus was not well known personally by most old-line Missourians whatever their theological persuasion. No

Missouri buddies knew him from cradle to ordination and be-yond as most Missouri ministers knew each other. The im-pacted Missouri subculture meant entire generations of clergy could keep few secrets about themselves from colleagues even if they had wanted to. Their strengths and weaknesses, their deeper motivations and aspirations, as well as their pretensions and game playing were known by scores of longtime classmates, in-laws, or fellow church executives. Missouri was not an envi-ronment which fostered a one-man ecclesiastical show. When the ship's captain comes up through the ranks, the crew knows well his feet of clay.

This Achilles-heel factor was missing with Jack Preus, and the significance should not be overlooked. It worked to Preus's advantage in several ways. Preus was himself psychologically free to play the prophet in Missouri, and many Missourians were not equipped psychologically to resist Preus even if they had wanted to.

The familiarity that would have instinctively limited a life-long Missourian wasn't there to impede Jack Preus. He could do and say things that—while not embarrassing or outlandish to him—would have been inconceivable for a product of the Missouri system. The biblical adage that a prophet is without honor in his own community suggests more than the fact that compatriots fail to recognize an in-house prophet. It suggests as well insights about the psychogenesis of prophecy. One of the boys who would be prophet at home finds himself paralyzed. Bold words and deeds just can't be mustered when the would-be prophet is looking into the eyes of his own kind. Targets of the prophet must somehow be the other—and capable of being objectified, categorized, and isolated. Otherwise the prophet freezes when he trys to bring down the wrath of God.

Missourians were poorly equipped to deal with Preus as their top churchman because they had no handles on the man's psychodynamics. They had to back off and watch and wonder what sort of man this was. Few had that cradle-to-maturity knowledge of Preus which might have allowed them successfully to get on the telephone and tease: "Come off it, Jack. You know better than that."

Long after he became Missouri's chief executive, Preus operated within this psychological buffer zone. For months he moved behind a personal aura which neither hard-line conservative ally or implacable moderate enemy knew exactly how to penetrate. Preus began his Missouri presidency, in this sense, as his own man. To an amazing degree, he has kept it that way. While conservative friend and moderate enemy both stood on the sidelines trying to figure out what made Jack run, Jack just kept running and left many Missourians behind.

But there was a reverse side to this situation. As an unknown outsider ascending willingly to the throne, Preus inevitably generated suspicion. It was easy for disillusioned conservative and skeptical moderate alike to attach the foulest motives to whatever Preus did or did not do. This curtailed Preus's freedom to play prophet. A churchman constantly defending his person as well as his ideology can understandably become distracted. Preus had to work double time to justify himself. An old-line Missourian right or left might have started with some benefit of the collective doubt. In any event, presiding over troubled Missouri in the 1970s would have been difficult even for an insider profoundly secure in his personal and ecclesiastical identity. It was more difficult for an outsider who was not insensitive to the implications of his lately come, adopted-son status. Moreover, if Missouri's blue bloods did not know Preus well, neither did he know them well. If he had surprises for them, they ultimately might have their share of surprises for him.

As instinctive teacher-entertainer, Preus theoretically could turn Missouri into a giant classroom for his brand of Lutheranism. That possibility surely was not lost on the conservative king-makers who selected him as their candidate. Yet the teaching and educational environment in whichPreus had most of his experience was a make-believe environment. Teacher and students agree to suspend reality. When the bell rings, it's over. The teacher doesn't follow the students home as avenging angel must do. Professor-turned-purifier Preus chafed under the "teaching" duties in the harsh, real world of polarized Missouri.

Other qualifications for the role of purifying prophet, which Preus's original conservative suitors might have seen in him, likewise had potential to cut both ways. Obvious from his background in other Lutheran communities were the Preus traits of boldness, toughness, and practical-mindedness. He was an ecclesiastical roustabout. There was little doubt about that. Church organizations beyond altar and pulpit were functional rather than sacramental for him. And unlike homes, denominational agencies didn't have to be very comfortable. One didn't live in them. One drove them like buses. When the buses could no longer function, one repaired them or abandoned them. Preus indeed seemed hell-raiser when "conscience" reasons compelled. But conservative party kingpins might have missed the obvious. Preus was bold and tended to risk all because he liked to build churches as well as purify them. He might be prone to suspend the churchly purification before all the theological termites were exterminated.

If a background of ecclesiastical independence was one relevant qualification of Preus, material independence was another. Preus was a financially secure man by any standard. It would appear he had personal assets in excess of one million dollars when he was anointed by his party although details of his wealth were not widely known then and are not widely known now. Clearly, Preus could afford to be a maverick, but he could also afford not to be a maverick or to be a different kind of maverick from one year to the next. An independent avenging angel might be risky in the end.

Besides all his other talents for the job, Jack Preus was a pleasant and pleasant-looking man. He could be jovial under almost any circumstances. He enjoyed meeting people, and he could put most of them at ease. He had a sense of humor and a winsome smile. What a perfect cover for the angel of vengeance!

Yet this was the most troublesome qualification of all from

the viewpoint of conservative party elements who, above all, wanted Preus to get on with his purifying mission. A politician was desirable, but not too much of a politician. A popular figure was needed, but not one who needed popularity. Yet the glad-hander in Jack Preus was no cover. "Pressing the flesh" was its own reward. He sought and enjoyed popularity. In the hurly-burly of shaking hands, kissing babies, and courting votes, Preus might forget all about the prophetic mission. He would be out there on the ecclesiastical hustings seeking the last hur-rah despite himself!

All the ambiguities of the Preus personality went into his role as Missouri's purifying angel and conservative prophet. Ulti-mately, he did what he felt was his prophetic duty. He did it his way, dancing through the maze to the frequent confusion of many Missourians. It was an interesting way and certainly not without its charm. If there is a special place in heaven for churchmen who never bored anybody, Jack Preus will be there among the ecclesiastical Harry Trumans. Preus of Missouri was all the more startling because his career peaked in the 1970s when many American church potentates wanted to be ignored. One-man shows were hard to find. It was a cooling-off period after the turbulence of the previous decade. Boredom was fast becoming the major occupational hazard of religion writers. Then, along came Jack Preus to shatter the stereotypes and to fight the good fight on a coast-to-coast front in a denomination that had traditionally attracted little attention outside midwest-ern Lutheran circles.

For an independently wealthy man to take on the role Preus did and survive in it, one would expect an atypical clergyman with an ambivalent personality. He would be a man of senti-mentality and conviction for his religious ideology and the church bearing it. Simultaneously, he would be cynical and opportunistic on levels of practical churchmanship. A man trying to make history in a hurry must move in a hurry. It would not be out of character for such a man to weep over the victims of his own rigid policies, both the tears and the devotion to policies being equally genuine.

Preus displays precisely this ambivalence. He has his own deep love and compassion for the Lutheran church he envisions. He begs others to celebrate with him what he sees as upright, holy, and useful in that church; yet he speaks as few men can of the foibles of churches and churchmen. Seemingly he could go from stand-up comedian doing church routines on Saturday night to preacher on Sunday morning, and he would be just as real in both roles.

Preus speaks of "preachers" with a sarcasm too heavy to be a mere rhetorical device for communicating with laity and reporters. His sardonic tone smacks of a certain contempt and carries a note of detachment. He speaks of "preachers" as if he weren't one. He runs on about the workings of Lutheran synods as if he wouldn't be caught in one. There is more than a hint that Jack Preus relates to the church ambivalently.

Both the attraction and the repulsion originated in part with his father, Jacob (Jake) Preus, who in turn was influenced by a remarkable Preus clan.

The Preus family tree has been traced to Hans Preus, a wealthy landowner at Eisfeldt in Germany. One son emigrating to Norway was Abraham Preus, who became Royal Commissioner of Weights and Measures. One of Abraham's sons was Jacob Preus (d. 1805), who became a Lutheran pastor at Haabel in southern Norway.

Jacob distinguished himself by marrying a remarkable woman, Anne Elizabeth Arctander. She ran a large parish farm, established a parish weaving industry, wrote poems and composed hymn verse, and bore Jacob a total of ten children. There is a legend, told in the privately published (1966) family history entitled *Herman Amberg Preus,* that Anne once saved her husband's career. Jacob had performed a hasty marriage of a couple who, unknown to him, had eloped. When Pastor Preus was suspended from the ministry, Anne persisted until she got him restored, by crossing the straits to Denmark and persuading the king to intervene on her husband's behalf.

The second son of Jacob and Anne was Paul Preus (d. 1867), who became headmaster of the Cathedral School in Kristiansand. Anne Rosine Keyser, his wife, was a bishop's daughter. Their family of seven children included two sons who came to America: Hans Nicholai and Herman Amberg Preus, Jack's great-grandfather.

Herman Amberg Preus (1825–94), who was educated at the University of Norway, taught briefly before accepting an offer in 1851 to become pastor at a Lutheran congregation in Spring Prairie, north of Madison, Wisconsin. He was one of the founders of the old Norwegian Synod in 1863 and was its president until his death. He had a parish of seven congregations within a twenty-mile radius of Spring Prairie.

Great-grandfather Herman was described as "orthodox to the very tips of his fingers." He was also polemicist to the tips of his fingers. Adolph Bredesen, a contemporary, noted Herman Preus's willingness to do theological battle by comparing him to the biblical builders of Zion: "Each did his work with one hand while gripping his weapon with the other" (Neh. 4:17). Herman didn't necessarily take the offensive, responding only when orthodox Lutheranism was being attacked; yet he "may have replied more sharply than was necessary and proper," Bredesen wrote.

Like his grandfather Jacob, Herman Preus had a bright and determined wife, Linka Keyser. Linka and Anne Elizabeth have led some Preus-watchers to conclude that there is a strong strain of matriarchy in the Preus family. That theory has been raised in reference to Jack and his wife, Delpha Holleque—as if Delpha somehow held the key to Jack Preus's thoughts and actions. She has been a steady restraining force on his life-style. While theologically more conservative than he, there is no basis for a matriarchy theory here or with the Preus ancestors. If Preus women have rarely been weak, they have never appeared to dominate their husbands.

The six children of Herman and Linka included Christian

Keyser Preus (1852–1921), who became pastor, teacher, and president of Luther College, Decorah, Iowa. C. K. Preus and wife, Louise Augusta Hjort, had eleven children. They included Jacob Aall Ottesen Preus, Jack's father, who was named after a well-known Lutheran uncle on his mother's side. Another child was Ove Jacob Hjort Preus, father of David W. Preus who became president of the American Lutheran Church in 1973.

Jack's father had two distinguished careers: politics in Minnesota and business in Chicago. After graduating from the University of Minnesota Law School in 1906, the tall, robust-looking Jake rose quickly to the top of state government and the Minnesota Republican party. After serving as secretary in Washington for Senator Knute Nelson, he was appointed state insurance commissioner. He won his first state elective office as auditor in 1914.

He was elected to a two-year term as governor in 1920 at the age of thirty-eight and reelected in 1922. When Nelson died suddenly in April 1923, Preus agreed to seek Nelson's Senate seat in a primary election. He lost to a populist farm-labor candidate, Magnus Johnson. Later Jake said the loss had been a blessing because he had been forced to file with no great desire "to become a fixture in the U.S. Senate."

Jake Preus appeared to have made a decision—even before this first loss—not to spend his life in politics. If played honestly, politics could leave a man proud but poor. Jake was determined not to die a poor man. He never sought public office again after completing the second term as governor in the spring of 1925.

After a few months as trouble-shooter for the Minneapolis Commercial Club, Jake became a broker for the old W. A. Alexander Insurance Company of Chicago. He became a vice-president and one of the most successful salesmen for the company, then the largest insurance firm in the Midwest. His clients included top establishment corporations. He achieved financial independence, the goal of his second career.

A man of simple Lutheran piety, Jake was thoroughly conservative in his basic beliefs although he never made a public issue of that as his sons were to do. Jake appeared to have been a dutiful communicant. By all accounts, he felt a deep and abiding need for the Word and the Sacrament, that is, preaching and Holy Communion, the liturgical heart of Lutheranism. He was an intensely moral man, proud and independent; yet he came to the altar for spiritual nurture.

Beyond his private devotion to Word and Sacrament, however, Jake Preus was anything but a subservient layman. All his life he was a tough-minded critic of the works and pomps of Lutheran churches and clergy. He knew their weaknesses inside out. If this familiarity didn't breed contempt, it fostered a skepticism and a reserve about church affairs that no son as astute as Jack could have escaped completely.

Jake was co-founder in 1917 of the Lutheran Brotherhood Insurance Company which pioneered the concept of insurance among Scandinavian Lutherans. Active in the Minneapolis-based firm until his death in May 1961, Jake considered it his crowning achievement. His devotion to the company revealed his deep ethnic, religious, and charitable fibers.

But the man who insures Lutherans (granted for their own good, not his) views churches and churchmen with a cold, calculating eye. The insurer must be unsentimental and objective. When board-room doors close, directors must speak frankly of practical matters. First Lutheran Church, anytown Midwest USA, wants a big loan. The Brotherhood must know the men behind the application forms. No to Pastor Ansgar. His sermons are so atrocious his members are dropping out like flies. No to Pastor Peder. He spends money as if there's no tomorrow. No to Pastor Jon. He's in the clutches of demon rum. No to Pastor Nels. He's been seen too often with his organist.

Undisguised paternalism toward "preachers" was involved in Brotherhood work from the beginning. Brotherhood founders needed to maneuver Lutheran ministers and synods of their day into accepting the concept of insurance.

Jake Preus liked to recount how this was done. Conservative Lutheran pastors, his own relatives included, condemned insurance as a form of gambling and as a sign of mistrust in Divine Providence. The hardheaded pastors were advised that this new service was not the dreaded insurance of the world's fleshpots. Suppose four brothers wanted to pool a little money each year to have an emergency fund for the widow if one of them died suddenly. Now isn't that a prudent family arrangement? Well, why don't we regard Lutherans as a big family where brothers help each other? The preachers tugged at their beards and allowed as how that wasn't so bad after all.

As an aspiring politician, Jake was a close associate and protegé of Senator Knute Nelson. Nelson, like other first-generation Norwegian-Americans, had an anticlerical streak. This was a reaction to the Lutheran state-churches of nineteenth-century Scandinavia, where the religious establishment could still legislate public and private morals. Nelson had deep sentiment for the Lutheran religion in the abstract but had no truck with clergy and synods he considered prone to poking into places they had no business. Jake Preus absorbed Nelson's views, or rather Nelson tended to reinforce what leanings Preus already had in that direction.

Jake had encountered pushy clerics. His father, Pastor C. K., had leaned heavily on son Jake to become a minister like his older brothers. Jake stayed in seminary a few months, one suspects grudgingly, but he dropped out to concentrate fully on law school. Jake frequently referred to himself as the black sheep because he hadn't become a minister, and that self-taunt had an edge on it.

Insensitivity by Jake's father apparently lasted to the end. Shortly before C. K. died in May 1921, Jake was being inaugurated governor at the state capitol in St. Paul. Old C. K. was in Decorah where a celebration was being held. The Luther College band came to play patriotic songs in front of the old man's home. A spokesman gave a little speech congratulating him on his illustrious son who was that hour becoming governor of the great state of Minnesota. Yes, C. K. allowed, it was a great day and he was proud. Still, he humphed, he could be really proud if at that hour Jake were being ordained a Lutheran minister.

As brother and relative of many Lutheran bishop-types, Jake got a stomach full of church politics as well. Prior to the merger of the major Norwegian synods in 1917, the Preus clan was active in the conservative opposition camp. Strategy sessions were held at Jake's home in Minneapolis. The caustic remarks he made in later years about synodical politics may have harked back to those days. Jake regarded church politics as a minor sideshow in life's circus. Secular politics was the real show. The self-importance implied in taking church politics seriously was annoying to Jake.

The financial dependency of early Preus families because of their service in the American church apparently was also an irritant to Jake, the epitome of the self-reliant Yankee. When Jake was eight months old in his mother's womb, his grandfather was literally kicked out of a parsonage because he took the wrong side in a raging theological dispute. Jake may never have gotten over what he called the "prenatal" image of his relatives out in the parsonage yard gathering up their furnishings like ragpickers.

One of the objectives of his aggressive business career was to make enough money so that his sons would be financially secure no matter what profession they chose. Jake looked back also. He paid old family debts that he discovered—some going all the way back to Herman Amberg Preus. Jake's will contained provisions for paying other family-related debts. This was a profound religio-family service of Jake done quietly and without trying to embarrass Preus clergymen. But when he drilled his sons on the necessity of paying debts promptly and handling money responsibly, there doubtless was a strong paternalistic undercurrent aimed at the clergy.

The pattern of his church membership commitments is another indication of Jake's ambiguous attitude toward the Lutheran establishment. Depending on how one views it, he belonged to several Lutheran synods or none. The ad hoc Lutheran ecumenism required for Jake's funeral tells the tale.

The funeral was held at a parish of the progressive American Lutheran Church—the right church for blue-blooded Norwegian Lutherans. The service was conducted by a minister of the hyperorthodox Little Norwegian Synod—the church on the wrong side of the ecumenical tracks. The surviving sons, Jack and Robert, represented the Missouri Synod, which wasn't Norwegian at all and ideologically was somewhere between the other two denominations.

The irony was that each denomination had about an equal claim (or equal nonclaim) to Jake Preus's loyalty. The balance ultimately would have to be tipped in favor of the Little Synod, however. Jake seemed most at home worshiping with Little Norwegians, and he enrolled as a member about three years before his death.

Throughout almost five decades as "Mr. Lutheran Brotherhood USA," Jake worshiped in congregations of all three synods and, when he traveled, perhaps in other Lutheran churches as well. But he apparently didn't hold "official" membership in any until the end. Nothing could have been more natural for Jake Preus, who wanted to expand the Brotherhood's services to all Lutherans and didn't want to do anything to antagonize the major Norwegian Lutheran clients of the Brotherhood. It was also natural because his personal faith did not stand or fall by the touchstones of particular synods.

Jake once told Pastor Julian Anderson of the Little Synod, "Let's just say my membership's in the Communion of Saints." He had reconciled his membership "eccentricities," as he called them, and felt no guilt. Still, Lutherans take membership matters seriously, as a kind of sacramental sign of one's religious commitment. Membership is a necessary item, like one's ecclesiastical social security number or driver's license. Jake's membership pattern thus could be seen as his little private joke on the Lutheran establishment or as rebellion against Lutheran protocol.

The father's satirical approach to synods at times touched

son Jack directly. After Jack's first year at Luther College, he broached Jake with his hope of entering the ministry. Well then, Jake announced, we'll buy you a church of your own. You don't want to haggle with synods!

All this is not to claim that Jake Preus was an ogre who despised the sight and smell of Lutheran clergy. Far from it. He could mix graciously with them for hours in his Brotherhood public relations work. He could and did enjoy their company. He often engaged them in a way which brought out their best and his. Ultimately, if he had a chastening attitude about Lutheran clergy and synods in his private moments, it was because he held in great esteem the good they could do. He expected as much from them in what they did as he expected from himself in his chosen professions. That was high expectation indeed and bound to be unfulfilled.

4

Young Man Preus

Stark personal and family tragedy has not been a direct part of Jack Preus's life. He had smooth sailing through infancy, childhood, adolescence, and young adulthood. He had wealthy, interesting parents. He was endowed with intelligence, sound health, and good looks. He had nonstop energy, a natural capacity to enjoy hard work, and a congenial personality.

Yet a picture of early security is too simple. Growing up under an overbearing and caustic patriarch like Jake Preus could not have been easy. Jake, who thrived on challenges, would have provided plenty of challenges to psychological survival. Jake was not consciously sparring with his sons, deliberately testing them, or ordering them around. Rather his example demanded big ideas about life and self from his sons. From boyhood, Jack and Robert grew up with men's burdens. Jake was their predominant peer group.

Nothing is harder than finding one's place in the sun if there's always a big shadow around.

Jack Preus was born January 8, 1920, in St. Paul, Minnesota. The birth was by Caesarean section. His mother, Idella, had weak kidneys which put a severe strain on her in the later stages of pregnancy. Idella Haugen Preus, described in the family history as "a Honeywell regulator to Jake's dynamic nature," was first-generation Norwegian-American. Her father, K. I. Haugen, was a merchant in Decorah, Iowa, for almost fifty years before his death in 1941. Idella raised two families. When she was seventeen, her mother died. As the oldest of six, she became mother of the Haugen household for a seven-year period until marriage to Jake in November 1908.

Jack was the third son. The first offspring, twins born in early 1910, died several months later of a then undiagnosable digestion malady. They pined away for lack of nourishment. The heartache of a mother over that loss would not pass quickly. When Jack was born ten years later, and Robert fourteen years later, there would be a tendency to lavish special care on them. Idella was a few weeks shy of forty when Robert was born on October 13, 1924.

The family lived in the hilly Prospect Park section of southeast Minneapolis, near the University of Minnesota. It was a comfortable but unostentatious neighborhood. The home, at 60 Seymour Avenue, had been purchased for six thousand dollars a few years before Jake became governor. It was a spacious, two-and-one-half-story residence. Declining the governor's mansion at the nearby state capitol in St. Paul, Jake kept the house on Seymour Avenue through his two terms and maintained it as a Minneapolis home after the family moved to Chicago. Cousin David eventually bought it from Jack and Robert in the mid-60s.

Remembered in the neighborhood as "Butch," Jack was an expressive, spunky youngster. He once bolted across the street, protesting in tears to Mrs. Theolanda Larson next door his gloom at having to go to kindergarten. "I'm not going to school —I'm all right the way I am."

The family appeared at ceremonial state functions. Jack remembered visits to the echoing Gothic halls of the capitol. There were the traditional publicity duties of a first family. For the 1924 Christmas seal campaign, the governor was photographed for the *Minneapolis Star*. He was holding newborn Robert in a blanket patched of cloth squares resembling Christmas seals. Little "Jackie," standing, wore a big smile as he held up a seal campaign poster.

When Jake began his insurance career in Chicago in 1926, the family moved to Highland Park, the lakefront suburb north of the city. After a brief period elsewhere, the family settled on Sheraton Road, a few steps from Elm Park Elementary where both Jack and Robert went to grade school. In this secure, cosmopolitan, waspish-turning-Jewish environment, Jack Preus spent his formative years.

He was to grow up outside the Norwegian Lutheran mecca of the Twin Cities and miles from Preus-clan territory of central Minnesota and northern Iowa. Periodic contacts were made with the Preus family on visits back to the Twin Cities and when relatives visited, as the family of cousin David did in 1933 for the Chicago World's Fair, but Jack and Robert grew up away from heavy ethnocentric influences. Norwegian Lutherans, all Lutherans, were a minority in Highland Park.

Except for the mystique that surrounded "Sire" Preus, as the immediate family called Jake, the Preus home in Highland Park appeared to Jack's friends as cordial, orderly, and secure. Mother Idella was always home. Rarely was she away at teas or society affairs. A day maid helped her with house chores, but Idella remained quietly busy at homemaking and seemed always ready to be a gracious hostess. She never scolded her sons or their friends, not so the friends ever noticed anyway. They observed how genuinely nice she was. She'd remember little things about them and took time to ask.

But the mood would change when the governor was around. If friends were over playing Ping Pong or pool or poring over their stamp collections when he came home, they knew they would have to be quiet. The governor seemed like a cranky big shot to them.

Later some of Jack's college friends were to get much the same impression of Jake. To nondignitaries and nonrelatives, Jake often gave the impression he was busy and couldn't get away fast enough. Jake struck them as a man easily respected but not easily loved, the classic old-European-style patriarch.

Over drinks with associates in later years, Jack communicated the respect and even the warmth that emerged at times with Jake, but he hinted also at the distance, describing his father as a good man in a business sort of way. Jack also remembered Jake's big hand reaching back to give him a terrible pinch when he and Robert were making too much noise in the back seat of the car.

Jake's temperament was influenced by a nagging health problem. He suffered from asthma, hay fever, and various sorts of allergies. There were periodic scares when he would collapse and seemed unable to get his breath; yet one suspects he would have been brusque even if he had not been so troubled.

Jack, no doubt, absorbed some of his skill at the sardonic put-down from Jake. One sample of a mild jibe is in a July 1943 letter to Robert, one of the few personal letters in the Governor Preus memorabilia at the Minnesota State Historical Society. Jake urged Robert to meet the family in Minneapolis so they could hear a weekend sermon by Jack, who had recently taken his first pastoral assignment. "You and mother will not be injured by it and I might be helped," he wrote of Jack's sermon.

Years later a Missouri district president was to remember a passing remark Jack Preus made privately in the midst of confrontations between Preus and the district presidents defying his conservative policies. "Don't ridicule me in public—that's what my father did."

But there was a sentimental side to "Sire" Preus also. When the sons were college age, he showered them with gifts. Jack was given two thousand dollars for all expenses when he left for college. Jake began to build up land holdings and investment portfolios for his sons. He could be sentimentally thoughtful, as when he brought bouquets of flowers to Delpha. He was a magnanimous grandfather. At holidays he delighted in his seventeen grandchildren—even if he remarked in mock displeasure to his business associates that his sons had taken on themselves the task of populating the world.

In his own way, he could express pride in his sons, as he did in a June 7, 1944, letter to Robert. His closing words: "You have no idea what a pleasure it was to see you. Mother and I should be the happiest people in the world if we could raise such fine boys and their father is such a rascal."

Although not the Tom Sawyer of his Highland Park neighborhood, Jack was not the choirboy-in-surplice either. He had a few close friends with whom he displayed a sense of adventure and humor but no great appetite for pranks. As would be expected of younger brothers four years apart, Jack and Robert were not inseparable in the early years. Each had their own friends.

The Preus boys were not particular celebrities because their father was a former governor. Some clucking occurred in homes of the Preus's friends when Jake's name appeared periodically on lists of high-paid corporate executives. But then, other Highland Park names were on the list because it was a neighborhood of heavyweights.

There were little byproducts of power, as when Jack and his boyhood and college intimate, Earl (Muff) Fritsch, drove downtown to Chicago to window-shop and lollygag around hotel lobbies. They would park in restricted zones near Jake's office at 135 South LaSalle, tell the nearest cop it was the governor's car, and go their merry way.

Though Jack and Earl, who was a member of the Evangelical Church, went to different high schools, they stayed close and later rejoined as roommates at Luther College. As younger boys go, they were hardly a wild team. When they tried, they found they didn't have the stomach for it.

In the winter of their third year in high school, they hatched a scheme to sneak in a bottle of gin to a basketball game at Earl's school, Deerfield-Shields Township High. This was more out of bravado than any overwhelming taste for gin. Jack had the bottle under his jacket. Just as they were getting their tickets at the gate from a hawk-eyed teacher, the bottle slipped and bounced unbroken on the floor. The teacher scolded them. They turned tails and went out into the cold.

The Preus family attached itself to the only Lutheran congregation in their vicinity, Redeemer of the Lutheran Church–Missouri Synod. A small congregation of less than two hundred members, it was hardly prosperous considering the neighborhood. The building was a humble frame structure. The pastor, William Suhr, was sincere and hard working, if somewhat abrupt. He worked diligently on his sermons, and if not creative, they were palatable dishes of conservative biblical faith. At any rate, Jake found Suhr acceptable.

The family attended regularly. While he was never active in the lay leadership of the church, Jake regularly offered the church board advice on financial and insurance matters. Jack and Robert, who had been baptized in the Evangelical Lutheran Church of their uncles, attended confirmation classes under Suhr. Both were confirmed at Redeemer. Jack was leader of the Walther League, the church youth organization.

As Missouri Synod president years later, Jack Preus was to be sensitive to charges he was essentially an interloper. He hit hard on the Missouri connections during his early years. He stressed he was a member of the Missouri Synod from 1926 through 1945, when he was ordained into the Evangelical Lutheran Church. But by all accounts except this public relations one, by the late '30s the family had begun a pattern of worshiping intermittently at various Lutheran congregations, and frequently among the Little Norwegians.

After the parents moved around 1940 to an apartment on Lake Shore Drive in downtown Chicago, the family attended three Little Norwegian churches, particularly St. Mark's on West Wabansia Avenue. Jake's cousin, Ahlert Strand, was pastor. For visits and vacations back at Twin Cities, and after the parents moved back to Minneapolis in 1958, the Little Norwegian Hiawatha Church on East Forty-Third Street was clearly Jake's favorite. At college Jack attended and taught Sunday school at First Lutheran of Decorah, Iowa, which was an Evangelical Lutheran Church affiliate.

A combination of family ties to other Lutheran institutions, Jake's membership "eccentricities," and an absence of Missouri churches in Decorah resulted in a marginal connection with the Missouri Synod after 1935. If Jack Preus had been nursing such close ties with Missouri during those years, he would have entered a Missouri seminary in 1941.

Preus enthusiasts might do better saying simply he was a "spiritual Missourian" whose growth into the physical Missouri was to blossom later. That case can be made better. Preus has never been a narrow legalist. He has been a free spirit when it came to synods. He is bound to stumble when he or his lieutenants try to alter his past to serve technical purposes. Trying to make Jack Preus look like an ordinary workaday Missouri pastor is like trying to make Oral Roberts look like a high-church Episcopalian.

Why not admit he is an ecclesiastical free spirit and celebrate that as a sign Missouri is no longer an ethnic ghetto? Enemies of Preus who raised the "Norwegian carpetbagger" notion in the first place only reveal themselves as narrow-minded snobs. These blue-blooded Missourians, not Preus, ultimately are the losers in that little game, but Preus apparently decided to play the game rather than expose it.

After a year in public high school, Jack was placed in Lake Forest Academy, a private prep school for boys five miles from his home. The academy's regime struck Jack as "compulsory this, compulsory that," but it was good academic training and provided a solid grounding for what was to become his specialty —classical languages. Instruction in Latin was particularly thorough.

Extensive travel and generous vacations were among the other amenities of wealth Jack enjoyed in his youth. As governor, Jake had helped create the Gunflint trail and recreation site in the far northeast corner of Minnesota, near the Canadian border. The trail angles northwest about fifty miles from the

Lake Superior port town of Grand Marais to a boundary lake also named Gunflint. In 1929 Jake bought more than two hundred acres of Ontario wilderness, fronting on sand beaches near the center of Gunflint Lake, and built a vacation lodge and a smaller cabin. Jake also had a modest home in Grand Marais. He came to these northern resort spots for clean air during the hay fever seasons. Often fall board meetings of Lutheran Brotherhood were conducted in Grand Marais. The Preus Ontario resort has remained the family holiday retreat through the years.

Jake and Idella enjoyed world travel, with Rome and Mexico City as favorite cities. Jack first went to Europe when he was six years old. Later in 1935, the peak of the Great Depression, the family of Jacob Preus traveled by ocean liner to Scandinavia.

Yet far from conspicious consumption in the family, there was frugality. Jake enjoyed making and investing money, not necessarily spending it. He was sensitive to paying any extra taxes—though just as sensitive to paying every penny of tax owed. His parsimonious traits were passed to Jack. Asked to recall Jack, every contemporary in the early years mentioned his frugality. "Tight as hickory bark," said one.

Jack delivered the ten-cent Sunday edition of the *Des Moines Register* on campus during the first months of his freshman year; yet his second year he was driving a car given by Jake. Jacob Stub, a cousin, recalled Jack moaned for weeks after he had to pay for replacing a girl's dress he accidentally ruined with acid in the Luther College chemistry lab. Stub also remembered that when Jack was an usher at Stub's wedding in February 1943, Jack wore a retailored white suit passed down from grandfather Preus. The suit was supposed to be white but was gray from wear and age. Jack recalled with pride that all the two-thousand-dollar kitty from Jake was not depleted when he left college. He has never purchased a car on credit.

Back-breaking common labor was another area Jack got accustomed to early. He took pride in the fact that at Luther

Seminary in St. Paul he worked in the nearby Puhlfahl Foundry. Long after many of his colleagues abandoned their foundry jobs, Jack was seen cutting across campus with slumped shoulders, hardhat, and soot-smeared face.

Earlier he had worked at the Western Foundry in Chicago, sweating, grunting—and presumably—cussin' along with the common foundry hands. During the summer months in his midteens, he had worked as a deck hand and driver for a grocery warehouse firm based in Mendota, with branches in Springfield and Quincy. He made the rounds, spending days away from home. The summer after his graduation from college, he managed a Bible camp at Long Lake resort area near Chicago. When the camp septic tank plugged up, he took shovel and attacked the mess. The country boy image and language of Jack Preus does have roots.

Understandably, there was little doubt where Jack would go to college. Great-grandfather Herman Amberg Preus had been one of three incorporators of Luther College in 1857. Grandfather C. K. Preus had been professor and president from 1898 to 1921. Jack's uncle, O. J. H. Preus was the college president when Jack entered in the fall of 1937. Jake had graduated from Luther.

Luther was a small parochial college in a small town in the northeast corner of Iowa. The college had about five hundred students. Decorah's population was six thousand, many Lutheran. Virtually all the students were Lutherans from Scandinavian backgrounds. The students, in the words of one professor, were "not always the smartest, but they were wonderful people." At this easygoing campus where every third person was apt to be related, Jack Preus touched base with the ethnic Lutheran nest he had experienced from a distance.

Classics and history were his majors. His Lake Forest Academy discipline helped him breeze through most courses. He had almost enough credits to finish in three years but was graduated magna cum laude in four years. Jack was prize exhibit for

Orlando (Pip) Qualley, the tough, tireless professor of classical languages and literature at Luther for almost fifty years. Pip Qualley rated Jack among the top students he taught, noting particularly Jack's retentive memory and analytical mind. "An inspiration and a challenge to me as a teacher," Qualley recalled. Jack Preus was the kind of student who could detect subtle patterns in language and apply them creatively. As far as Pip Qualley was concerned, Preus had the potential to be a biblical scholar.

The studious linguist was hardly the Jack Preus fellow students saw around the Luther campus. They saw a handsome, energetic, free-wheeling quipster. They saw an honor student who always had a wisecrack, who often had time to grab a beer at Dutch's Tavern, who always knew what was going on around campus, and who always had the latest rumor and gossip. Maybe he was an egghead in class, but everywhere else he seemed one of the boys.

"When the 'ripple of snickering' runs through the boarding club or a classroom," reported the January 1941 Luther College *Chips,* "you can bet your last dollar the honor student Jack Preus was the immediate cause."

What others saw was a "presem" (preseminary) student who wasn't heavy on piety but would join their game of counting the number of times the pastor at First Lutheran licked his lips during his sermons. They saw an athletic trainer who scurried around the bench during football, basketball, and baseball games. Not that he was an avid sports fan, that wasn't it at all. They saw a fellow wanting to be where the action was and on the inside of all campus events.

His senior year Jack was elected student body president. He had a way of sniffing where the action was, and he was always there—as he was for the legendary "Carsten Brein Affair." Some Luther students had gone up to friendly rival Concordia College in Morehead, Minnesota, for a visit. The students were put up in the homes of Lutheran families. One Luther student overindulged and vomited in his host's bedroom. He went undetected, but Brein, a Concordia College student, was accused of having named the culprit to authorities.

Several weeks later the Concordia choir was at Luther, and with the choir was Carsten Brein. Some Luther students spotted him in a recreation room. A lynching mob gathered. Brein was cowering in the corner as threats were bellowed at him. Jack Preus was at the head of the mob trying to turn it back, but he wasn't all that successful at diffusing mobs. It took a dean, eventually, to assure no bodily harm came to Brein.

But Jack was never completely one of the boys and girls; he always generated a certain psychological distance. Some got the impression the governor's son was trying too hard. He wasn't for real. He came on too strong. His jokes cut you off too quickly. Jack Preus did not appear to be at ease with himself or the world around him.

Preus was to say years later he wasn't at ease because the Norwegian piety fostered a double standard of life on campus. "Three-fourths of the students went out to get drunk while the other fourth stayed behind in prayer meetings, and I didn't feel comfortable with either group," he said in typical Preusian hyperbole.

If he was transmitting mixed signals, his decision about whether to enter the ministry might have been one cause. Jack had entered Luther College without a firm commitment to the ministry. By the end of his first year, he had taken the step of entering the preseminary academic program, but this was an academic routine rather than compulsory spiritual regime. The real decision could be delayed until after graduation. It was to be late in his third year, after what associates recall as considerable agonizing, before Jack Preus decided. Some associates still didn't believe it. They felt Jack would never go to seminary and if he did he wouldn't stay.

With encouragement from his various clerical uncles, with the natural weight of the traditional Preus clan commitment to church work, and with his own leanings in that direction, Jack at Luther began to think of the ministry and his potential in it.

He enjoyed many of the externals of ministry.

Still, the route of law school followed by politics or business, the route Jake had taken, looked every bit as appealing. Certainly Jake wasn't pressuring him. Jake didn't have to pressure; his presence and his hints were enough. (Jake was to indicate later to others that he envisioned Jack as politician and Robert as theologian.) Most of all Jack wondered about the demands on his life-style should he become a minister. He knew he'd have no serious trouble with the basic morality required of a Lutheran minister, but having to live up to everybody's pious expectations could be a problem. It could cramp one's freedom. Maybe he just wasn't pious enough for altar and pulpit.

The person who seems to have influenced Jack most in his final choice for the ministry was his wife, Delpha. She was close to him from February 1938 when they began to date regularly until graduation the spring of 1941.

Delpha Holleque (sounds like HA-li-kway) was born of middle-class Norwegian parents in Great Falls, Montana, in 1919. Her father, Oscar E. Holleque, later resettled the family in Austin, Minnesota. He worked for the town's major employer Hormel Packing Company, providing an economically secure home. Delpha's family was not heavily pietistic, but the pastor of their congregation, St. Olaf's of the Evangelical Lutheran Church, was aggressively pietistic. He insisted grape juice be used instead of wine for communion service.

Delpha attended public high school in Austin. She was a scholarly, shy, serious-minded young woman. She graduated valedictorian of her class. Golfing, hiking, and canoeing, rather than dating, seemed to be her favorite pastimes. Luther, eighty miles south of Austin, was a natural choice for college. She studied Latin and English and completed teaching and library administration requirements. She was a close match to Jack in the technicalities of Latin if not, according to Delpha, in ability to grasp meaning and flow.

If Jack was perceived as "Mr. Joe College," Delpha was perceived as "Miss Goody Two Shoes." She was prim, proper, and pious—and respected for that by some. But she was too reserved and too upright for some. One reason for Delpha's image was that she was among the more cultured of the women students who were still relatively new at Luther. The college had gone coed in 1936. There was resentment that women had intruded on this all-male enclave, but ultimately Delpha lived up to her image. She was strait-laced.

There was mutual attraction between Jack and Delpha after they became aware of each other through Linne Science Club activities in the fall of their first year. But Delpha proved a challenge and a mystery to Jack, according to roommate Muff Fritsch. During most of his second year at Luther, Jack was upset by Delpha's apparent reserve and coolness toward him. He sensed she felt he wasn't virtuous enough, too worldly, perhaps. Frequently that year when he returned to his room after an evening out, Jack would engage Muff in conversation into the wee hours. He was trying to sort out his relationship with Delpha. Young man Preus, it seemed, was deeply troubled by a person he couldn't walk away from yet couldn't win easily.

Fritsch and others couldn't escape the feeling Jack was opting for the ministry as an integral part of his wooing Delpha. Delpha encouraged Jack in his leanings toward the ministry, but, she recalled, she never told him outright to become a minister. She "accepted Jack on his own terms." Any coolness toward him was natural feminine diffidence. The ministry was not on any conscious white list Delpha had as a condition for their relationship. Jack remembered talking extensively with Delpha about this and other spiritual matters. But of his decision, Jack recalled, "The only person who got me into the ministry was God." To which some college buddies would likely respond, ". . . and Delpha."

Whatever the case, Jack was still uncertain of his vocational choice in early March 1940 but decided shortly afterward. Morris Wee, a Lutheran pastor in Madison, Wisconsin, encountered a vocationally unsure Jack Preus by chance. Wee was speaker at a Lutheran Student Union conference the weekend of March

1–3, 1940, at Luther College. After his Saturday evening address, Wee had to catch a late train at nearby Calmar, Iowa. A chipper young man, popping up to the podium, offered Wee a ride to Calmar. During the long ride and wait for a 1 A.M. train, Wee listened to Jack Preus reflect aloud on what could, what should he do with his life. Two options then as before were the ministry or politics after the fashion of Jake. Wee strongly encouraged a choice for the ministry, impressed as he was after this brief encounter with an attractive, enthusiastic, and forceful young man from solid stock. Wee parted, asking Preus that at the communion service that Sunday morning to commit himself absolutely to the Lord before reaching a decision. Within a week, Wee got a postcard from Jack Preus with a simple message that it would be the church.

To ask why and how a man is called (by God) to be a minister is to pose theological questions. To ask why and how a man chooses the ministry is to pose a question open to a journalist. Preus's decision was not spontaneous and facile. Here was not the case of the governor's son, the quasi celebrity, and would-be playboy, up and deciding one day to devote his life to the Lord and damn the consequences. Preus counts the cost in what he does if not in everything he says.

With substantial personal investment in decisions, Preus does not easily or quickly abandon commitments. Yet there is the vacillation when tough decisions come. Like other decisions later, Jack at Luther didn't or couldn't flatly decide something important. He demurred. He arranged for others to nudge him into the brink. He got help from Delpha, Pastor Wee, and the ghosts of famous Lutheran ancestors.

If anything is consistent about Preus, it is this pattern of begging to be pushed. At times it seems a game of ecclesiastical "please don't throw me into the briar patch." It is as if Preus knows three steps are required to get from point A to point B. He takes two and one-half steps briskly and with fanfare. Then, strangely, he waits for external realities to force him to take the last half-step.

Preus teases fate, and fate makes his decisions and closes off his options. Like the politician he is, Jack Preus lives out a coyness in everything. "I will under no circumstances seek this office," he declares to reality with his fingers crossed. "But I would serve if drafted."

5

Awesome
Seminarian Preus

When thousands of Americans his age were gearing to fight the Second World War, Jack Preus was gearing for his own theological war at Luther Seminary in St. Paul. Ironically, his seminary career, from the fall of 1941 to early 1945, coincided roughly with American involvement in the war. It was as if young Jack Preus, uneasy because he wasn't in uniform, did his patriotic duty vicariously by theological combat. At least Jack had the comfort of knowing he had committed himself to seminary well before Pearl Harbor. Some at Luther and other seminaries suffered deep pangs of conscience wondering in their heart of hearts whether they were really dodging the draft.

Different struggles were in store for Jack during his seminary days. He was experiencing a mild theological and a severe ecclesiastical identity crisis that was expressed by theological aggression. When in doubt, attack. When one's theory is unsettled, test it boldly against one's environment. When pushed and shoved in one's mind, push and shove back. How can one discover whether the ground he stands on is firm unless deep borings are taken? The sure way to find oneself theologically is to fight the other and see who wins. If might doesn't equal theological right, at least it makes for theological clarity. Polemics is the lifeblood of theology.

Jack Preus got into the habit of anchoring his personal theology by dueling others. He has been doing that ever since, and apparently long after his own theological universe was secure. But ultimately at seminary it was more his synodical identity Preus was attempting to sort out. Did he really belong in this synod of his forefathers? Was this composite synod, formed in 1917 by merger of three Norwegian Lutheran traditions, any longer truly the synod of his forefathers? That more than theology was the burden he carried into seminary. His theological position on the great issues of Lutheranism was already hardening if not quite hardened. Preus at seminary was not learning new theology so much as learning methodology to contend for the old theology imbibed from birth.

The overwhelming image seminary classmates have of Jack comes out something like this: Sitting near the front of class, he had his desk piled nose-high with reference books. With one hand on the Bible, the other hand on the Triglotta, the massive Latin, German and English translation of the scholastic-era Lutheran Confessions, he waited for just the right moment. Then seminarian Preus brandished the right quote to challenge a professor or to turn the discussion back in a more conservative direction. He was not alone in contending for the gospel of the seventeenth-century scholastics, but he is remembered as brightest, toughest, and most eager. He took his polemics seriously.

Luther Theological Seminary was in the St. Anthony Park section of St. Paul, then a city of industrial smoke, trolleys, and flour mills. The seminary had the flavor of an inter-Lutheran theological supermarket because the students and faculty were products of several Scandinavian traditions and independent educational institutions. Luther was operated by the 900,000-member Evangelical Lutheran Church, created by the 1917 merger of the Norwegian Synod (the early Preus tradition), the Hauge Synod, and the United Norwegian Lutheran Church. For a successful merger, the various synods had to commit themselves to theological compromise and balanced political representation in their institutions, including Luther Seminary.

This composite synod was working smoothly, but diversity and some tension remained at Luther and elsewhere. Students were fed into Luther from four friendly rival colleges: Luther, Decorah; Concordia, Morehead, Minnesota; Augustana, Sioux Falls, South Dakota; and St. Olaf, Northfield, Minnesota. Graduates of these colleges tended to form cliques when they came to Luther.

Class schedules and pedagogy at Luther made it look something like a one-shift knowledge factory with a lenient boss. Classes were held from 8 A.M. to noon, Tuesday through Friday. Monday was off, "preachers' day" it was called. Holidays were not rare. Many students were married and had other jobs and interests. The professor-feed, student-regurgitate method was predominant. Because of political requirements of staffing a union seminary, not all the professors were academic stars. Survival of the blandest rather than survival of the fittest seemed the rule to Jack Preus. Family oral tradition has it that Jack later told University of Minnesota professors: College and seminary was a farce. Give me something tough.

During his first years, Jack was single. Creating much the same image he had in college, he seemingly was one of the boys. He was sharp intellectually and always determined to prevail, but he was not big man on campus. There was no big man on campus—only big men within the various traditional groupings. Jack was a ringleader in a smaller circle of students who tended toward ultraconservative theology but nonpietistic practice. He was the cavalier, independent-minded house critic who attracted a limited following on the strength of his personal talents and jocularity.

A major influence on Jack's theological formation was uncle Herman Preus, theology professor at Luther Seminary. Uncle Herman was an archetypical Preusian churchman. He was well trained, having studied on the continent in the 1920s and later earned a Ph.D. from Edinburgh University. Relentlessly conservative, he was committed to the notion that the Golden Age of Lutheranism had left a never-to-be supplanted legacy of truths. Students once challenged his nothing-new-under-the-theological-sun approach by pointing out this meant God could never again send another Martin Luther to speak a new message. Professor Preus responded calmly he'd leave that question in the hands of the Holy Spirit. He had conceded nothing. He had hinted that a new Martin Luther might be a contradiction in terms, something like God trying to make a square circle. Uncle Herman may well have been a closet Missourian; yet he was a cultured, urbane churchman who taught love and loyalty for one's synod, in his case the Evangelical Lutheran Church. He preached and generally practiced good ecclesiastical manners. In frequent bull sessions over coffee, Uncle Herman communicated with nephew Jack. While lessons on rigid orthodoxy stuck, Uncle Herman was far less successful in breaking Jack ecclesiastically.

Jack has summarized his seminary period as unhappy in comparison to his college days. Partly the nagging backdrop of the war, he said, but also "at that time I began to realize that the Missouri Synod was different and that I was not at home in the Evangelical Lutheran Church." He really had no synodical identity prior to seminary, he said, and now he was seeing how the one he had inherited by birth was operating. He didn't like what he saw.

Driven into deep theological reflection, he plunged into the Bible and the Lutheran Confessions, he said, but what stood out most was the impact of C. F. W. Walther's *Proper Distinction between Law and Gospel.* He read that book at least four times during his first seminary years, he said. An amorphous Christian before, Jack said he became "both a Lutheran and a Missourian" thanks to Walther's book.

Law and Gospel was an eminently practical guide to the Lutheran distinction between the law, which serves to convict persons of their utter sinfulness, and the gospel, which alone has the function of redeeming. Law is the hanging judge; gospel is the reprieving governor. Law imprisons. Gospel frees. A religious commitment lived in terms of fulfilling the law is sub-Christian. A religious commitment lived in terms of accepting the gospel is genuine Christianity.

Both law and gospel were from God, and both were necessary currencies in the Christian economy, but they should not be mingled in preaching, policy, and practice. Knowing when to stress one or the other was important for a Lutheran minister, Missourian Walther said. If a scrupulous prone sinner was deluged with the law, that would drive him to despair. Preach the gospel to him. But if a person had no conscience or a bad one, he needed the law thrown mercilessly at him. The gospel would only confirm him in sinfulness.

Walther's insights, gleaned from earlier Lutheran tradition, did not constitute epochal Lutheran theology for the historians, but Preus was duly impressed. He termed Walther's work "the most important book ever written by any Lutheran in America."

It is not mysterious why Jack Preus was impressed with *Law and Gospel.* It was sound, vital, and biblical theology. More significantly, it was clear, simple, and practical theology. The book was compiled many decades earlier from Walther's Friday night lectures to Concordia Seminary students. It was manuallike with no ifs, ands, or buts. In this sense, the book was theological law and order. Preus, the searching seminarian, found it immensely refreshing, an oasis in a theological desert.

Much of Jack's theological sparring in seminary was lightweight. He would post on the bulletin board a theological point. Another student would come along, rip it off, and tack up a counterpoint. He pestered various professors with presumed final-word quotes from the Bible or the Triglotta. He took his lumps, as when professors, among them G. M. Bruce, would calmly tell him to flip to another passage which frequently took the steam out of Preus's quotation.

But it was a different story with George Aus, professor of systematic theology. Jack dueled more or less seriously with Aus. Certainly Aus took Jack's, and later Robert's, attacks seriously. The issue was how the individual Christian converts or is converted by God. This is an ancient and essentially unresolvable theological puzzle because it involves questions of man's free will. Does God alone bring man to faith and conversion? What part does man play in coming to faith and in conversion?

For conservative Lutherans the issue flows from Scripture passages stating man is spiritually inert and God alone is the agent of salvation. This was about all the super-orthodox Lutheran view would tolerate. The strick monergistic or single source (God) theory of conversion was championed by Jack Preus. Professor Aus, like some others, tended to discuss the mysteries of conversion by emphasizing man's role. Didn't election and conversion have to be two-way? God speaking and inviting, surely, but also man listening and responding. Synergism this view was called although the then-current Lutheran definition of synergism as a humanistic-based heresy would certainly never have been conceded by Aus.

George Aus was a small, articulate, and apparently hypersensitive man. "A little more than five feet of dynamite," one student wrote. Then about forty, Aus was an energetic, thorough, and popular teacher. He had been born, reared, and educated (Ph.D.) in New York City. He came out of a pastorally oriented, moderately pietistic tradition, making it natural for him to speak of man's role in Christian phenomena. Aus had been at Luther only two years when Jack Preus arrived and began making his presence felt.

Jack recalled his campaign against Aus as "nothing compared to what students dish out these days." Aus spoke of it no less than thirty years later as virtually a theological terrorist attack. He developed ulcers, he said. He came close to leaving. Apparently, he wasn't the fire-eater he seemed. More likely, he just hadn't met out East any nail-eating Norwegian Lutherans like Jack and Robert Preus. Whatever the case, the brothers Preus struck a certain terror in Aus he had not fully digested after three decades. Aus, who died in early 1977, never lost the feeling he experienced an inquisition.

Jack Preus was unofficial boss of a harmless theological goon squad at Luther. About eight or so orthodox-tending students, including cousin Nelson Preus, frequently compared notes on alleged liberal professors, chiefly Aus. The group was not malicious or vindictive, Jack included. Most were not zealots. They were just "concerned," conscientious Lutherans. Presumably though, Jack was taking these matters more seriously than he let on to the others. Two and one-half years after graduation, when most of them had long forgotten theological crazes in seminary, Jack issued his open letter bolting the synod because of "false teachings" at the seminary. It was clear to many that Preus was referring to Aus's opinions.

The Preus goon squad would frequently stay up late to prepare for the next day's class with liberal teachers, primarily Aus. On one level, they were simply superstudents digging jointly for the truth, but they took time to rehearse ways and means to trip or trap Aus. Their efforts had a seriocomic flavor. At one prayer meeting, the superorthodox students prayed that Aus would take a job offer he had from another institution. When Aus heard about these sessions, he suspected Preus-inspired heresy hunting. When Preus later made his public charge, Aus felt his intuitions weren't so offbase after all.

Although the role of Uncle Herman in Jack's crusade was hard to determine, he was clearly antithetical to Aus. There were differences in style and personality. The two men were symbols of two opposing theological currents at Luther. As one fallout of the controversy, Herman and Aus were pitted against each other. To head off potential factionalism at Luther, seminary and church officials appointed a committee to interview the two professors. In May 1948 the church president Johan Aasgaard officially accepted a committee report claiming no irreconcilable disagreements existed despite the obvious differences in emphasis. The case was officially closed.

Uncle Herman clearly supported Jack's efforts to keep Aus theologically honest by conservative standards. Jack frequently consulted him and got advice for his classroom dueling with Aus. But was this primarily a case of Jack egging on Herman, or Herman egging on Jack, as many assumed? Luther president Todd Gullixson early on told Herman to call off his troops on the assumption Herman was directing a family campaign against Aus.

If others tended to play up Herman's role and play down Jack's, Aus did not. Aus's intuition told him it was not the elder uncle using the young nephew but the nephew using the uncle. The reaction of Aus is interesting. After he encountered young Preus in battle, Aus felt he was fighting the five-star general and not a common foot soldier. Unlike the others, Aus did not assume Jack was pawn, even at his young age. Jack was master. Later in Missouri, opponents would shake their colleagues in exasperation trying to convince them that Preus calls all the shots all the time. He is rarely a true victim of circumstance. Anyone who has looked deeply into the whites of opponent Preus's eyes never again underestimates him.

For several semesters after graduation, Jack taught New Testament Greek part time at Luther. He kept an interest in the great election-conversion controversy although the mantle had passed to brother Robert. Jack and Robert began dealing with Gullixson, seminary president. With a gravelly, quavering voice and a stern partriarchal look, Gullixson was definitely old school and paternalistic with seminarians and young clergy, but behind his gruff exterior, he was clever and supple. He was committed to making the 1917 merger work and to furthering unity among Norwegian Lutherans. Theoretically, he would seem to have been a natural ally of the Preus faction because of his background. He came out of the orthodox Norwegian Synod, and he had been a classmate of Jake Preus at Luther College; yet Gullixson and the young Preus brothers clashed.

After Jack graduated, he met with Gullixson to discuss the escalating controversy. Jack long remembered the three points Gullixson made to try to convince him to abandon the Aus matter. Gullixson allowed as how Aus might be overstating his case on conversion, but Aus was still fairly young and fairly new at teaching. Lay off, Gullixson said, and give him a chance to develop his theology. Second, the seminary president said, Jack ought to realize the Evangelical Lutheran Church was committed to an irenic approach in all things. The church was big enough in spirit to tolerate differences. Third, Gullixson thought Jack Preus ought to know he was jeopardizing his career in the church by all this contention. He ought to cool it for his own good.

The Gullixson rationale could not have been more offensive to the crusading Preus. Preus thought, and told Gullixson as much, that it was a strange way to run a church seminary. Hiring a professor with an undeveloped theology was like hiring a pilot untested at the aircraft controls—very dangerous for the passengers. Allowing differences in theology on crucial issues in what was supposed to be a confessional Lutheran assembly? Why that bordered on dissipation, dishonesty, hyprocrisy. As to jeopardizing his ecclesiastical career, didn't Gullixson know that real churchmen served the truth? Bringing up job security at a time like that was crude. Jack was all conscience, all idealism, not unlike the liberal Seminex students in their day, Jack was to say later. After that conversation he knew he would get nowhere with the Evangelical Lutheran Church.

Both Jack and Robert appear to have been mortified by what they saw as Gullixson's paternalism. Cousin David, then living with Jack, recalled the exasperation of Robert particularly. The Preus brothers felt Gullixson was treating them like boys. Go get some experience, then come back as men and we'll talk theology, they heard him saying. Why wouldn't Gullixson take their theological concerns seriously?

When it comes to contending for their theology, the Preus brothers will suffer long, but they will not long tolerate being ignored. Agree with us if you can, disagree if you must, but don't ignore us and our theological claims!

The Preus brothers might not have bolted the Evangelical Lutheran Church had Gullixson given them what they seemed to want—a chance to fight and a fighting chance. They did not want, necessarily, for Aus to be thrown out immediately as a heretic; nor did they want the church to purify itself overnight. They wanted some assurance they could contend in real, not mock, battle for their position. They wanted some little foothold where they would have to be listened to and taken seriously, but Gullixson did the one thing certain to drive the Preuses a thousand psychological miles from Luther. He announced, in effect, "No fighting here under *any* circumstances." To the Preus brothers that was like banning serious theology from Luther.

Jack and Robert began synod shopping. Missouri was one place they shopped. In late 1946, they drove to Concordia Seminary in St. Louis. Jack was then almost twenty-seven; Robert, twenty-two. They were to see Theodore Graebner, then near the end of a brilliant, forty-year career as Missouri professor, essayist, and apologist. Once a member of the old Norwegian Synod, he had taught at the Lutheran Ladies Seminary in Red Wing, Minnesota, where Idella Preus had been among his students. Jake Preus and Graebner had long been friends, and it is not inconceivable Jake had some hand in the St. Louis meeting.

The Preus brothers outlined their quarrel with Luther Seminary and the Evangelical Lutheran Church. They made certain Graebner understood their objections to the (alleged) synergism of Aus. What should they do, particularly Robert who was still enrolled? Graebner was cautious, but he eventually urged Robert to quit and come to Concordia. Jack should also consider joining Missouri.

But between the lines the Preus brothers, Jack, at least, heard a much less encouraging message. Graebner's feeling tone revealed he believed Missouri had enough dissenters without importing new ones. More basically, Graebner showed no interest in the synergism issue, the current Preus theological passion. Graebner, it turned out, was another Gullixson. As they headed back to the Twin Cities, the Preus intuition told them they

might be ignored in Missouri as well if Graebner was any
weather vane.

Before their feeler in St. Louis, the Preuses had been in
contact with the Little Norwegian Synod, the purist Lutheran
sect in Mankato, sixty miles southwest of the Twin Cities. The
Little Norwegians had banded together after the despised 1917
merger. They had survived although hardly thrived as their
membership of less than twelve thousand indicated. They ran
a junior college, Bethany, in Mankato. They nurtured their
faithful in about seventy-five congregations, mostly in Minnesota. They were linked with Missouri and other conservatives
in the old Synodical Conference, a loose federation for mutual
support, theological study, and mission. From their fortress in
Mankato, the Little Norweigans scrutinized the Big Norwegians (the Evangelical Lutheran Church) and railed against
them when they saw any abuse of sound Lutheranism, which
was quite frequent.

Despite their standoffish mentality toward the Big Norwegians, they were apparently not above prestige-seeking and ecclesiastical nose-thumbing if that could be done without compromising pure doctrine. They had a rare opportunity when
they heard that Governor Preus's sons were having trouble at
Luther. Capturing the brothers Preus would be safe, sweet
one-upmanship on the Big Norwegians.

Doubtless Jack and Robert were genuinely attracted to the
Little Synod for its bold consistency in doctrine and practice.
They had one uncle, other relatives, and friends in the Little
Synod, but it is also true that the two ranking luminaries in the
Little Synod, Sigurd Christian Ylvisaker and Norman Madson,
courted the Preus brothers.

S. C. Ylvisaker ("Doc Y"), yet another of Jake's classmates
at Luther College, carried a Norwegian aristocratic name even
more awesome than the Preus name. "The Preuses speak only
to the Ylvisakers and the Ylvisakers speak only to God," went
the class-conscious maxim. S. C. was the only Ylvisaker to side
with the Little Norwegians, and he seemed to devote the rest

of his life to proving that the Little Synod was not second rate. He was an accomplished scholar, with a Ph.D. from Leipzig University, where he had studied under the world-renowned Old Testament specialist, Rudolf Kittel. "Doc Y" was the only Little Norweigian with a doctorate. He headed Bethany College from 1930 until 1950. He was squeezed out as a professor two years later in an in-house coup led by Paul Zimmerman, who years later emerged in Missouri as Jack Preus's chief theological investigator.

Norman Madson, a former football player, was the down-home preacher and practical executive type. He was dean at the college and headed the tiny Bethany Seminary initiated in 1946. He was hard working and aggressive, but he kept a sense of humor and never lost his ability to preach rafter-raising sermons. Jack once told Robert after they heard Madson preach on 1 Peter 2:9 that the two should join the Little Synod if it meant they could preach like Madson. Ylvisaker and Madson were the stars. "Doc Y" was the quarterback, Norm was the fullback, folks used to say. Between them, the Little Synod plodded forward.

Quicker than Jack to reach definitive theological judgments and act on them, Robert made the move first. He had never been a member of the Evangelical Lutheran Church. That technicality wasn't in his way. He left Luther at semester break in early 1947, only months before he would have graduated. He enrolled at Bethany Seminary, bringing the student population to six. Robert was the first graduate. There was great rejoicing in Mankato. Robert graduated amid some pomp. Ylvisaker was beaming, Madson aglow. Surely God's hand was on the Little Synod if their first seminary graduate was the son of the former governor of Minnesota bearing the great Lutheran name of Preus.

Jack did more pondering before a headlong plunge into the Little Synod. He weighed the pros and cons. He listened longer to his uncles, including Herman, who advised against it. Jake let his sons know he thought it was a monumental mistake. The

Little Synod would be a dead end. They should get into the Missouri Synod where they would have expansion space. Other associates told Jack he was committing ecclesiastical suicide by throwing in with the Little Norwegians. Delpha supported Robert. She didn't push Jack but indicated she was impressed by the Little Synod doctrinal coherence.

Ylvisaker had indicated there would be an opening for a Greek and Latin teacher at Bethany that fall. But there could be no formal job offer, "call" as the Lutherans say, while Jack was still technically a Big Norwegian. Jack made his move in the summer. He published his open letter against "false teachings" at Luther and resigned from the Evangelical Lutheran Church. The call came from Bethany. Jack accepted.

When almost one hundred of the Preus clan gathered at Spring Prairie, Wisconsin, that summer for a reunion, Jack and Robert were already bearing witness for their new synod's theology. Cousin David remembered the two made a point of limiting their participation in group prayers to avoid religious "unionism." There was no compromising the truth, even, perhaps especially, among family. Some of the Preus clan revealed their negative thoughts about the two brothers' move. One aunt remarked to the effect that she supposed they could serve the Lord *even* in an outfit like the Little Synod.

Jack's letter to fellow clergy was brief and blunt. He listed the "false teachings," carefully citing a Scripture passage for evidence. Sample heresy: "That man has free will in spiritual matters before conversion, contrary to 1 Cor. 2:14, Rom. 8:7 1 Cor. 12:3." The Bible called for "false prophets" and "errorists" to be shunned "wherever they may be found." He had tried to correct the serious situation at Luther but had failed. He saw "no other course open than to sever relations with the individuals involved and the synod which upholds them." He was acting from a troubled conscience, he wrote, and begged others to understand. "Please do not regard my attitude as unloving or pharisaic. Christ does command us to be perfect Matt. 5:48, and while we certainly can never attain this goal it would be sinful for us not to strive for it."

There is no indication Preus intended or expected to generate a big flap, much less any schism, by his open letter. A handful of others left in roughly the same period but apparently not directly influenced by young pastor Preus. On the other hand, there is no evidence he was ideologically opposed to causing a split or bringing the 1917 merger crashing down.

His action generated some comment and a little heat in some quarters. "Some people seem obsessed with the idea that they are the keepers of the Holy Sepulchre, and that other people must pass their muster before they can be accepted as grade A Lutherans," remarked one Lutheran columnist. The committee to clear Herman Preus and George Aus was set up as a direct result of Jack's letter, but the Big Norwegians just weren't interested in a theological civil war.

It came down to Jack Preus's giving an explanation for what he was doing. He was bearing witness to the truth as he saw it, the abstract theological truth sans ecclesiastical considerations. His move came as no great surprise to those who knew him although many were surprised he planned to join the Little Synod rather than a larger conservative body like Missouri. Apparently no official liaison came by day or night to try to get him to change his mind.

Despite all his superficial ties to the Evangelical Lutheran Church, Jack Preus had never been an integral part of it. He had drifted into what was nominally the church of his forefathers. Then, in the posture of a prophetic reformer appealing to the higher patriotism of the fathers and the Bible, he more or less demanded this church live up to his expectations.

Preus was only twenty-eight, but some of the patterns were to hold for later years. He is a would-be reformer who will not be ignored, a conservative polemicist who selects his opponents because they are vital and effective "liberals" not simply because they are "liberal." Aus stuck in Preus's craw and mobilized him, much the way another New Yorker, John Tietjen, was to do twenty years later in Missouri.

Other patterns did not hold. Preus was never again to dance such a politically naïve number. Never again was he to take the offensive without a firm foothold in his politico-theological environment. He learned that abstract truth changed nothing. What mattered was powerful men in high church office committed to realizing the truth politically.

6

Scholar, Teacher, and Pastor

While struggling with his synodical identity, young Jack Preus was taking on lasting personal and professional identities. From 1943 through 1957, he became husband and father in his private life. He became professor, language scholar, and polemicist in his professional church life. He was to have several rounds at pastoring congregations and one turn at recruiting and fund raising, but these phases of church work did not get into his blood as did the academic, polemical, and "political" phases.

When Jack and Delpha left Luther College in spring 1941, they agreed to write each other. No promises beyond that, Delpha recalled. She went to Mora, and later Sleepy Eye, Minnesota, to teach and direct library in high schools there. Jack went to seminary in St. Paul, but he visited Delpha several times. They were engaged in the summer of 1942. They married at St. Olaf Church in Austin on June 12, 1943.

After the wedding, Jack began serving a year-long pastoral internship at Lake Nokomis Lutheran Church in Minneapolis. The couple got a small apartment. Jack's pay was about forty dollars a month; Delpha worked part time in a grocery.

The financial independence Jake was eventually to bequeath to his sons came gradually. Jake gave them pocket money, and there was an understanding they could get help in any emergency. In a June 1944 letter to Robert, Jake wrote: "When this runs out let me know or if you need any more money let me know as it is entirely unnecessary for you to draw on your own funds." The two sons had some income from the farms Jake had given them in their senior year of college. Jake also periodically bought stocks to help the sons build a personal investment portfolio.

Jake never doled uncautiously. When he doled, he was always trying to teach. In an August 1943 letter, he informed his sons he was giving them each fifty shares of Braniff Airways stock. But he didn't want them to sock the shares in a drawer; he wanted them to understand and follow the development of Braniff. He sent a recent financial statement and pointed out items they should observe.

Yet during those years there apparently was not much income considered expendable by the Preuses. When Jack was doing full-time graduate work later, mother Idella asked Robert in a letter (August 1946): "Did you take Jack and Delpha to supper some place? You know he hasn't a great deal of money these days."

Lake Nokomis was a solid, 1500-member parish with plenty of pastoral and teaching chores for a young intern pastor. Jack served under Pastor Roy Olson, who had known Jake and had met Jack at a Bible camp. Olson, impressed, had requested Jack for an associate. He rated Preus high on overall competence and ability to work with parishioners, especially with youth, his primary duty as an intern. Jack was adored by the people. When his internship ended in mid-1944, he served an additional seven months and apparently could have gotten a permanent call there.

He was well liked despite, or maybe because of, the fact he brought his feisty spirit from seminary to the Lake Nokomis pulpit. Early on he was asked to fill in for Olson at the main Sunday preaching service. Not wanting to let an opportunity pass without making an impact, Jack preached a harangue against liberalism. He brought to the pulpit several popular

Christian books and read passages containing liberal ideas. With a flourish, he banged shut the last book, peered out at his flock and asked, "Now you don't believe that crap, do you?" While it might have gotten an older, or a different, man in trouble, it was accepted as Jack's refreshing spontaneity.

He could give the women something to whisper about occasionally. When one woman in the congregation once came around fishing for compliments for her Sunday school children, he cooled her rather quickly with a remark about only geniuses and problem children standing out, so her children must be somewhere in between. He wore his sauciness well from the beginning of his church career.

In June 1944, Patricia Louise, the couple's first child was born. Within ten years the Preuses had six more daughters and a son: Delpha Marie (b. '45); Caroline Elizabeth ('47); Sarah Annette ('48); Idella Susan ('49); Mary Helen ('50); Jacob, Jr. ('53) and Margaret Naomi ('55).

Father Jack was exceptionally busy during the period after his first daughter's birth. He was working at Lake Nokomis, completing studies at Luther Seminary under an accelerated wartime schedule, and beginning part-time study in classics at the University of Minnesota. The busy father was to become a pattern. He became a good-hearted, pliant parent who earned a healthy respect from his children. He gave direction; yet he was not the disciplinarian and worrier Delpha was. He was not the pressure-cooker parent Jake was, but Jack has been a very busy man much of his adult life. He remarked to associates in St. Louis that during family crises he had unfairly burdened Delpha with parental responsibilities.

When Jack graduated from Luther Seminary in January 1945, he had two job offers, one from a church in Washington state and the other from Trinity Lutheran Church in South St. Paul. He never considered leaving the Twin Cities because he was a graduate student and because he still had unfinished business with Aus and Gullixson. He took the small, poor congregation in South St. Paul. He was ordained a pastor in the

Evangelical Lutheran Church at a group ordination service at Central Lutheran Church in Minneapolis on January 28, 1945. It was not an auspicious start, worldly wise, for a man eventually to head a denomination of three million. Trinity had about two hundred members and no future because it was soon to be merged with a neighboring congregation. Trinity was in an industrial corridor with most of its members living along Concord Street a few blocks from the Mississippi River. Trailer trucks rolled by day, shaking the fronts of the Concord Street homes. Freight trains rolled by night behind them, shaking the back stoops.

With the gusto he showed later in taking on any new venture, Jack Preus went to work. He added some new members. He preached spirited sermons although he had toned down from his early days at Lake Nokomis. He maintained his folksiness. When he made home calls, he adjusted to the style of his hosts. At times he sat, short-sleeved with an elbow atop a garbage can, visiting on the back steps. Jake once came to worship at Trinity, which was cause for pride at the little congregation.

Jack's ministry at Trinity was the last blessing, a kind of steak-and-champagne dinner before the execution. Trinity congregation hated to see him go. Jack had to prod the search committee charged with finding a new pastor because they didn't seem to want to accept the fact he was leaving.

Restive in pastoral work, Jack resigned the Trinity position after eighteenth months' service. He longed for more career options. The prospect of seminary or college teaching loomed larger in his mind. He wasn't disillusioned by Trinity, and he had enjoyed his work; yet Trinity had become symbolic of what Jack Preus didn't want—a relatively unchallenging, thankless, and obscure pastoral career. He was going into graduate work full time, and he was waging his doctrinal war at Luther. Those played into his decision as well.

Ultimately, it must be said also that Preus easily becomes bored with routine assignments, not that he lacks persistence when he believes much is at stake or when he enjoys a project.

He can spend hours wrestling with the translation of a slippery Greek or Latin word, but if the personal and professional challenge has faded from a project, Preus quickly begins to consider other options.

Sensing his son might be on the verge of switching careers, Jake took an active interest during Jack's university days. Jake arranged for Jack and Delpha to move to the Preus home on Seymour Avenue. He supplied funds. He urged Jack to complete his master's degree and follow through immediately with the Ph.D. Jake wanted Jack to pursue a secular academic career, or failing that, an academic career with the church.

In choosing the University of Minnesota's classics department in the fall of 1946, Jack was not plunging into the great American academic mainstream. As was the case in most state universities in the postwar period, glamour fields at the University of Minnesota were in the physical sciences, social sciences, and professional schools. The waning classics department was struggling to stay alive while other departments were flourishing. There were three full-time classics professors, one part-timer, and no surplus of students. Jack was something of a celebrity because he was the first doctoral candidate in classics there in almost two decades. It was another of the big-fish-in-a-little-pond features of Jack's early career.

His master's work, completed in spring 1947, involved language analysis of the writings of St. Jerome, the prolific, epochal Church Father of fourth-century Christianity. Jack analyzed how St. Jerome rendered in Latin the controvertible Greek word *daily,* the only adjective in the Lord's Prayer. He stayed with this topic for his subsequent Ph.D. analysis, completed in 1951 under Professor Donald Swanson.

"What Preus did was to verify that St. Jerome was indeed a careful, professional and cosmopolitan translator of the Bible from Greek to Latin. Preus demonstrated that St. Jerome's translation was perhaps the best among scores of them then floating around," Swanson recalled.

Years later, Preus (assisted by Delpha) was to concentrate his

Latin-to-English translating skills on Reformation-era scholars, chiefly Martin Chemnitz (d. 1586). He translated Chemnitz's *The Two Natures of Christ* (published in 1970) and Martin Luther's *Commentary on Romans* (1972). When the public relations war heated up after he became Missouri president, moderates were to observe that Preus was more language "technician" than true classics scholar. Real scholarship, they scoffed, amounted to more than transposing communication of another era into a contemporary language. Someday computers would be translating Latin texts as efficiently as the Jack Preuses of this world. It was a cheap shot and misleading. Preus apparently knows the theology of the early Church Fathers much better than his detractors give him credit for. He seems capable of using his knowledge incisively in one-shot polemical theologizing, if not long-range theological exploration. The moderate pooh-poohing must be understood as a reaction to the Preus apologists who were making him out to be a Nobel Prize scholar and theologian.

During Preus's full-time university study, the couple experienced a family crisis. Delpha was stricken with polio in an epidemic in the fall of 1946. She was placed with other victims at the Fort Snelling compound where the Sister Kinny rehabilitation program was used. She was confined from late September until just before Christmas.

Delpha long remembered the bittersweet test used to determine if patients were fit to leave. If a person could raise herself from a prone position on the floor without help, she was cleared to go home. Still, it was many months before Delpha recovered to near-normal. She lost permanently the use of some thigh and leg muscles. She walks with a slight limp noticeable only when she is exhausted.

Meanwhile that fall, Jack was homemaking along with cousin David. Recently returned from army duty in Japan, David was then in law school. He and Jack cared for the two Preus daughters, one less than a year old when Delpha entered the compound.

Jack remembered Dave as good housemate and good with the Preus babies, despite the distraction of his "clunking around the house all year in his army boots." Also, Jack said mockingly as he recalled the period later, David "wasn't quite sure whether Shintoism or Christianity was the true religion." Dave remembered Jack being swayed (unduly in David's mind) by Ylvisaker's and Madson's overtures and the Little Norwegian propaganda generally, but mostly what he remembered was mutton. They ate most of the mutton marketed that fall in the upper Midwest, David recalled. Jack was an avid shopper, driving all over town for bargains. His favorite buy in meat was mutton chops for under twenty-five cents a pound.

When Jack completed his master's degree, it seemed he would soon have the academic world by the tail. He was offered a teaching assistantship at the university. He had the outlines of his Ph.D. program worked out, a program he could have completed by mid-1949. He had no immediate financial pressures because of Jake. With an M.A. degree in the postwar education boom, he could have secured teaching jobs easily in both religious and secular settings. He had two other teaching possibilities when he accepted the Bethany College position.

Preus was later to concede that he had made a mistake by going to Bethany and the Little Synod—if for no other reason than he had to string out his Ph.D. work too long and under less than ideal conditions. He had to commute periodically from Mankato, and later, Luverne, but the lure of teaching and the prospect of finding a compatible synodical nest won out over other considerations.

The thrill of captivating a classroom audience, the challenge of imparting information and molding minds without boring students, the opportunity to inform while entertaining, perhaps rather to entertain while informing, the sense of building a little community with Professor Preus as the shepherd—all these played into the Preus ego-involvement in teaching.

Some of the best teachers are actors with high ego needs, just as dynamic preachers are actors with higher than normal ego needs. Teaching and preaching are intensive social processes demanding feedback. Selfless teachers and preachers who operate as if they had no personal investment in their presentations induce sleep; yet an egomaniacal teacher distracts, much the way an egomaniacal actor overplays the role and focuses attention on himself rather than on the play. Preus was somewhere in between but, as in all he did, leaned toward too much personal involvement. Some students always sensed a hidden agenda in all Preus classes, an agenda that called above all else for Jack Preus to emerge popular.

While at Luther College, Preus first assumed a teaching role. He was a substitute catechism instructor in 1940, recalled Leigh Jordahl, then Jack's pupil and later associate and friend of the Preus brothers during Little Synod days. Collegian Preus would often sit *on* the table with his legs crossed under him. He told campfire tales and used earthy analogies to communicate what could have been rather boring fare—Luther's Small Catechism. Preus lulled the pupils into not only learning but enjoying it. For Jordahl the ninety-minute sessions passed quickly.

During early seminary days he tutored for the family of the Puhlfahl Foundry owners. At Lake Nokomis church he conducted youth classes. After graduation from seminary he taught beginning New Testament Greek for war veterans entering Luther Seminary. His first full-time teaching position was at Bethany Junior College, where he taught Greek, Latin, French, and religion from the fall of 1947 through the spring of 1950.

Bethany and Little Synod offices were situated in a hilly section of Mankato, a residential and educational community of about twenty thousand. Bethany, which incorporated a secondary school as well, had about one hundred fifty students. It was the smallest of four colleges in the town. The staff of sixteen faculty carried heavy schedules, Jack included. He taught a twenty-hour routine. The Preuses lived in a duplex near the small campus but summered at the Preus resort at Gunflint Lake.

Young Mr. Preus was a bouncy, blustery, playful instructor. He greeted all with a cheerful "Hello Brother" or "Hello Sister." He knew students by their first names. He could tease them inside and outside the classroom—as when he ceremoniously blew cigarette smoke in the faces of freshmen he knew were breaking the nonsmoking rule. He ran an orderly but never tight classroom. Students got the feeling he never spent a lot of time organizing, but he was always somehow prepared and in control. True, students could get him diverted onto virtually any topic under the sun. A sure-fire way to get him into a spirited discussion was to pose hot topics in inter-Lutheran affairs, but they knew he knew they were diverting him with his consent.

Instructor Preus imparted the necessary technical skills and "content" in his courses. If his students couldn't produce, they could expect low or failing grades. Mr. Preus was no pushover. He was no respecter of students with important relatives—as David Ylvisaker, S. C.'s son, found out when Preus once socked him an *F* on a Greek exam. Yet Preus remained instinctively a generalist who loved to ramble and parade his considerable knowledge of contemporary issues.

A Bethany yearbook of that era has a caricature of a pug-nosed Preus, in robe and throne of a Roman emperor, glaring down in mock discipline at a quaking student-peon. A thumbnail sketch attempted to catch the flavor of "Brother Preus's" rambling classes, noting Plato's discourses fell by the wayside when someone asked if there was such a thing as a Greek umlaut or whether those were flyspecks on his book.

From fall of 1958 to spring of 1962, Preus had a second period of full-time teaching at Missouri's Concordia Seminary in Springfield, Illinois. Although Preus was hired to teach Greek and Latin, his courses later included New Testament interpretation. Most students there entered ministry later than they would have in standard training programs. Preus adjusted his teaching style to meet this new and older clientele. The students were stimulating and "bears for work," he wrote in a

December 1959 letter. He managed well to get all his nuts-and-bolts work in, but he remained the free-wheeling generalist and facile lecturer-entertainer.

Later in troubled times, Preus liked to make it known how much he enjoyed teaching and translating. He relished getting up early to pore over his texts. Midway through his second term as president he hinted he might not run again so he could get back to his beloved academia. Is Preus really an academician? Clearly he could and did fit the role of handshaking front man for an educational institution, but Preus's "Oh to be back in the classroom" lament doesn't strike quite true. He has not arranged his life to be a professional educator. He enjoyed teaching. He knew its satisfaction, its security, and its freedom, but he knew its limits for him. Professor Preus was temporarily self-nurturing the incipient church-politician Preus.

While a Little Norwegian, Preus served in his second and final pastorate. He broke off his teaching career at Bethany to take a tiny problem congregation in Luverne in a far-off corner of Minnesota. He took the job because he was already feeling claustrophobia from the tribal atmosphere in Mankato and because it was a chance to prove himself in the field. An energetic man was needed in Luverne to make inroads into a Big Norwegian monopoly. If Preus worked miracles there, he could come back to Mankato with a feather in his cap. Perhaps significant also, the Little Norwegians had a rule that the synod president and other officers had to be pastors.

Like much of Preus's career, the Luverne ministry was cloaked initially in controversy. Like other Preus controversies, though, the thorny Luverne situation was not created by Preus. As elsewhere, he rushed headlong into a burning building. He may have fanned the flames, but he did not start the fire.

Luverne, in Rock County in the rich agri-business corner of southwest Minnesota, was a community of five thousand. As one of those prosperous heart-of-America towns where people took staunch pride in their material and churchly achievement, Luverne supported twelve churches, half of them Lutheran.

There were two Big Norwegian churches, Our Savior's and Immanuel. By the late '40s both had less than one hundred members. Folks in both believed a merger was appropriate, and a good time for it would be in 1950 when the aging pastors of both congregations were to retire. The only trouble was, Lauritis Peder Lund, the crusty, dictatorial pastor of Immanuel, had grown to despise the Big Norwegian Synod for its alleged liberalism. He wanted to leave his congregation as a legacy to the Little Norwegians.

Pastor Lund railed against the proposed merger, threatening hellfire for those who would approve it. About 60 percent of his congregation voted for merger nonetheless. Pastor Lund stood his ground. With the open support of the Little Norwegians in Mankato, he organized a splinter group. The bitterly contested question then was the ownership of the Immanuel church and two-story parsonage. There was a desperate search by both parties to establish legal ownership.

The cornerstone, presumably containing a strongbox with the original charter, turned up vandalized one day. It had been chiseled out. If there ever was one, the strongbox was missing. There was a document for the parsonage. It was owned, not by any church entity, but by the pastor and several other trustees. The only competent trustee surviving was Lund, who signed possession to the splinter group. The majority, who had assumed the congregation was owner, felt they had been bilked out of their parsonage. They hired an attorney to see what claims they had. Chiefly through the attorneys, a shaky compromise was eventually worked out whereby the majority conceded their share of the parsonage.

Enter Jack Preus. Through Lund, Little Norwegians in Luverne had first heard about Jack when he published his open letter against Luther Seminary. Earlier that summer of 1950, he had been hired as pastor in nearby Jasper where another of Lund's congregations had voted to join the Little Synod. Now the Little Norwegians wanted Preus to anchor the potentially more prosperous splinter group in Luverne. A legend persists to this day that the Jacob Preuses occupied the disputed parsonage at 735 Freeman Avenue under cover of darkness. Jack Preus was a squatter for the crafty Little Norwegians! It was hardly as devious as it seemed and came about by chance as far as the Preuses were concerned.

On rather short notice, the Preuses had been notified they could move into the parsonage. A caravan of pickup trucks would be sent to Mankato to move them, but the Luverne group and the Little Synod had some problems assuring Jack of the undisputed legal ownership of the parsonage. The move was delayed several days until attorneys gave clearance. When the clearance came, the trucks headed for Mankato. It was a stormy day in southwest Minnesota. The trucks waited and waited until the rain slacked off to begin the three-hour drive to Luverne. They arrived about midnight. An electrical storm had disrupted power service; so Jack, Delpha, and company were groping around the parsonage with candles and kerosene lamps. Some promerger folks witnessed this scene. A rich, if false, legend was born.

A ministry launched under these circumstances obviously took a while to settle down to a normal pastoral routine—by which time Jack Preus was again restive and looking around for other opportunities. He was soon fishing for a job teaching Latin at the local public high school. He was busy working his way up the Little Synod hierarchical ladder and taking trips to Europe and the Gunflint Lake lodge. He was complaining to some parishioners how tough it was to give up the three months' summer holiday he was accustomed to as a professor.

But before Preus left Luverne in the fall of 1956, he had served the Little Norwegians well. Besides Luverne and Jasper, he pastored a small congregation in Ellsworth. He proved to be an aggressive, efficient, and faithful minister—the all-American, Protestant, church-builder type. Within two years of his arrival, the congregation, renamed Bethany, had dedicated a new $45,000 church. Preus built up membership by approaching fence-straddlers in the controversy and by engaging inactive

Lutherans and other nominal members of some faith. He worked hard among the remnants of a disbanded Methodist church in the area.

Preus was "sheep-stealing" and busting up Lutheran families, some critics said. Rather it appeared he was just the hardest-working pastor in town. The charge of "sheep-stealing" came in part from what Preus believed was his legitimate claim to church records of the old Immanuel congregation. Those records were needed for normal inquiries made by former members although Preus was not above partisan preaching. He clearly let his flock know they had joined the true Lutheran church on earth, and he let them know what was wrong with the other Lutherans around.

Pastor Preus took firm control of spiritual and doctrinal concerns for his Little Norwegian flock. He let them know the theological flaws of other Christians, Missourians included, but he was no dictator in the administration of the churches. He was graciously democratic when it came to the overall operation of his congregation. He was new-school in dealing with lay persons. He won their lasting respect even after he shocked and saddened them later by what many saw as his opportunistic move into the Missouri Synod.

Missourians unsympathetic to Preus later pointed to his meager pastoral experience as one cause for his alleged ruthlessness in the great Missouri doctrinal war. Preus was no pastor, they said, he was a politician. They thought him incapable of dealing pastorally, of letting heart go out to heart so each could influence the other.

Preus bristles at what he considers this phony liberal argument. Of course he's pastoral! He will walk the extra mile to win over any reasonable dissenter. He will bend almost to the breaking point to keep peace. He will concede any day the shape of the bargaining table. He will meet any time, any place with any ground rules to negotiate peace. He's not a petty tyrant, he's a pliant pastor.

How is it Jack Preus sees himself as the Curé of Ars reincarnate while his opponents see him as Tomás de Torquemada reincarnate? Ultimately, Preus and Missouri opponents have such radically different theological world-views that neither can be "pastoral" in face-to-face exchange. Short of that impasse, there is another dynamic at work. Preus has a basic streak of political machismo. From this comes his operating definition of *pastoral.* A Preus pastor painstakingly lays out "the truth" as he sees it. He patiently draws a picture of "reality." He may rightly or wrongly claim he had nothing to do with creating that reality and would prefer another, but his duty as pastor is to interpret that reality for his flock.

Of course, Pastor Preus doesn't browbeat, he doesn't tell the subject what to do. The political realities of the situation dictate what the subject must do. Preus sees pastoral counseling as a kind of man-to-man "reality therapy." Do this not because I say so, not because you like it, not because you agree with it, but because it is what any reasonable man would do when faced with this reality. You may have thought reality was on your side, but it obviously isn't; so brace up like a man. No whining here. Swallow your medicine. Resign in seventy-two hours because that's what any reasonable man would do.

Among others, Herman Neunaber, a one time Missouri Synod district president, believes Preus is tragicomic in the role of pastor. It was December 2, 1975, at Preus's presidential office in St. Louis. Neunaber was the first of eight moderate district presidents scheduled for ouster if they continued sheltering the self-exiled rebels of Seminex and supporting their theological claims. The deadline was only days away for this potential crisis, with its threatening implications for the whole church and its obvious effects on Neunaber and his churches.

At first, a globe-trotting Preus had tried to delegate the required "pastoral counseling" with Neunaber. Now they were face to face. As in the Tietjen-Preus breakfast meeting at New Orleans, Preus was ill at ease. He handed Neunaber a twelve-page questionnaire. If Neunaber could see fit to answer those questions in writing within the next couple of days, this mess could be over shortly. Neunaber scanned the questions. He felt they were loaded, and he rejected Preus's request. More basically, Neunaber wondered, did Preus believe a written test was "pastoral counseling"?

Preus was mildly irritated, and he groped for several minutes. He poured Neunaber a cup of coffee, then in a rare lapse, drank it himself and launched into an hour-long discussion of the "reality" of Missouri. He had just returned from the mission fields in South America and Africa, he said, and his heart ached to do more for the great work of missions. Oh, to spread God's Word! Missouri was a vigorous church with such a heavy responsibility to spread that Word. It could do so much more if this infernal doctrinal bickering could be once-for-all ended. The majority in the church wanted it to end, and he knew Neunaber wanted to help end it. The synod at convention had set down reasonable ways to solve matters. Why couldn't Neunaber come around for the sake of peace and mission?

Several times during his talk, Preus interrupted to ask if Neunaber believed Preus had said enough. It sounded like asking "Have I done enough pastoral counseling now? Have we talked enough? Can I stop now?" Laying out theological and churchly "reality," it seems, was much easier for Preus with the good layfolk of Luverne in the '50s than with hard-bargaining Missouri district presidents in the '70s.

What is so bad about the Preus pastoral approach? Because it doesn't conform to moderates' rarefied definition is no judgment against it. Moreover, the Christian church has been operating for two thousand years on "reality therapy" of one kind or another. Gullixson had tried his version on Preus thirty years earlier; now Preus was trying his on Missouri moderates.

Yet Preus does appear weak at personal pastoral relations. Missouri moderates and critics say Jack Preus, heart, soul, body, and mind, is never all there sitting across from you. There are too many Jack Preuses in search of who knows what destinies. Unlike conservative leaders in other churches who have pastorally diffused their "liberals," Jack Preus has not convinced Missouri moderates he really believes the "reality" of which he speaks.

In almost seven years, Preus personally has made few, if any, converts. Of course many Missourians are on his ideological side because that is closer to traditional Missouri than the moderates. But Preus has made few converts. Everybody pretty much stands or leans where they were standing or leaning in 1969 in their personal reaction to Preus. Those who felt he was rank politician with something always up his sleeve still feel that way. Those who felt he was a churchly equivalent of the blue-suede-shoed salesman still feel that way.

7

From Norway
to Missouri

"Gossip and envy are the bane of a small synod," Robert Preus wrote in a brief account "From Norway to Missouri" which was published after he left the Little Norwegian Synod for a teaching position at Missouri's Concordia Seminary in St. Louis. More than an abstract observation, it was his way of hinting why he had left in late summer of 1957.

If Jack Preus had written a similiar article after he left in 1958, he could have added his own list of Little Synod flaws. Later, he was to do so privately to his new Missouri colleagues. He was caustic where Robert had been vaguely polite. Jack would describe the Little Synod to Missourians as inbred, back-biting, peevish, sluggish, hopelessly unimaginative. It was the lost tribe of Western Christendom.

Often his remarks came in the context of trying to ingratiate himself with Missouri's elite and show how much he loved Missouri, but at times he roasted the Little Synod when he had no other axes to grind. He never disowned the ultraorthodox cargo of the Little Synod, exactly, but it appeared he had come to disdain the vessel bearing the freight. When Jack Preus effects an ecclesiastical separation, sooner or later he circulates a bill of particulars.

But while the Preus brothers were in the Little Synod, they

were among its most vigorous defenders. They were among the more strident critics of other Lutherans, Missourians included. The phenomenon of the neophyte outpoping the pope helps explain the Preus brothers' posture in the Little Synod, and for that matter during the rest of their career. But ultimately the Preus brothers have not been so much converts destined to adjust to various synods as they have been synods unto themselves. It was a foregone conclusion among the whittlers at the barbershops in Decorah, Iowa, and in other Preus strongholds in the upper Midwest that the Preuses were born to rule. They always rose to the top.

What happened to the Preus brothers' marriage with the Little Synod, a marriage so passionate in 1947 but so strained ten years later? For one thing, it had been a teen-age marriage. The Preus brothers were growing out of their earlier visions although not out of their orthodox theological commitments. For another, the Preus brothers' honeymoon ended as the two potentates who wooed them, Ylvisaker and Madson, began to fade. Some elder sons in the synod began to see the Preus brothers as fair-haired boys whose loyalty needed to be tested by the ecclesiastical equivalent of military latrine duty. They needed to pay their pecking-order dues like everybody else, maybe even pay more. The Preus brothers seemed to have gotten shabby treatment considering their credentials and talent. They may even have been a threat to their new colleagues. After 1952, with Ylvisaker retired to Texas, the two were the only Little Norwegians with Ph.D.'s.

Finally, the Preus brothers, who once believed their own chauvinistic tirades, discovered that enemy Missouri wasn't the dreaded theological wilderness after all. Jack, particularly, got to know a wide range of Missourians for the first time. He found they weren't the liberal devils he thought.

But for the early years in the Little Synod, the Preus brothers led the verbal raiding parties against outsiders. Both quickly began publishing barbs in the synod's *Lutheran Sentinel* biweekly journal. Robert was still in seminary (April 1947) when he wrote a blast against a proposal by a Big Norwegian that pastors be selected under the episcopal system rather than by congregational vote. "Unlutheran, false, heretical and papistical," he thundered, adding that the "Roman papacy . . . was and is the very Anti-Christ." Fresh out of the seminary, he was out after Lutherans who would join the World Council of Churches. A pernicious, wicked, sinful, even "satanic movement," he wrote of the council.

Later he warned against the dangers of the Boy Scout creed with its pledge to respect the convictions of others in matters of custom and religion. No Christian could ever make that kind of pledge! In February 1948, Robert, on the attack again, noted he got tired of correcting heresies appearing in other Lutheran publications, but he got even more tired of heresies being there in the first place. So he'd just have to continue.

Jack began to wield an acidic pen for the *Sentinel* in the fall of 1948 when he took a potshot at Luther Seminary for hosting a Presbyterian lecturer. Didn't Luther officials know that the Presbyterian creed had serious errors? In later months he huffed against President Harry Truman for his well-known use of "low-minded talk." He scored the "buffoonery of Masonry." He spoke of the "terrible dangers in the teachings of Roman Catholicism," whose exaltations of Mary were lapses into "the darkest paganism." He warned of cozy complacency, the "danger of turning Christianity into Churchianity."

In June 1950 he attacked the editor of the Big Norwegian *Lutheran Herald* magazine for allowing an article with alleged heretical views on scriptural inerrancy. His conclusion may well be an enduring apology for Jack Preus.

> We dislike attacking people in this way; but for the sake of our own members who are often led to believe that nothing serious is at stake, for the sake of those (other Lutherans) who read our paper and need to know the truth, and for the sake of our sister synods and Lutheranism at large, we feel constrained to tell the facts. God's word is under attack, and there is no use in evading and equivocating. The time has come for us to stand and be counted.

Preus got long-range mileage in the Little Synod out of a 1948 essay entitled "What Stands Between." He read it at the '48 synod convention and the following year published it. He revised it in 1956 as a forty-page pamphlet under the title "A Closer Look."

This essay was a polemical piece expanding on his infamous open letter. Preus cataloged all the alleged false doctrines of the Big Norwegians. They embraced or tolerated heretical views on the Lutheran doctrines of conversion, the nature of human will, original sin, justification, conversion after death, Hades, millennialism, the anti-Christ, creation, and the authority of Scripture, he wrote. Moreover, they had permissive practices on "unionism," lodgery, and women's suffrage in the church—all contrary to the Bible, in his view.

The one theme in this much-traveled essay that still rings true to the Preus of today is the theme on Scripture. "To undermine the Scripture is to destroy the church," he wrote. Verbal inspiration of the Bible must be maintained. The notion that "merely the inspiration of ideas" is involved "destroys the Bible as an authoritative book."

Not one to conclude anything on a pious exhortatory note, polemicist Preus urged action. Verbally, he crossed ecclesiastical lines to incite riot. A Big Norwegian should "correct the doctrinal errors if he is in a position to do so, or else separate himself from the church body. We are sure that many laymen, when they learn the true state of affairs will rise in protest against such conditions."

What must be said in defense of the Preus theological sallies then as later in Missouri was their raw simplicity, logic, and candor. A detailed analysis of what the Big Norwegians actually had on their theological books in 1948 would doubtless reveal Preus had technical grounds for chastising. They weren't living up to what they proclaimed. Preus had noted, for example, that the classic Lutheran Confessions explicitly identified the papacy as the anti-Christ of the Book of Revelation. Horror, declared an outraged Jack Preus, none of their pastors taught that any more!

Churches are ceremonial, human institutions that have to cling to their past while struggling always to reinterpret that past. Churches, like societies, have scores of laws on the books that are ignored and ideas that are discarded or suspended indefinitely. Of course, churches have inconsistencies. The more "confessional" a church, the more apt it is to have a closetful of inconsistencies—unless it is a tribal sect.

That is why Preus theological candor looks to many Lutherans like rank legalism and not totally candid. Churches are not brittle assemblies or wartime armies in which absolute correspondence of theory and practice can prevail. Churches cannot be frozen. Theological traditions cannot be reprogrammed once a year to insure not a single inconsistency exists.

If liberal Lutheran churches sin by theological laxity and hyprocrisy, by paying lip service to "confessions" no longer confessed, the Preus Lutheran church sins by demanding an inhuman purity. Lutheran critics fume at Jack Preus because they are convinced he knows better than to lead a churchly revolution based on such theological "scruples."

"A Closer Look" got so much mileage it even embarrassingly trailed Preus into the Missouri Synod. The manager of the Bethany book store in Mankato wanted to sell back copies of it in early 1963. Bethany College president Bjarne Teigen was asked to review the pamphlet to drum up sales. His review got widespread circulation through a reprint in *Lutheran News* (later *Christian News*), a right-wing weekly published by an independent Missouri crusader.

Big Norwegians by this time had merged into the American Lutheran Church, which was involved with Missouri in sensitive inter-Lutheran consultations. To Fredrik Schiotz, church president, it looked like Preus, then head of Missouri's Illinois seminary and an ambassador for those inter-Lutheran talks, was spoiling for a fight as in the old days. But Preus told Schiotz he had no hand in the reprint of his old pamphlet. Moreover, according to Schiotz, Preus said he had since changed his position. A few weeks later, *Lutheran News* published a letter Preus had sent to an Ohio pastor wherein Preus claimed his theological position had not changed in the slightest.

There followed some corporate tap dancing by Missouri Synod officials to try to smooth over this flap. Preus eventually declared it had resulted from a "misunderstanding" between him and Schiotz. Preus disassociated himself from *Lutheran News,* which had started the flap by claiming that Preus was inconsistent, but he didn't formally disown his positions in "A Closer Look." To the *Lutheran News* editor, Herman Otten, a closer look at Jack Preus had revealed he wanted to assure the Missouri hierarchy he wasn't a troublemaker yet wanted ultraconservatives to know he was still their man.

At the 1953 Little Synod convention, Robert Preus preached a strong isolationist sermon. Speaking of "Our Mission As Remnant," he said that Little Norwegians should never be ashamed of their war on false doctrine, that "poison to the soul." They should never be ashamed of being a remnant in a Lutheran mainstream gone afoul. Truth was not decided by counting noses. He then chastised Missouri for allowing itself to be shamefully compromised in union talks with liberal Lutherans. "Repent," Robert said to Missouri. He was twenty-eight and speaking boldly about sensitive intersynodical matters. Too boldly for a young newcomer, some thought. Ironically, Jack had made hay with his essay, but Robert's devotional confirmed his image as reckless upstart from which he was never to recover during his days with the Little Synod.

Robert Preus, taller, leaner, more intense-looking than Jack, was ordained in October 1947. He served as pastor of Mayville, North Dakota, and Bygland, Minnesota, congregations in his first church assignment. He married Donna Mae Rockman of Minneapolis in May 1948. The couple were to have six boys and four girls, born between March 1949 and June 1965. Robert returned to Minneapolis after two years as a pastor, apparently to build his academic credentials. He took graduate courses in classics and history at the University of Minnesota but never completed a degree program.

He began a Ph.D. program at the University of Edinburgh

in Scotland in 1950, completing work in 1952. In his dissertation he analyzed the concept of biblical inspiration held by the seventeenth-century Lutheran dogmaticians. Published in 1955, it became a standard in its field. Later, on leave from Concordia Seminary, he received another theology degree from the University of Strasbourg in France. Unlike Jack, Robert was to write many theological tracts through the years and to earn a reputation as first-rate dogmatic theologian.

There was mild questioning when Robert came to Concordia because the Edinburgh degree was considered one of those "continental quickies" eventually challenged by the American academic establishment. Ironically, the questioning came from conservatives, not liberals, but there was never a theological credential campaign against Robert during Missouri's great war. He was tolerated, if not embraced, by liberal associates as the blunt truth-seeker. Whereas Jack got something of a reputation as politician first, last, and always, Robert got a reputation as theologian first, last, and always. Robert had a high trust level. What he said about one, he would say to one.

When Robert returned to Minneapolis from Edinburgh, there were openings at Bethany and at Emmaus congregation in North Minneapolis. He was passed over on both. He took a call at the synod's Harvard Street Church near Harvard Square at Cambridge, Massachusetts, and was there about three years. Some said he was homesick for the Midwest and that he resented the isolation of being far from Mankato. But he kept abreast of synodical issues and published critiques, including ones against Missouri, in a newsletter.

He moved back to the Midwest in 1955, accepting a pastoral job for three small congregations near Trail, Minnesota. He was not unsuccessful as a pastor, but he was marking time for a teaching offer, any decent teaching offer the Little Norwegians had.

Meanwhile, Jack was faring better, and both brothers were active in a campaign to "suspend fellowship" with the Missouri Synod. Despite the fact that Jack took the Luverne detail, he was making progress in the pecking order. He was elected to his first board position—for Christian day schools—in 1948. He got some nominations for president of Bethany college at the 1950 convention and was elected to a two-year term as vice-president in 1954, normally a step to the presidency. He was on the speaker's circuit for pastoral conferences and church anniversaries, and he gave illustrated lectures of his European trips. The Luverne pastorate didn't take him out of circulation.

The role the Preus brothers played in the Little Synod's "suspension of fellowship" with Missouri because of presumed doctrinal laxity was as substantial as it was ironic, in view of their leap into Mother Missouri's lap months later. It was not nearly so ironic, it turned out, as the fact that Missouri's neutral managers accepted them. The Preuses had preached, propagandized, and politicked for the suspension months before the vote. In retrospect it looks much like the Preuses were throwing eggs at Missouri just to get Missouri's attention.

Jack and Robert Preus in mid-1954 could have counted on two hands the number of workaday Missouri clergy they knew well. They had gotten—and faithfully transmitted—many of their horror stories about Missouri from Ylvisaker and Madson.

At the Little Synod convention in early summer 1954, Jack and Robert were among seven delegates who were champing at the bit. Late in the convention the seven introduced from the floor a motion to suspend fellowship with Missouri. This was unusual because unwritten protocol required that only official committees broach weighty matters. Most were on the appropriate committee, but they had not been able to report it out. There was the hint of railroading also because of the lateness. The motion was tabled until the next year, but Preus brothers and company had achieved the classic political move of getting the issue to stew and build momentum for twelve months and to assure its place on the agenda in 1955.

At previous conventions Jack had been elected to the Unity Committee, and in 1954 he became part of the Little Synod's Synodical Conference delegation. This is how he met Walter

Baepler of Missouri's Springfield, Illinois, seminary. Jack was a member of the Doctrinal Committee which introduced the suspension motion. He was long a part of every key group responsible for developing the rationale for suspension. When the vote was taken on June 24, 1955, the Preuses were among the sixty-five who voted for, not the ten who voted against. Jack had also been party to a presumed compromise agreement, worked out only days before, which Missouri representatives assumed would delay any such vote by the Little Norwegians until at least the 1956 convention.

Yet neither should the Preus brothers' role be exaggerated— as if they tooled the unwilling Little Synod into action. At most, the Preuses helped the synod take earlier an action that was inevitable given the realities. Jack may even have begun to have second guesses. His experience with Baepler and other Missourians had revealed Missouri to him. Here were essentially conservative but practical, gracious men running a big ship. Little Norwegians must have looked amateurish in comparison.

Robert's affair with the Little Synod came to an end in late spring 1957. Bethany Seminary needed a full-time professor, the obvious place for Robert. Academically, he ran circles around the only other candidate. Bethany's board, mostly elder-son types, picked one of their own. Robert was pained by the obvious freeze out.

He visited his high-school and seminary buddy, Leigh Jordahl, then teaching at St. Olaf College in Northfield. Jordahl suggested Robert inquire at Concordia Seminary in St. Louis. It was on an accreditation drive and gobbling up Ph.D.'s. Jordahl told Preus he could take a summer job, and if Missouri was as bad as he thought, he could back out.

Robert Preus made his second trip to Concordia in mid-1957. He was hired virtually on the spot.

Jack meanwhile had returned to Bethany as a full-time "student canvasser and fund solicitor," a new position he had recommended. He tried to squeeze in teaching, but he was saddled most of the time with the other job. It was paltry fare for an ambitious thirty-six-year-old. Theoretically, the job was ideal for a glad-handing jack-of-all-trades. Preus, in effect, was the public relations department for Bethany College. The eight job qualifications fit him, including one about ability to travel and "to thrive on a certain amount of irregularity." He drove thousands of miles during his two years on the job. He saw firsthand the seamy side of some Little Synod parishes and schools. Occasionally, he would get so upset by an inefficient or dictatorial pastor that he would telephone college president Bjarne Teigen urging that something be done.

But Preus never pushed too hard. He had enough trouble keeping the crustier synod pastors off his back. Around the spring of 1957, public-relations-man Preus started a little campaign of Bethany students peddling chocolate bars around Mankato to raise money and reinforce the college's name. Some old-school pastors objected on the ground it was a cheap come-on and a worldly gimmick. Teigen, in Colorado, recalled an anxious Preus, telephoning from Mankato urging him to get back as quickly as possible to help Preus stave off an assult being mounted for an upcoming pastoral conference. Public-relations-man Preus, literally and figuratively, had to eat his chocolate bars.

As student recruiter, Preus had a difficult time getting Missouri students. Teigen remembered that Preus avoided Missourians in the area like the plague, presumably because the Preus name had been connected prominently with the suspension move. Preus remembered his troubles were caused by the Little Synod hard-liners who established a policy that because fellowship had been suspended Missouri students couldn't sing in the Bethany choir. How was a fellow to do much recruiting with that kind of nonsense going on? Preus wanted to know. It was not an untypical Preus reaction. Later, he was to blame the hard-righters for going too far in a revolution he had helped create in the potentially explosive Missouri Synod.

For a while Preus could hide his frustrations. He remained good-natured Jack to most, but the one qualification for the job —"understanding the temper of the people of our Synod, their

customs, ways of thinking and the potentialities of our Synod"
—was becoming a joke for him. Sometime in late 1957—after
enduring one too many boring pastors and one too many appeals for the $10,000 Bethany tuckpointing fund—Jack Preus
wanted out of the box that Jake and others had warned him
about.

Jack visited Jordahl, reflecting on his options. He defended
Robert's move to Missouri but indicated he was unsure he
could do that. He mentioned several universities where he was
making inquiries—Hampden-Sydney in Virginia, Iowa University, Iowa City, and perhaps the University of Minnesota.
When Jack left, Jordahl believed that Preus would soon be
leaving the Lutheran ministry for good.

Recruiter Preus was on the road recruiting a job for himself.
He called on Martin Neeb, Sr., then president of Missouri's
Concordia College in Fort Wayne, Indiana. A nattily dressed
and eager Jack Preus asked about openings. He wanted very
badly to teach, he told Neeb. He wasn't interested in synodical
affairs of any kind. He was gagging on synods, he said. The
Little Norwegians were backward. They had a single soul with
a Ph.D., and what was he doing? Serving as a traveling salesman!

Walter Baepler of Springfield had first broached to Jack the
possibility of coming to that seminary in late 1957. Baepler
wanted Preus on the faculty, but the seminary president was
cautious about hiring any outsiders for fear of criticism. Baepler
ached for Ph.D.'s because he was in the process of turning the
seminary from a hip-pocket-run Bible school into an academically recognized institution, but he had to move cautiously so
Missouri didn't get the notion he was populating the place with
a lot of slick strangers.

Baepler had remarked to Alfred Fuerbringer of the St. Louis
seminary that he preferred to hold off calling Jack until Robert's appointment proved satisfactory. Baepler telephoned
Preus on March 1, 1958, with an offer. Three weeks later he sent
an official offer in the mail.

When they heard Jack Preus was leaving the Little Synod, a contingent from his church in Luverne drove to Mankato. There were rumblings around campus that the Luverne group was hopping mad, ready to scald Preus and remind him of his past bad-mouthings of Missouri, but it was a rather cordial meeting under the circumstances. When the good folks from Luverne couldn't talk Preus into staying, they said goodbye and happy hunting. Then as later, the Preus ability to differ with friends without losing them was impressive.

"A great deal of prayer and anguish" went into his decision, Preus wrote in a late April letter announcing his departure. He wasn't cut out for canvassing and wasn't doing "as good a job as needed." Preus begged his action not be seen as a repudiation of Bethany College or the Norwegian Synod. He professed "the deepest love and respect for both institutions," but he felt he could "serve God and the cause of true Lutheranism in the Missouri Synod."

It had taken Jack Preus more than a decade to realize, admit, and undo a youthful mistake. That is the revelation of his Little Synod career. His Missouri critics point somberly to his days there, trying to conjure up all sorts of images—Preus was a fanatic; he was a storm trooper against Missouri; he came into Missouri to destroy it; he is a rootless, unscrupulous opportunist.

But the revelation of his Little Synod days is much more simple. Preus seems like a stubborn man with limitless creativity to avoid a genuine mea culpa and act on it. That's what his ten years and nine months in the Little Synod was all about. Jack wanted to prove Jake was wrong, but Jake was right. So were the dozens of relatives and college and seminary buddies who saw the obvious that Jack wouldn't or couldn't see. He was not made for the Little Synod.

Old buddies who had visited an almost desperately friendly Jack Preus at Luverne and who had urged him to swallow his pride and come back to the Big Norwegian Synod or go to Missouri had gotten a quick no or change of subject. A distant relative had even approached Fred Schiotz with the message that Jack Preus might come back to Big Norway if he were invited. Schiotz had said his door was always open, but Preus would have to make the first overture.

A man persisting for eleven years in a basic mistake, in a form of self-exile, really, is not weak. What endurance would he have once he corrected his mistake and found his true church home? If Preus was a terror in Little Norway where he didn't belong, wouldn't he be a superterror in Big Missouri were he did belong?

8

Eager-Beaver
Seminary Builder

Jack and Robert Preus could not have picked a better time to join the Missouri Synod. In the late '50s Missouri was expanding. The boom in American religion in that decade had been particularly kind to Missouri. Seemingly unlimited growth was envisioned, especially for its colleges and seminaries.

Along with expansion came new patterns of meritocracy and a worldly wise openness. Missouri continued to pay homage to its traditional doctrine, but the ideological guard was relaxed. Neutral church bureaucrats were in key slots. They displayed little hesitancy about outsiders simply because they were outsiders.

Far from sneaking into Missouri, the Preuses were embraced by the bureaucrats. Almighty Ph.D. was the passport to mobility in Missouri. This held for a time whether newcomer was right or left. It was heyday for bureaucrats who were allowing no parochial concerns to obstruct the building of their respective empires. The bureaucrats knew what was best, not the masses with their baser ethnocentric, chauvinistic instincts.

Only the late Pastor Alvin Fehner can make any "I told you so" claim about the Preus brothers, if any Missourian is prone to making any such claims. Then a pastor in Mankato, Fehner wrote St. Louis shortly after Robert Preus was hired. Fehner's instincts told him anybody from the Little Synod, Preus especially, ought to be checked out thoroughly before being hired permanently. Fehner's letter read like provincialist sour grapes to church bureaucrats, and the letter was dismissed.

Rich ironies abounded in this brief but crucial reign of the neutrals in Missouri. The Ph.D. mongering peaked in the waning years of John Behnken, the simple-hearted Texas pastor and Missouri's president since 1935. Behnken was a babe in Academe. As late as 1960, he revealed his ignorance that one got a Ph.D. *in* something. Behnken had been taking it literally. A Ph.D. was a master of philsophy, a well-educated man.

Ironically, also, the same ideological neutrality that resulted in a St. Louis seminary too liberal for the constituency was how the Preus brothers got into Missouri so easily and moved up so fast. Certainly Missouri had stomachs needing academic beef. When Alfred Fuerbringer hired Robert Preus, the students were snickering at the Concordia dogmatics theology teachers. It is true also that Behnken welcomed the Preus brothers because they were conservative. On paper in 1957, the theology of the Little Synod and Missouri was more alike than different, and many professors were imported during that era who never had the radicalizing potential of the Preuses.

Yet the irony remains that the Preuses owe their careers in Missouri to the same bureaucrats the Preuses presumably want to ban from the church along with the moderates. The Preuses became living proof of the very philosophy they espouse over against the neutrals and moderates: If a church gets too tolerant, it asks for trouble.

But no sign of the Preus brothers' potential to shake the foundations was seen for almost a decade. Robert had hinted, in his "From Norway to Missouri" article, of possible adjustment problems down the way. He said it was going to be difficult living in a big church where he wasn't sure what all his colleagues were teaching, but he settled into a busy, happy academic career at Concordia Seminary. He and Fuerbringer, who was later to become an archenemy of the Preus regime, remained on good terms for a decade despite theological differences. Certainly, Jake and Idella were delighted. At a meeting in Minneapolis a few months after Robert came into Missouri, the elder Preuses profusely thanked Fuerbringer for "rescuing" their son from the Little Synod.

Jack Preus, during his early years, was minding his ecclesiastical manners while taking stock of his new synodical home. He was professor and then president of the Springfield seminary. For all most Missourians knew, he was just a busy young man on an educational mission. That appears to be all he was—until he began to see the lay of the politico-theological land.

Getting into Missouri's Springfield seminary was the first good opportunity Jack Preus had had in his young church career. He was ecstatic at first. It was like a homecoming. His early years there were among the happiest of his life, he recalled later. He was teaching in a large conservative seminary in a large conservative Lutheran body, natural habitat for him. He had the freedom of the academic world without ecclesiastical demands. He could relax for the first time.

The family settled in an older home on South Glenwood Avenue. Trinity Lutheran Church and parochial school in downtown Springfield was the family church center. Delpha became active in the school, among other things organizing the school library. She and Jack were faithful participants in parent-teacher assemblies.

Trinity principal Martin Wessler noticed immediately one of Jack's enduring social trademarks. He cannot sit still at a meeting, particularly when he has a passive role. At school meetings his limit was about fifteen minutes before he was up scurrying about. Later as Missouri president he could tolerate about an hour before he'd be on his feet. He created the impression of the strung-out executive always making or receiving phone calls. He left board rooms so frequently uninitiates assumed he had bad kidneys. He was to maintain a habit of coming late and leaving early and—if he wasn't the main speaker—of shooting the breeze with the boys in the back row.

To his seminary colleagues, Jack was the casual one. He invariably bummed cigarettes, told the better jokes and stories at faculty bull sessions, brown-bagged lunch, and rarely indicated any interest in church matters. He showed no signs of a would-be crusader for doctrinal purity. No one seemed to know ultimately what to make of him, but he had a way of ingratiatiating himself with many colleagues. Each felt he was Jack Preus's best buddy. As he has always been, Preus was one of the boys, yet always a step ahead, never exactly in step.

Walter Baepler died in October 1958 only a few months after Jack arrived. The following May, George Beto was elected Concordia Seminary president. Texan Beto and Preus hit it off instantly. Beto, more than any other, launched Jack Preus in Missouri. Through Beto, most Missourians heard favorably of the Preus brothers for the first time. Beto's phrase "They have minds like steel traps" made the rounds.

Beto was a whirling dervish riding a brilliant career as college president and civic leader in Austin, Texas. He was thick with Texas Democrats and presumably could have moved even higher than he did eventually in Texas politics. He was not unlike Jake Preus, whom he got to know and admire. He was one of the sharpest goal-oriented bureaucrats during the expansionist era. He landed at Concordia like a Texas tornado. He was intent on making it a first-rate institution and intent on making it and himself well known in the all-American city of Springfield, the capitol of Illinois and home of one hundred thousand.

In contrast to the traditional "theoretical" Concordia St. Louis, Concordia Springfield (now at Fort Wayne) was the "practical" seminary. Latecomers to the ministry and students with weaker academic qualifications (high-school equivalencies were accepted until late '50s) traditionally trained there. It always played second fiddle to Concordia St. Louis where it was viewed more or less as a trade school. At the height of the depression in 1935, Missouri's convention voted to close the institution but relented the next day. Baepler started quietly working on its ugly-duckling status when he took over in 1953. He established such essentials as a business manager-accountant and the rudiments of administrative staff. Moving forward on these reforms, Beto soon had the community believing the only difference between Concordia St. Louis and Concordia Springfield was the one hundred miles down Route 66.

Beto quickly integrated Preus as trouble-shooter and confidant. Preus filled in key slots when others were on leave. He appeared for Beto at routine ceremonial functions. Preus knew "the right moment to move for adjournment of faculty meetings and he knew when I was ready to move onto another topic," Beto recalled. Preus had talent for sizing up persons. "Menschenkenner," Beto called it.

Although Jack's catering to Beto struck some as sycophantic jockeying for power, many colleagues saw no obvious ambition in Preus. He seemed too free spirited to want any job laden with burdens although it had become clear he was no slouch. When Beto resigned suddenly in early 1962 to become head of the Texas prison system, he recommended Jack for interim president. Beto was somewhat surprised Preus took the job because he assumed, as others did, that Jack wanted to remain footloose. For all Beto knew he was recommending an independent-minded bureaucrat like himself. Preus became acting president in March. He passed up a trip to Europe with his family that summer to stay close to developments.

At the 1962 Missouri convention in Cleveland, several Missourians cautioned soon-to-be-elected president Oliver Harms against approving Preus. Frederick Geske, longtime Minneapolis pastor, approached Harms prior to the election with a warning that Preus's loyalty potential might be low because of his recent switch from another synod. Nothing personal, Geske noted. He liked Preus. Still, crucial jobs like the seminary head ought to go to tested Missourians. Harms listed noncommitally.

Presidents of Missouri seminaries were elected from candidates nominated by congregations and screened by a faculty committee. Jack received more nominations from the field than all others combined, and he was high on the faculty list. Curiously, in late August he received an offer to be president of Missouri's Concordia Teachers College in Seward, Nebraska. Preus suspected this offer was planted by moderate bureaucrat Walter (Pat) Wolbrecht, the powerful executive secretary of the synod and later archenemy of Preus. Two weeks later, Jack was elected Concordia president by the four-part electorate of President Harms, the synod's board of higher education, the Central Illinois district president, and the seminary board.

Jack went to St. Louis headquarters to sniff the air. He met with President Harms, asking Harms for direction. Harms encouraged Preus, then forty-two and with little administrative experience, to take the Springfield appointment. On September 18, Preus announced his acceptance with the words ". . . the future is extremely bright and I am expecting great strides forward."

In an editorial a few weeks later in the seminary journal, the *Springfielder,* Preus declared Concordia was "not a place for theological one-upmanship or for immature smart alecks." He said Concordia must lead, but not lead astray. Have vision, but always the scriptural vision. Be pious, but not pietistic. Be orthodox, but not obscurantist. Be academic, but not pedantic.

From October 1962 through June 1969, Jack Preus ran Concordia, with its 375 students and 35-member staff. He carried through without serious flaps the major reforms initiated by his predecessors. When he left, Concordia had a standard four-year seminary program recognized by the National Association of Theological Schools.

If Preus had any churchwide image, it was as eager-beaver seminary builder. *Correspondent* magazine, published by the German-Lutheran insurance firm, Aid Association for Lutherans, gave Preus a front-page spread in fall 1965. Typical of the image he was gaining among Missouri laymen, the gushy account of a "bubbling" Preus was headlined: "Busy Springfield President Sets High Standards for a School with a Pastoral Heart" and "Young Theologian with a Ready Wit Supervises a Highly Serious Project."

Seminary-head Preus worked smoothly with his six-member

board of control, particularly with fellow Norwegian Harold Olsen, an attorney and long the bustling "Mr. Lutheran Layman" of Springfield, and Lewis Niemoeller, prominent pastor and Central Illinois district president. Preus never leaned on board members, and never worked for his causes behind their backs. He laid out his preferences on policy questions, winning most but losing some. Unlike Beto, Preus rarely sprang surprises, but he was never accused of being meticulous. While chairman Niemoeller recited opening devotions, Jack often scribbled his "president's report" on the back of an envelope. When detail or further-study items were discussed by the board, Jack nodded without taking notes. Those items later often had a way of getting lost. Preus rarely revealed any overriding theological concerns. To out-of-town board members, he seemed moderate by Missouri standards. He mixed with Protestants and Catholics in quasi-religious settings—not particularly acceptable behavior for hard-line Missourians.

The line about a college president needing to be a ball of fire by day and a bag of wind by night fit Jack Preus. He entertained faculty, students, and visiting dignitaries. He could be gone for days, but he bore in quickly on his return and had his house in order by sunset. As later, his tremendous energy combined with an ability to call signals at the line of scrimmage made his administration carry smoothly.

Preus may even have topped Beto on the civic circuit in Springfield. He was active in Chamber of Commerce, Rotary club, and Capitol City Plan Commission. He was one of four citizens most active in lobbying in late 1966 to bring a four-year state college to Springfield. Political columnist Eugene Callahan noted after the successful campaign that Preus "will take a backseat to few in the understanding of politics." In a city where politics was stable and politicians a dime a dozen, Preus had been noticed.

Meanwhile, he was not a model administrator, as his deans and business manager discovered. They had to spend time undoing some promises Preus made too casually. Preus has often been criticized for his inability to communicate a firm no. Martin Luebke, dean of admissions, had to fend off Preus-inspired applicants unfit for the army, much less ministerial material.

One Missourian in the field was led to believe he could expect job offers from Preus, but, according to a member of the seminary board of control, Preus had never even put his name in the hopper. There were reports of others getting similar impressions of job opportunities from Preus. Once Preus accommodated his buddy Fred Precht with a convenient class time but had to relent when virtually the entire faculty would have been forced to readjust their schedules.

During the worrisome drive for accreditation in the mid-'60s, Preus was sending mixed signals when the tough decisions came on cutting courses. Lorman Petersen, Preus's accreditation trouble-shooter and academic dean, believed his boss was playing both ends against the middle. Preus was encouraging Petersen to make the necessary revisions but at the same time supporting professors (mostly older, mostly conservative) angered by the revised curriculum.

Yet Preus seems to have come through Springfield with his personal credibility and respect intact with most faculty and students. The required critiques written by faculty and students for the accreditation process were mild. Preus got fair to good ratings overall although some revealed they saw far too much ad-lib decision making.

If he was ad-libbing, it worked. As an inexperienced executive in a highly volatile era for higher education, Preus's record was exceptional. He knew the pulse of his institution, and he defused stress situations. He got positive publicity for his seminary. He had no student flare-ups. No professional renegades got a foothold in his school although Jack was beginning after 1966 to play with fire from the right. As to academic progress, Concordia Springfield had begun to attract brighter students who once went to Concordia St. Louis, which ironically ended the decade with a student revolt of sorts. In early 1969 students there forced faculty and administrators to implement curricu-

lum changes during a three-day "peaceful revolution."
But behind the external success were internal patterns indicating the emerging church-politician Preus. There was the pattern of rule by personal popularity. Preus sought and gained intense popularity on a community and an individual basis. His relationship to both students and faculty involved endless polltaking and apparent fishing for assurances. Students and faculty, in informal sessions with Preus, were pumped for their reactions to everything on campus.

He also relied on a certain amount of inside information. John Heussman, librarian who later moved to a secular job, thought Preus knew everyone's secrets. He was always one step ahead. A friendly female librarian who chatted frequently with faculty members kept Preus up to date on faculty concerns. Preus also had student leaders reporting to him almost weekly. They were flattered, and they freely unburdened. Later, some came to the conclusion that Preus must have been unsure of himself to have sought such nonstop feedback.

Notable also was the highly competitive, machismo-flavored attitude Preus displayed toward the St. Louis seminary. His pep talks were reminiscent of a frustrated football coach accusing his team of being sissies in the face of the champs. He appeared to have a very personal stake in besting the lofty number one St. Louis seminary.

Doubtless, he was spurred by the elitist attitudes emanating from Concordia St. Louis. Years later he would allude to smarting under the passing remarks of Arthur Repp, Fuerbringer's lieutenant at the St. Louis seminary and presumed gray eminence. Rambling to a student in April 1974, Preus recounted that Repp once put down Concordia Springfield in an address there. Preus claimed he publicly unbraided Repp. Repp backed down, even apologized, Preus said. He had learned a lesson, he said. The goliaths at St. Louis could be successfully confronted.

Preus seemed to take more than an abstract theologian's interest in the first great liberal-conservative debate in Missouri during that decade—the Norman Habel Genesis debate. Habel, a Bible interpreter at Concordia St. Louis, had composed a "for discussion only/not to be quoted" paper dealing with the Genesis narrative of Adam and Eve's fall from the Garden of Eden. It was a cautious defense of Genesis as "symbolic religious history." Adam and Eve may or may not have been real persons. The serpent may have but probably didn't talk. The important things were the religious truths symbolized by the story, truths determined not by the words themselves but by analogies drawn from Near Eastern religio-cultural knowledge. Habel had first presented his argument to Missouri district presidents and professors in November 1963. It was debated for the next four years, and reaction to it became one way of distinguishing hard-line conservatives from upfield moderates.

Preus gave indications privately he regarded Habel as a symbolic archenemy. In late February 1964, he was then in the process of weeding out three professors at Springfield, among them rising star Richard Jungkuntz. Preus was sounding out Jungkuntz on the possibility of changing ideologies so he could team with Preus to demolish Concordia St. Louis in theological battle. "Help me gut Habel," Jungkuntz recalled Preus's words.

Yet there was enough ambiguity in Preus's Springfield administration to raise the question whether he was more expedient administrator than conservative true believer. Everything he said for public consumption was party-line conservative. But with the more "liberal" students he displayed a cavalier attitude toward the finer points of pure doctrine and enforcement. He often told militantly liberal students in dutch with true-believer faculty and students that *he* wasn't troubled by their views. He simply had to keep the peace. Conservative publisher Herman Otten kept getting these reports on Preus, who never cleared them up to Otten's satisfaction.

Jack even aided his brighter "liberal" graduates once he felt they had learned their lessons in ecclesiastical politesse and would not embarrass him. Craig Settlage, editor of the student newspaper *Quill,* raised conservative ire repeatedly. Far from browbeating Settlage, Preus molded him with keep-the-peace arguments. Preus did not try to convert his liberal-learning students as a true believer presumably would have. When Settlage later took a year's graduate study at Yale University, Preus helped him secure difficult grant money. Despite expressed views left of Missouri center, Settlage was graduated and was placed easily in the ministry. Preus could take administrator's pride in his products regardless of their ideology.

Preus's weeding out of Jungkuntz and two other "liberal" profs, Curtis Huber and Bernhard Kurzweg, later was interpreted widely as evidence that Preus at Springfield was the relentless conservative purist opposed to all moderates on principle. A closer look indicates Preus may have acted out of ego factors and personal convenience as well as ideolog. Moreover, the way Preus disposed of these men reveals more than the fact he did it.

Only a month after he became acting president, Preus sent a letter to Carl Hoffmeyer of Hamler, Ohio, one of several self-appointed guardians of the faith then floating in Missouri. Hoffmeyer, with Otten, ferreted out "liberals" and mailed them doctrinal fitness questionnaires weekly until they got nibbles. Preus wrote (March 14, 1962) Hoffmeyer that Jungkuntz and Huber did not hold various alleged heresies. It was obviously a hurried response, apparently to get contending parties off his back. It was not a totally accurate report of the two men's manifestations to Preus of their beliefs on such matters as the "factual inerrancy" of Scripture, Jungkuntz recalled later. The Preus letter was hardly the way a would-be crusader might be expected to begin a career for theological purity, and it showed Preus was tolerant of the two at first.

Later the two professors, along with Kurzweg, formed a loose, left-leaning cadre which Preus at first found uncomfortable and eventually intolerable. Holed up in "Heresy Hall," the three seemed more a threat to Preus's personal peace of mind than to Missouri orthodoxy. Moreover, the three were not unpopular teachers. It was the Aus pattern again: not "all liberals must go," so much as "all-star liberals must go."

Otten increased his pressure also. He threatened to publish Preus's letter to Hoffmeyer to blow Preus's image with the hyperorthodox. Preus scoffed that Otten had no power over him, but eventually Otten came away with the understanding he would lay off Preus if Preus would indeed start cleaning the "liberals" out of Concordia Springfield.

By grapevine Preus let it be known that the contracts of the three would probably not be renewed. Then these faculty members got several job offers elsewhere which they eventually took. Preus alternately encouraged and discouraged them from taking the other offers—even after he had communicated to them they were unwelcome in their existing postures. To moderates and bureaucrats, Preus wasn't firing anybody or even squeezing them out. To conservatives, he was cleaning house. Preus later was very sensitive to even lighthearted suggestions he had "fired" or even edged out some professors.

The episode also revealed an enduring Preus pattern of disposing of opponents while trying to remain friends, and with no apparent attempt to scuttle them entirely. He insisted that the departing Huber come to dinner at the Preus home. He got weepy and sentimental as he lamented the loss of Huber to his team. Although he was to send out mixed signals on Jungkuntz and later under Preus administration at St. Louis Jungkuntz was dismissed as head of the synod's theology commission, he once argued for a raise for Jungkuntz, and he displayed no obvious vindictiveness. Preus does not appear to have a mean streak although he can be testy when he feels his enemies are treating him meanly or attacking him personally. Again, a kind of ecclesiastical machismo was at work. Can't men forget about a few hard punches during the process, shake hands after the match, and part friends?

When he met in St. Louis as a member of various synodical agencies during the mid-'60s, Preus was known more for his ants-in-pants jitteriness than as a crusader for conservative causes. He sat through many meetings of the synod's top theological agency (Commission on Theology and Church Relations) without raising objections to scores of liberal-leaning interpretations and reports adopted during that period. He chose not to enter battle or even reveal he was a potential antagonist at Missouri headquarters.

Preus had written an editorial in the Springfield seminary journal in 1963 outlining the growing divisions in Missouri. Ways to resolve problems were "complete surrender to Scripture, a willingness to forgive and love our brethren, the avoidance of evasion and the espousal of honesty, the shunning of ecclesiastical politicking and double talk" and avoiding "impatient individualism which fragments the church." If he fell short of practicing all he preached, he certainly avoided "impatient individualism" from his entrance into the synod until 1968. He was member in good standing in the church club.

At the apex of the liberalizing trend in Missouri in 1966, Jack Preus stood on political center. He could have moved either way at that juncture. No bridges had been burned beyond repair, only bridges built. He was trusted by most conservatives and not distrusted by most neutrals and moderates. In eight years he had learned which political stance was appropriate in Missouri and when. He had learned it better than many lifelong Missourians.

9

Coyness Becomes Jack

Four men in the conservative party soon to be in power in the Lutheran Church–Missouri Synod met in late fall of 1968 at the home of Jack Preus in Springfield to launch a publication called "Balance" prior to the synod's convention the following July. As they were settling down to business, Preus asked John Lutze, who was then pastor of Immanuel Lutheran Church in Downers Grove, Illinois, who had driven two others down from Chicago, where his car was parked. Right out front, he was told. Well that might be bad, Preus said. No use arousing suspicion needlessly. Why not move the car away a bit just to be on the safe side.

While once Preus had been bull, now he was fox. Discretion had become the better part of valor as he entered his first great politico-theological campaign. He was beginning to build one-way bridges, but he wanted to stay cautious, and he did. Not even all his Springfield seminary board knew in advance he was the heavily primed dark horse for synod president.

But a politician never wastes his effort on a hostile environment. He must be picking up vibrations. Missouri by the late '60s was emitting mating calls for a crisp leader. Missouri was begging for a Jack Preus, a radicalizing leader, to clear the air of uncertainty lingering after a decade of superficial liberalization. The leader might have been from the left to consolidate the gains of the progressive movement. He might have been from the right to reverse them, but a business-as-usual man was not in the cards.

The Missouri that elected Jack Preus might be portrayed by a hypothetical parallel from the Catholic church of the late '60s. Suppose after the epochal changes of the Second Vatican Council, the American Catholic church was suddenly a democratic institution needing consensus on everything from abolishing Latin masses to electing rectors for seminaries. The result would have been, at best, a terrific ecclesiastical tug-of-war and, at worst, ecclesiastical chaos with demagogues right and left vying for control. The right would have had a deep well of anxiety to tap. The left would have had a progressive momentum to tap. But the Catholic progressive momentum could not have carried the day without decisive leaders and a herculean political effort, if it carried at all.

Roughly that is what developed in the Missouri Synod. Dazed conservatives woke up around 1966 and discovered Missouri was, after all, a democratic institution changeable through politics. Many conservatives were upset, and a few were at the point of bolting Missouri. But before they did anything drastic like pull out, they were going to give the moderate-liberal administration a good old-fashioned run for the money.

Facing rumblings from the right, incumbent president Oliver Harms banked on the progressive momentum to carry Missouri unimpeded into the '70s. He attempted to carry the day with business-as-usual techniques. Not that Harms rolled over politically and played dead on the key issues in Missouri between 1962 and 1969. Far from it. He worked hard and spoke plainly in favor of the most troublesome proposals then before Missouri. He boldly reported out of his administration a convention proposal to join the Lutheran World Federation, despite poor chance for its acceptance. He supported fellowship (intercommunion and board ecumenical ties) with the more liberal American Lutheran Church. Fellowship was being opposed by conservatives on the ground that too many Missouri doctrines would be compromised sooner or later by that new relationship. Harms pulled all the stops to make it acceptable for Missourians by the 1969 convention.

About six months before the 1969 convention, Roland Wiederaenders, Missouri elder statesman and then vice-president, told Harms that the great middle of Missouri was uneasy, the right on the move. Wiederaenders predicted Harms would not be elected and that fellowship would be defeated, but Harms could turn things around by announcing a delay of the fellowship vote. This would assure his reelection and give him time to achieve consensus on fellowship later, Wiederaenders told Harms.

No, Harms responded. A delay was not needed. Sure, there were rumblings. He was getting them every day, but he doubted there was any serious threat of his being dumped. He'd stay with the timetable.

Born in 1901 into a farm family in the tiny central Missouri town of Cole Camp, Harms was a product of the synod system from his third grade to election as full-time vice-president in 1959. He had been pastor and district president in Texas for thirty-three years. He was a stately, white-haired, well-groomed patrician with a trusting and eternally optimistic heart.

But Harms was not without his flaws. Some said he should have been more self-critical. Not unlike the master of a troubled Southern plantation, Harms did not want to admit that his administration was losing its grip on the Missouri Synod. He was no politician for troubled times. He failed to see the signs of the times, or perhaps he failed to act when he saw the signs. If he had been a politician, he would have pushed the fellowship question to a vote at the 1967 convention when most observers believed he had the votes. Harms may not have been a politician at all. He spoke and acted out what he felt was the simple truth. Assuming everybody else was always doing the same, he was victimized literally right and left. He never dreamed the conservative politicians would pull all the stops to dump him, and he never dreamed his moderate friends would turn out as far left as they did. The rise and fall of Oliver Harms had the sense of the tragic about it.

Roland Wiederaenders, veteran Missouri executive, associate of Harms, and keen observer of the dynamics of the body politic, watched this tragedy unfold. Wiederaenders was a theological conservative, but he took a pragmatic and irenic approach to the exercise of synodical authority. He had thought much about synodical authority, some said, because he had hoped he could have his day as Missouri president. He was an "old Missourian," steeped in what some considered the hopelessly romantic expectation that apolitical and gentlemanly consensus could be reached on disputed questions.

Wiederaenders had indicated early that he believed the Harms administration, of which he was a part, was headed for trouble. About eighteen months after Harms was elected Missouri president, Wiederaenders told the council of district presidents: "We have not dealt honestly with our pastors and people. We have refused to state our changing theological position in open, honest, forthright, simple and clear words. Over and over again we said that nothing was changing but all the while we were aware of changes taking place."

What developed from this see-no-change, hear-no-change, speak-no-change policy was ecclesiastical disaster, Wiederaenders was to say in January 1974 at the peak of the Concordia Seminary crisis. "Quite generally our pastors and almost entirely our laity became more and more confused. Confusion led to uncertainty. Uncertainty led to polarization. Polarization destroyed credibility. Loss of credibility destroyed the possibility for meaningful discussion. The loss of meaningful discussion set the stage for a head-on collision."

The credibility problem was created in part by Harms's inadequancies as a theological trouble-shooter at Concordia Seminary, Wiederaenders believed. Isolated complaints from the field about Concordia's drift to the left had been heard during John Behnken's presidency. Behnken had been no match for the professors when he tried to deal frontally, and at times antagonistically, with them. Aware of this, Harms once told Wiederaenders that he was going to control the leftward-moving Concordia professors by the buddy-honor system. He was going to "love them into line," Wiederaenders recalled Harms's words. When he got complaints from rank and file on particular professors, Harms dutifully met with the professors in friendly and informal sessions. He invariably came away convinced the professors still believed the Missouri ideology of an "inerrant" Bible more or less the way he did. He believed that old Missouri doctrines prevailed.

Wiederaenders recalled attending one of those sessions where, he said, he witnessed thinly disguised snickering by several leading professors after Harms had departed from the room. The implication was that the professors considered Harms easy prey for their sophisticated theological suasions. Concordia professors who recall those sessions recount a different spirit. They cherished those times with Harms as forthright teaching and ministering sessions, not as opportunities to mislead, they said. If there was ever mirth after any of those sessions, it was more in the spirit of celebration at winning a brother to their view, or at least convincing him of the wisdom of tolerance on a disputed question that needed more time to jell.

Through the turbulent '60s, Harms seemed to maintain the posture that there was no change at all in old Missouri doctrines and only minor theological changes, that is, changes in how those doctrines were being articulated. Later he was to acknowledge significant theological change and eventually to come to the more realistic assessment that there had been no change in basic Lutheran doctrine.

Missouri was to become so polarized that conservatives and moderates could not agree on the working definitions for *doctrine* and *doctrinal*. Harms was one of the first who seemingly allowed himself to get caught in the semantic cross fire.

Using a position paper developed during the '60s and eventually approved rather routinely by the synod convention in 1969, moderates didn't like to talk about "doctrine*s*" at all but rather about the one "doctrine of the gospel" around which were clustered all the essential "articles of faith." If the traditional Christian articles of faith were maintained, so was the "pure understanding" of the gospel doctrine.

Conservatives tended to use the atomistic language of the seventeenth-century dogmaticians. That terminology suggested that numerous "doctrines" were all of equal importance in the one doctrinal constellation and thus roughly equivalent to what the moderates meant by "articles of faith." So an inerrant Bible or the prohibition against ordaining women, for examples, were essential doctrines or doctrinal issues for conservatives, but neither doctrinal nor articles of faith for the moderates.

The language of that 1969 synod-approved document "Review of the Question 'What is a Doctrine?' " clearly favored this moderate usage and the more flexible moderate position implicit in it. Moderates had come a long way because they were, in effect, defining the terms of the debate. If that document had been consistently applied, moderate professors from Concordia could never have been accused at New Orleans of "false doctrine," only "mistaken exegesis." The document had stated: "A mistaken exegesis of a passage or section of Scripture does not constitute false doctrine, provided it does not conflict with any part of the Christian doctrine."

To suspicious and fearful conservatives, however, Oliver Harms's insistence, first that there were no changes in Missouri doctrine*s* but then later that there was no change in basic Lutheran doctrine, was a signal either that he had come out of the closet at last as a full-blown "moderate" or that he had been fooled by the moderate professors all along. Conservatives generally felt betrayed in this way by Concordia professors and other "liberals." "Liberals" first seemed to be screaming there were no changes in doctrines. But after the Preus revolution smoked them out, "liberals" were boldly admitting their changing views on doctrines but demanding tolerance on the ground that basic doctrine was not at issue.

Ironically also, Harms's greatest administrative help was also his greatest political liability—chief Executive Secretary, Pat Wolbrecht. Savvy, tough, and resolute, Wolbrecht was doubtless one of the best executives Missouri ever had. He had moved up the ranks as pastor and educational administrator to the second highest executive post in 1961 when he was forty-six years old. Wolbrecht had a reputation in many quarters of Missouri as highhanded "boss" who strongly influenced Harms. Even his friends were sensitive about that image. At the 1965 convention in Detroit they advised him to stop striding across the podium platform like a churchly Napoleon. Insiders report that if Wolbrecht was "boss," he was filling vacuums Harms didn't or couldn't fill. Wolbrecht never took command where the commander was active. If it looked like he was hyperactive, it was more because the commander was underactive on more than a few fronts, these observers indicate. Leaning moderate on all issues, Wolbrecht also had his ideological enemies in high places.

With moderates making bold gains at Concordia St. Louis from 1958 through 1962, the surprise was that the conservatives weren't more mobilized from the beginning of the '60s. One irritant was Martin Scharlemann, a New Testament professor as brusque as he was creative. Scharlemann, former military chaplain, punctured all that passed in review of his critical eye—from "liturgical leaning" Lutherans to Billy Graham crusades. But he played with fire when he turned his critical brilliance onto Missouri's reflexive allegiance to an inerrant Bible. In a series of essays for colleagues, he argued against a Bible so brittlely errorless as to be inhuman and magical. He was going to "defend the paradox that the book of God's truth contains errors." Many Missourians would have needed to read no more.

Scharlemann and Concordia were quickly under attack from the right, under pressure from the middle. The storm clouds swirled until the 1962 convention when Scharlemann "withdrew" his essays and apologized for the disruption. He acknowledged "inadequate formulation" but pointedly did not retract. He remained independently moderate until John Tietjen was elected Concordia Seminary president in 1969, at which point Scharlemann began turning loyalist conservative. An early manifestation of conservative dissent came in May 1961 when a group called State of the Church, Inc., met in Milwaukee. With the nude statues in their room of the Hotel Schroeder draped to avoid offending pious eyes, this assembly of about four hundred Lutherans heard warnings against communism in the National Council of Churches and modernism in Missouri. The following year about one hundred fifty met in Chicago. After both meetings, "documentary" books were circulated purportedly proving the various abominations afoot in Missouri and American Christianity. When the group attempted to get a propaganda booth at the Missouri convention in 1962, they first were granted space at about ten times the normal fee. Later Wolbrecht denied the request. Missouri officials eventually published a condescending critique praising the group's motives but dismissing their concerns.

A more broadly based group of conservatives met in St. Louis in late April 1965 under the name Faith Forward—First Concerns. This ad hoc assembly, including ten Missouri district presidents, wanted essentially to prod Harms into enforcing traditional Missouri views on inerrant Scripture. They emphasized they were not antiestablishment. Preus attended this meeting. Later, organizers claimed some seven thousand Missourians had signed their letter of concern to Harms.

Their success can be gauged by the progressive high watermark reached a few months later at the Missouri convention in Detroit, when the majority adopted the ecumenical "Missions Affirmations" platform and approved synod membership in the Lutheran Council. Some conservatives then resigned themselves to the progressive majority and made their uneasy peace with it. Some converted to the moderate-liberal wing, but a hard core went underground after the failure of Faith Forward—First Concerns and were to emerge victorious four years later.

Meanwhile, with the clergy seemingly powerless to alter the liberalizing momentum in their ranks, conservative laymen were faring better. The Lutheran Laymen's League, the dutiful men's auxiliary always there with hats and funds in hand for their clergy, had been moving leftward with the church. But in 1965, with careful politicking, conservatives elected Robert Hirsch as president. Hirsch, a blunt, law-and-order attorney and politician from South Dakota, read the riot act at a September board meeting. League staff, publications, and programming veered right. Several league executives and league hangers-on later began hobnobbing with Jack Preus and promoting his candidacy for clergy president of Missouri.

Clergy and lay protests were mounted in 1965 against the scheduled appearance of folk singer-activist Pete Seeger at a Missouri youth convention in Squaw Valley, California. Initiated by outsiders but quickly appropriated by Missourians, the protest prodded Harms into asking the synodical youth boards to cancel the Seeger appearance, but the boards held firm for Seeger. Some pastors and parents prohibited their wards from attending. About eight hundred protest letters were received, among them a Springfield seminary protest signed by Jack Preus.

Round the Cherry Tree, a religious play scheduled for a Missouri Sunday school convention the next year, was the target of a more successful pressure campaign. The play made light of the doctrine of the virgin birth, conservative activists charged. After careful study, Harms announced the play intended to show that Christians accepted the virgin birth by faith alone, but he backed down anyway, reducing *Round the Cherry Tree* to optional status on the schedule.

For a time, John Warwick Montgomery, polemicist, jousted for conservative Missourians. A converted agnostic with a Ph.D. in library science, he became a Missouri clergyman while at evangelical Trinity Seminary in Deerfield, Illinois. He interrupted a busy schedule of theological dueling (with such notables as Thomas Altizer of God-is-dead fame) to strategize and

coin slogans ("gospel reductionism") for Missouri traditionalists to use against moderates.

In early 1967, Montgomery teamed with self-willed Missouri
conservative Waldo Werning, then director of stewartship for
the South Wisconsin District, to "expose" John Elliot, "liberal"
professor then at Concordia St. Louis. The Preus brothers had
a brief theological romance with Montgomery, but for unexplained reasons, no lasting alliance was formed. Before the 1971
Missouri convention, Montgomery put Jack Preus on notice,
through an article in the national evangelical magazine *Christianity Today:* Preus had better halt the theological drifting
quickly or Missouri was doomed as conservative giant.

But when historians assess power and influence in Missouri
in the '60s, no man right or left will be more important than
journalist Herman Otten. Before the ink was dry on his final
exams at Concordia St. Louis in the late '50s, Otten was accusing professors of heresies. He took his claims up as high as
President Behnken but got nowhere. Instead, he was denied
certification for ordination by Concordia on the ground his
attacks showed unbecoming conduct. Otten got a pastorate
anyway, at tiny Trinity Lutheran Church in New Haven, sixty
miles west of St. Louis and, appropriately, on the bluffs of the
Missouri River. Although he was to influence the mighty Missouri Synod as much as any individual, he never became a
certified minister. He liked his independence under the conservative Preus administration just as much as under a moderate
administration.

Otten, a lean, ascetic man, was unflaggingly devoted to a
literalistic Bible and to enforcing virginally pure allegiance to
the letter of all Missouri doctrine. He began publishing a biweekly newspaper in late 1962. Named *Lutheran News,* it became *Christian News* when made a weekly in 1968. Although
its national circulation was never above 20,000 (compared to a
peak of 550,000 for official publications), the paper had wide
impact. It was "must" reading for all who were trying to keep
ears to the Missouri ground. Otten sought to "expose" mostly

moderates and neutral bureaucrats but taunted conservatives also if they failed to walk his fundamentalist tightrope. Headquartered in an old frame parsonage filled with books and cotton-haired Otten offspring, publisher Otten established an incredible endurance record. With little editorial help and uneven financing, Otten got to the New Haven post office with 540 consecutive editions (twelve years) before he missed one in early 1976 because of a knee injury.

Otten counted on assorted radical columnists, news of moderates piped in by alert conservative agents, and miles of reprints from all sources to fill his cluttered sixteen-page editions. His notations on reprints inspired wags to remark that Otten wasn't born but "photographically reproduced." The jokes, however, weren't on Otten. If his newspaper didn't always get action, it rarely failed to get reaction. Otten perpetually had the establishment on the defensive. He kept traditionalists informed and inflamed—even if they were still politically unorganized.

The hard-core remnant of the Faith Forward—First Concerns group gradually gave up trying to change the Harms administration. They began to politicalize their thinking. About fifteen conservative organizers among them Waldo Werning of Milwaukee and A. O. Gebauer of Chicago, plotted political goals for the 1967 convention in New York. Conservative candidates for elected synodical positions were to be screened, nominated, and eventually promoted among voters at convention time.

A year before the convention, for example, Gebauer telephoned Larry Marquardt, Chicago area Buick dealer and recent conservative Methodist turned crusading Missouri Synod conservative. Identifying himself only as a Missouri pastor, Gebauer quizzed Marquardt on his views. Six months later Gebauer called again, identified himself, and asked if Marquardt would be a candidate for a board position at the Missouri college in River Forest, Illinois. Marquardt agreed. He was elected. Conservatives, overall, made modest inroads at the convention, but most came to realize they would have to work harder.

Under the name United Planning Council (UPC), the hard-core conservatives held regular sessions about every two months at the O'Hare American Inn in suburban Chicago. The informal sessions usually ran a day and a half. The UPC had no officers, printed agendas, or treasury. Identity of members was kept secret because, it was felt, the establishment would paint them as renegades and blacken their reputations if it were known they were openly working for political changes.

Werning and Gebauer were among the most dutiful UPC members. Other faithful participants included three Missouri district presidents: Edwin Weber of Michigan; Karl Barth of Wisconsin, and Ellis Nieting of Iowa. There were several relatively obscure pastors, including a Canadian named John Korcok, Richard Musser of Milwaukee, and John Lutze, pastor from Chicago.

Marquardt was one of the few laymen involved, but for a time Glen Peglau, with Lutheran Laymen League connections, was a member. A Brazil district president who was later discovered by the Preus administration to be black-marketing American currency in Brazil and indulging in bookkeeping irregularities, was among about fifteen others who had direct or indirect ties with the UPC core.

Jack Preus was perhaps the best-known Missourian in the UPC, but he was hardly kingpin. By one account, he missed several meetings between 1967 and 1969 and, typically, arrived late and left early at others. But Preus was there when the crucial decision was made—whom to run for synod president.

By the late '60s, Jack Preus was again toying with the idea of relocation. He was playing out his routine roles but with his heart and mind beginning to stray. He had mastered the challenge of operating a large seminary and he had proved himself on the Springfield civic circuit. He was to signal later that the personal challenge of the Springfield presidency was fading. Preus was growing restive. He began to listen to the would-be

ingmakers, among them Peglau, urging him to make a run for
ne big office.
Combined with restiveness, Preus also had his family
nances fully squared away for the first time. Mother Idella
'reus, who had spent the final years in a Springfield nursing
ome, died in January 1968. A family trust fund established by
ake and composed of stocks and bonds valued at approxi-
1ately five hundred thousand dollars was disbursed, half going
Ͻ Jack Preus. His investment portfolio, developed from that
hare, consisted of New York over-the-counter stocks which
vere screened, he said, as are church funds to preclude any
10rally embarrassing investments such as in munitions or li-
įuor firms.

But the bulk of Preus's total assets is in land. He owns a
·70-acre farm in Benton County in west central Indiana, where
he soil is highly rated for corn and soybeans. (The average
narket value of an acre of farm land there is two thousand
lollars minimum, and average net income to owners from an-
1ual crop yields is one hundred dollars an acre.) Preus assumed
ɔwnership of most of the farm in April 1941 and received the
emainder (160 acres) from mother Idella in February 1967. He
s co-owner of a 160-acre plot in Burke County in the North
)akota coal-mining belt. He is co-owner (since 1960) of the
virtually priceless (because private ownership has since been
·estricted) family lakefront property (221 acres) at Gunflint
∟ake in Ontario.

As he contemplated his first, and potentially risky, church
ɔolitical campaign, Jack Preus did not have financial worries.
His total assets made him perhaps the wealthiest person ever
o be elected to a Lutheran presidency in America. There has
ɔeen speculation that Preus bought some votes on his way to
St. Louis headquarters. There has been speculation on how the
our issues of "Balance" were financed prior to the Denver
:onvention. Yet when Preus says, "I never spent a dime on
ynodical politics," there are reasons to believe it and there is
10 evidence to indicate he did so. The significance of the Preus

wealth lies elsewhere. With it came a personal independence to enter the synodical fray without any long-range worries about finances for his family.

When Jack Preus was first anointed as the conservative party candidate varies according to UPC sources. Perhaps some jockeying went on outside official sessions to explain the discrepancies. Ed Weber, the flat-topped, basso-voiced district president from Fraser, Michigan, and Preus were the frequently discussed choices. Earlier, Wiederaenders had been approached, but he rejected the conservative party overture. Weber was considered the more doctrinally stable, but Preus was regarded as the more able and attractive candidate overall.

By several accounts, there was an unofficial agreement in mid-1968 between some UPC members or hangers-on that Preus would be the man. Later, there were rumors that some political patronage deals had been discussed to get Preus the inside track. But other UPC sources recall the official anointing of Preus later, in March 1969, four months before the convention. They were unaware of any inside deals.

Accounts vary also on whether Preus was an eager or reluctant candidate at the March session. With the enduring Preus pattern of coyness, presumably he was a most reluctant candidate. One UPC member recalled that a half-day was spent discussing various candidates. Preus emerged with the consensus at about noon. Although he never flatly declined, Preus protested mightily during the next twenty-four hours. Weber was the best man, Preus said. Preus was happy at Springfield. Harms was unbeatable. And so on.

"We converged on him that evening in the motel room, trying to demolish every argument he put up," recalled a UPC member. Finally, Preus agreed with the words: "Well, if you fellows feel that strongly about it and you think I've got a chance to get elected, I'll do it. But frankly, I think I'm being offered as a sacrificial lamb."

A pact stipulating precisely what Preus had to do if elected was never formulated by the UPC. Feeling the campaign was a long shot, most never got around to talking about who Preus should hire and fire, but there was a generalized understanding on several points. Fellowship with the American Lutheran Church was to be opposed and thwarted. Pat Wolbrecht's power would have to be reduced. Concordia St. Louis would have to be cleansed of "liberalism," and "liberals" if necessary. All synod agencies and schools must be returned to traditionalism. Jack Preus knew what was expected of him.

Before the July convention, Preus was urged to get exposure, but the campaign relied on local and regional workers to spread the message. Every voting delegate was to be approached on behalf of the conservative ticket. Plans were made for soliciting the delegates again as they arrived for the Denver assembly. Preus recalled later that he didn't take the UPC candidacy seriously. He does recall breaking openly with the Harms administration on the major issues and speaking out.

The UPC studiously avoided any official link with Otten and *Christian News,* but unofficially there were leaks and contacts. Weber was Otten's choice for president, but Otten was persuaded of the political necessity of endorsing Preus to avoid splitting the conservative vote. Independent radical that he was, Otten sniffed at the UPC secrecy and politicking from smoke-filled rooms. He almost told the unofficial envoys to go back to their smoky rooms, but he played ball. Three weeks before the convention, Otten ran a front-page story subtly endorsing Preus. Two other preconvention editions either endorsed Preus outright or contained favorable stories. *Christian News* was dubbed "Jacob's Ladder."

Meanwhile, independent Missouri moderates had been expressing concern. At a rally in Connecticut in March 1968, convened by astute but histrionic-prone Richard Koenig of Boston, warnings were sounded about a "resurgence of fundamentalism" in Missouri. Cited were the Preus brothers, Werning, and Lutheran Laymen's League worker Eugene Bertermann. Soothsaying moderate Richard Neuhaus of Brooklyn wrote in July 1968 that Jack Preus's election was "one fantasy not impossible of realization."

Moderates were not above politicking. They might well have

assured a Harms reelection with a countercampaign, but Harms never gave the signal, saying later he never considered "stooping to politics" on his own behalf. The basic reality was that most moderates just didn't see any serious threat. All odds were on a Harms reelection and a hard-fought, perhaps unsuccessful, campaign for fellowship. At a Chicago meeting several months before the Denver convention, moderate kingpins were generally optimistic. Even the night before the Preus victory, when about thirty delegates met for a free-wheeling assessment session, alarms were ignored. The grand ol' man of progressives, O. P. Kretzmann of Missouri-related Valparaiso University in Indiana, discounted fears of a right-wing revival.

Richard Jungkuntz, who had become the synod's all-purpose theologian, was on the plane to Denver when he first got a queasy feeling about impending revolution. He went immediately to Harms aide-de-camp Arnold Wessler, suggesting Preus's record from the Little Synod be made available to the local press. Wessler and others told him to relax. Preus was no threat; Harms was invincible. Another associate with queasy feelings urged Harms to somehow delay the election until midway through the convention.

UPC and associates had done the best they could. Bypassing the establishment convention committees, a UPC coordinator Wilbert Sohns, Denver-area pastor, had reserved in April the Albany and DeVille Hotels as conservative headquarters and the readily accessible Centre Theater for a worship service featuring (new president?) Preus and Weber. (This later had to be moved to Sohns's suburban church because of flak.)

UPC leaders, disturbed to find many delegates had not been previously solicited, stepped up the politicking. Voters were met at the airport with "hospitality" vans. A two-page directive (labeled "confidential/do not reproduce") contained among other advice: "Forget about the mountains and relaxation until the vote has shown that God has given the blessing he promises." There were truckloads of promotional materials and no shortage of foot soldiers and sympathizers supplied with insig-

nia for ready identification (fishhook lapel pins).
The irony was that the UPC never expected victory with any
certainty. A Denver meeting had been scheduled to plan what
to do after Preus *wasn't* elected. Moreover, the UPC was hardly
the sophisticated machine later fantasied. The Centre Theater
episode was a blunder. Delegate soliciting had been effectively
thwarted in many areas. When a St. Louis daily boldly printed
that the Preus victory had resulted from one of the most sophisticated and heavily financed campaigns in American church
history, more appearance than fact was being reported.

Ironically, the political nonevent raising the biggest hullaba-
loo at Denver was literally a joke—and as much a surprise to
the UPC as to anybody else. In what may well be a first in
American church history, a "Preus for President" advertise-
ment appeared July 11 in the *Denver Post*. The small ad (costing
forty-four dollars) had been placed and signed by one "A (poli-
narios) E. Batiansila," identified as a Missouri pastor from
Keene, New Hampshire. Sure enough, there was a Batiansila.
He had been a 1965 graduate of Concordia Springfield and a
friend of Preus. Conservative, he wanted Preus president. But
the ad was simply a "conspiracy of fun" hatched by him, his
wife, and a fellow pastor. They had first checked with Denver
party caterers on hiring mock campaigners, with derby hats and
canes, to pass out "Preus for President" buttons. Expense pro-
hibiting that, they telephoned the *Post* and placed the ad.

The Batiansilas, on vacation in the Midwest during the convention, had a big laugh when they heard about the monumental flap over their ad. Presumably it could have hurt Preus, who
indeed later called Batiansila several times, grilling him as if he
might be a liberal double-agent. Preus eventually laughed at the
whole episode but pleaded with Batiansila not to carry out a
mock threat to buy a St. Louis newspaper ad welcoming Delpha
Preus as the "First Lady of Lutheranism."

An anxiety-ridden Missouri Synod convened at Currigan
Hall in downtown Denver on Saturday morning, July 12.
Harms, who had delayed a cataract operation, read his presi-

138 Preus of Missouri

dent's report. The delegates were restive, not listening to Harms, as if in guilt at what they were soon to do. With the text noticeably close to his face, the preconvention rumors planted about Harms's health were doubtless given added impact. After his defeat some delegates greeted Harms with a telltale and genuinely surprised "My, you're looking well!"

Election of president was the next business, beginning with the "nominating" ballot. This was normally a pro forma ballot, resulting in a majority for the incumbent. Preliminary results were available to insiders rather quickly that year because of an IBM sorting system.

Harms got the bad news of the first ballot even before Pat Wolbrecht, in a surprise move, discarded his routine report in favor of a frontal attack on the Preus-for-president politicking. In a blistering denunciation, Wolbrecht lamented "the full bag of propaganda devices" and rank politicking which had shamed and divided the church. Heavy soliciting of delegates was against the spirit and probably the letter of synod law. Church politics ought to be done "by the light of day and subject to public scrutiny by all." Then, with a theme contradicting this smoke-filled-room image, Wolbrecht complained that "never before in the annals of the Missouri Synod has there been an open, avowed and public candidacy for the top office of the church."

Jack Preus and many others insist to this day that the Wolbrecht speech was a contributing factor in Preus's election because it backfired. All the talk of Wolbrecht being the "boss" and gray eminence behind Harms took on searing meaning when Wolbrecht used the convention podium for his anti-Preus speech. Preus became the underdog everybody was rooting for. This theory sounds good but holds no water. Delegates had already cast the first ballot which had failed to elect Harms. He was the only "liberal" on the ballot. That meant the strongest conservative would almost surely emerge in later balloting. Politically, Preus was the strongest candidate.

After a lunch break, Preus asked for time at the podium to respond. He said the politicking had not been done at his direction. He said the items in *Christian News* had appeared, deplorably, without his consultation and knowledge. He agreed politicking was undesirable for the church but added that both sides were guilty. The deeply felt reaction to issues, not personalities, was the cause of the politics.

"Nobody runs for the office of president of the Missouri Synod . . . I am no more a candidate for this office than any other eligible pastor in the Missouri Synod. Every man is eligible, and it is up to the delegates to decide what they want. It is not my intent to inject myself into an office which the church has not asked me to serve," Preus said.

True, no one "ran" for office of president. Missouri had no mechanism for that. The man does not seek the office, the office seeks the man. The Missouri myth conjures up notions of "the office" as living entity, with arms, legs, and a mind of its own. Preus was speaking truth because the myth was still intact although under heavy strain. He was denoting an ecclesiastical reality about Missouri.

But Preus's connotation that he drifted into Denver just like any other humble Missouri pastor was surely politician's license. When he implied he was no more candidate than thousands of others, the implication bore little resemblance to reality, as did the implication he was virtually a pawn in a spontaneous "draft Preus" movement. He may indeed have been unaware in all cases of how he was being promoted, and he did not technically promote himself. He did not "run" for office, but he knew better than anyone else at the convention that he was not just another "eligible pastor."

Why should Preus go to such lengths to convince Missouri that Missouri was choosing him rather than he choosing Missouri? Surely more was involved than "political" considerations. Preus apparently wanted to be pushed over the brink. He genuinely seeks to be convinced he is acted on rather than acting. When he said his intent was not to inject himself where he was unwanted, no man ever spoke more honestly. Preus intends always to be wanted.

After his remarks, the nominating ballot results were an-

nounced. Five men were in the running, including Harms,
Preus, and Weber. The second ballot was taken. Persisten
rumor (vote totals were not made public) has it that Preus fel
short of the majority by only one vote. Interestingly, Weber fel
out on that ballot. When a third ballot was taken shortly before
the dinner break, most moderates had grown fearful indeed.

Word was out to insiders even before the announcement o
the Preus victory at the beginning of the Saturday evenin
session. "Liberal" district president Bertwin Fry of Clevelanc
was at a microphone greatly disturbed over the fact that some
committee members might have been unwittingly deprived o
their vote. Fry knew of one such case. Harms dismissed the
appeal. The election of Preus was announced. Harms callec
Preus to the podium. Seated far in the back of the auditorium
he began that "longest walk." Before he took more than a dozen
steps, two delegates challenged the election because of the
heavy politicking. Jack Preus remembered with searing clarity
Fry and the two others. He indicated more than seven years
later that he was deeply hurt by what he saw as these first o
an endless series of attempts by "liberals" to embarrass him.

When Harms ruled the obvious, namely that the Preus elec
tion was valid, most of the twenty-six hundred conventioneer
let loose a thunderous applause as Preus neared the podium
They seemed to be releasing a cheer supressed for a decade
Harms's friends were openly weeping. Moderates were angerec
at the apparent snub of Harms and at their helplessness, a
new and frightening experience after a decade in the ascend
ancy. Some were in virtual shock.

"I am simply overwhelmed," a dry-mouthed Preus told Mis
sourians. He said he could not accept until he resolved hi
doubts about the "propriety" of the events surrounding hi
election. He'd need a chance to consult with his Springfiel
seminary board, as well, he said.

The consultation with the Springfield board, held shortl
afterward, was a pep rally for new President Preus, not a discus
sion of whether he should accept. That was never seriousl

discussed. Also interesting was the line of folks who came by before that meeting started to offer congratulations. Among them was Herman Otten, with a greeting something to the effect of "we did it." Nonetheless, Preus appeared genuinely anxious about what the future might bring if he decided to accept, recalled Martin Wessler, who made the long trek back to the hotel area with Jack and Delpha. Among other things, Preus wondered if moderates would dig up his Little Synod past, and if so, would that hurt his credibility with average Missourians? Delpha was numb, seemingly terrified for the future.

At about eleven o'clock that evening, elder statesman Wiederaenders, Missouri vice-president since 1962, heard a knock. Jack Preus wanted to talk. Wiederaenders offered a drink and they talked until about 2 A.M. Preus said Delpha was unhappy about the election. He also was very uncertain and anxious. He never dreamed of being elected, he said. He just wanted to throw a scare into Harms. What should he do? If he decided to accept, would Wiederaenders serve with him?

Wiederaenders confronted Preus with the facts of the heavy campaigning, the long preconvention scheming, the sharp partisans who had worked to elect Preus. Surely there were a lot of political debts hanging. "Jack, you're obligated up to your neck."

Preus protested mightily. The election was a complete surprise. He knew nothing about any elaborate campaigning or to whom he was supposed to be obligated.

Roland Wiederaenders eventually served as vice-president under Preus for four years, but he pondered long and deeply through the months he saw Preus in action on the psychological dilemma of a man who does not intend to deceive but nonetheless issues conflicting messages.

Early Monday morning Jack Preus announced his acceptance. "In the belief that through the vote of this convention God has called me to the presidency of our church, I feel that I have no choice but to accept," he said.

Missourians at Denver began to moderate, no doubt partly

from collective guilt over having rebuffed Harms. After several rounds of heated earlier debate, the vote on fellowship with the American Lutheran Church was called late Wednesday. Minutes before the balloting, Preus had spoken in favor of an indefinite delay, but he ultimately urged all to vote their conscience. He promised to abide by the convention decision whatever it might be.

Marquardt and several other right-wingers were shocked at the apparent ease with which Preus "capitulated" on the fellowship issue. Preus should have bluffed, at least, they thought. If the president-elect had stood firm, delegates might have been forced to kill the proposal to avoid the embarrassment of passing legislation the chief executive had promised not to implement.

Most conservatives had moderated along with the convention. They were battle weary. Although some wanted to blaze on, most had had enough for one convention. No overkill, they warned. No more overt politics, some even said. There may even have been some guilt surfacing. Most realized also that should fellowship pass it could be turned around as early as the 1971 convention.

The vote margin, 522 for, 438 against, indicated Preus would likely have been stung had he tried an all-out confrontation on fellowship. So mysterious Missouri had elected a conservative but rejected what was ostensibly his anti-ecumenical platform. The guilt theory is usually offered to explain that. Missouri delegates were not so much voting for fellowship with the American Lutheran Church as salving their consciences over Harms. They couldn't send him away in total abjection; so they voted for his platform.

Preus continued to sound a moderate trumpet. He promised there would be no "head rolling" or "hatchet party" against moderates. *Christian News* had a divisive effect, he said. While hardly a "repudiation," the statement made him appear critical of the radical right. He promised to do his part for healing divisions. Jack Preus left Denver with the image of comforting angel rather than avenging angel, but he revealed the shape of things to come for those reading between the lines. The real issue, he told delegates and reporters several times, was not fellowship. The real issue was the proper understanding of and adherence to the doctrine of the inspiration and inerrancy of Scripture. That's what was troubling him. That's what should have been troubling all Lutherans, Preus said.

10

President Preus

If indeed the Preuses were born to rule, Jack Preus initially did not find his destiny easy. He stumbled and groped internally. He briefly experimented with civil religion during the pre-Watergate Nixon administration. He was out of grace at his own headquarters. He had poor relations with the district presidents. He became enfant terrible in high inter-Lutheran circles.

First he said he could live with moderate Pat Wolbrecht, then changed his mind and tried to fire him. Preus tended to personalize the ideological struggle with moderates. Taking the smallest protocol rebuffs as conspiracies to taunt and humiliate him, he saw a moderate behind every tree. He came close to publishing a sweeping attack on leading moderates in the Missouri Synod.

He was suspicious of the press which had greeted him unkindly and, in some cases, unfairly. Curiously, he wavered between stonewalling and telling all, a pattern that applied to much of his early administrative style toward the church as well. He was either saying nothing or saying too much. He had a mysterious way of being out of town when conflagrations occurred. He began a pattern of trying to unify a polarized church by, in his own words, "talking out of both sides of [his] mouth." He began using a stock "this controversy will soon be over" pose which got to be pretty old after seven years of escalation toward schism.

Delpha was engaged in a confrontation with a St. Louis Lutheran high school during the early months in St. Louis. Conservatives limped at the 1971 convention. Ad-libbing his way, Preus seemed in over his head. Apparently genuine, he privately broached the possibility of resigning.

But if Preus didn't wear the crown gracefully, he wore it effectively. He achieved the agenda he had set, mobilizing Missouri to enforce traditional views of the inerrancy of Scripture. His first four-year term ended in raw political success. Reelected handily at the New Orleans convention, he went on to put the St. Louis seminary under foot and conservative machinery in gear virtually everywhere.

New Orleans was so outrageously successful one wondered if Preus was posing as peevish stumblebum to divert moderates. Apparently not. The personal hurts and insecurities were genuine. "They [moderates] came mighty close to driving me out," Preus remarked years later. Preus had proved smarter, tougher, and more committed than his opponents in winning the ecclesiastical prize of Missouri.

The Preuses moved to a new home in St. Louis the summer of 1969. A modest thirty-one-thousand-dollar house in a near northwest suburb and within range of airport noise was purchased for them. With all Preus children away four years later, Jack and Delpha moved to the high-rise Mansion House Apartments on the Mississippi riverfront and a few steps from synod headquarters.

Jack brought informality to his new $28,000-a-year (later, $32,500) job. He came to his office in Hush Puppies and red short-sleeved shirts. When advised to dress presidentially, Preus bought cut-rate suits to his adviser's horror. But Preus soon took naturally to pin-stripe, Protestant executive dress. His frugal unpretentiousness endured. Never demanding fancy hotels, he often stayed in homes of hosts when he traveled. Enemies could never charge him with regal living off the presidential office although both moderates and conservatives suggested he preside more and travel less.

With few friends in high places, the keys to his early survival were treasurer Milton Carpenter and canon lawyer Herbert Mueller. Layman Carpenter, then sixty-four, was an old-school Democratic politician, serving first as comptroller of St. Louis and later as revenue director of the state of Missouri. But he was waning, having been defeated in a primary for U.S. Representative in 1968.

Elected synod treasurer in 1962, Carpenter had expanded the position enormously. He was an assiduous fiscal agent but carped and dealt too secretively for some Missourians. He was pragmatic and advised Preus accordingly.

Carpenter supported the "spoils system" in that he believed a synod president should pick executives. He once compared this to statehouse politics: The Democrats were defeated, now headquarters should adjust to the Republicans; yet he daydreamed of an efficient, apolitical system. He alluded admiringly to the Mormon system of twelve men with absolute authority elected for life. No political instability or inefficiency there. Missouri presidents by contrast had to negotiate with autonomous boards and think always of reelection. Carpenter noted that Missouri presidents (Preus included) were the only officials in the Western world who would travel two thousand miles to speak to twenty constituents.

Prone to centralization, Carpenter fit well in the Preus authoritarian administration. He became a Preus loyalist. He rarely missed an opportunity to make Preus look good although Carpenter realized better than most that Preus was not the smooth politician that he was criticized for being.

Herb Mueller, Chicago-area pastor and secretary of the synod since 1965, had moved to St. Louis after the Preus election. Kindly, fastidious, and elder-brother type, Mueller was known to have been disturbed by the free-wheeling '60s. He assumed the role of procedural and canon law expert, carrying clout in the critical Commission on Constitutional Matters, the appeals court for the Missouri Synod. Disgruntled moderates were to conclude Preus could do nothing that wouldn't be declared constitutional as long as Mueller was around.

Disdain was mutual between new president Preus and most liberal-leaning executives. Preus sensed they were Wolbrecht's allies, unfriendly and bitterly anti-Preus rather than sentimentally pro-Harms. Preus saw some as whiners prone to cutting him down behind his back and watching gleefully as he stumbled. He complained often in the early days of the cruel fate of being elected president without power to name his own cabinet. He hinted privately he might try to establish the practice of requesting resignations from all department executives.

Preus told editor-executive Harold Rast in midfall 1969, "All you guys want me to do is bare my bottom so you can take a whack at it." Preus long remembered Wolbrecht's effrontery in inviting him to a party at Wolbrecht's for moderate newcomer John Tietjen when no similar party was planned for Preus. Delpha particularly bristled at that.

The only headquarters "reception" for the Preuses was in late September. It was a Kool-Aid and cookies affair squeezed between board of directors' sessions. Having to drive herself in, Delpha missed an exit and wound up in the East St. Louis stockyards on the wrong side of the Mississippi River. Arriving annoyed at that, she then had to endure cold-fish handshakes and plastic smiles. Some staff had managed to be busy elsewhere. Others slipped through the reception line and quickly departed. Most staff stayed within their departmental groups and only a few gathered round the Preuses.

Many headquarters executives could see only a crass, glib ward heeler whose politicking had put out gentleman Harms. Preus seemed not to want or respect their views. He had his own agenda for which they were largely marginal. When he attended monthly, morale-booster meetings, he often came late and left early. Frequently pacing in the front of the room, Preus fielded questions as if he were a hurried wartime general needing urgently to move to the next front. He once had a coughing spell just as a question was posed. Walking out for a drink of water, he returned and asked the stunned questioner to repeat. Literally, Preus could take them or leave them.

The monthly staff sessions grew irregular after the New Orleans convention. They occasionally produced apparent breakthroughs which, however, invariably degenerated. At the end of an enthusiastic exchange in the spring of 1974, hearts were warmed because Jack had spoken so openly and had come so close to promising an end to conservative politicking and stacking of boards. Then it was announced that Robert Preus had just been elected president of Concordia Springfield seminary. "Well what do you know about that!" Jack responded with a reflexive grin.

As at Springfield, Preus always had an open door for one-to-one sessions. There he fared much better, building the trust and tolerance he eventually commanded among the staff. Overall, he wooed most into passive neutrality and some into loyalty.

With his thirteen-member lay-dominated board of directors, Preus sought and gained good relations although initially he displayed annoying jitteriness and insecurity. Preus has always managed to make sense with leading-laymen types, largely because of his pragmatic instincts toward church administration. At work also was a fierce Missouri loyalty, an "our president right or wrong" attitude, and an incredible financial stability holding through all the brinkmanship. If the money had dried up, Preus might have had trouble with his board of directors. Previous presidents had limited this board, essentially a fiscal control unit, but Preus brought it to the fore in his ecclesiastical forays. While he never exactly had this board on a leash, it supported him when the crunches came.

The initial Wolbrecht-Preus relationship was ambiguous. Wolbrecht, as did some others, seemed to think Preus could be tamed. Preus seemed to think Wolbrecht could be tamed. Wolbrecht recalled a long flight in August during which Preus was trial-ballooning. "Pat, you cooperate with me and we can run this church for a generation," Wolbrecht recalled the message.

Because of the typical Preus art of surprise, it was soon clear who was tamer and who tamee. Wolbrecht was in a Houston hotel room with Preus in early September when Preus got a phone call. Offhandedly, Preus remarked the call was from an applicant seeking Wolbrecht's job. Yet before a late September board of directors' meeting, Preus promised Wolbrecht he would fight to keep him. On the second day of the board session, the agenda was devoted to a Preus request that Wolbrecht be terminated. He was, but the board reconsidered after Wolbrecht mentioned legal counsel. He survived the reconsideration by one vote.

Wolbrecht got a long-distance call one evening the next week from a maudlin, apologetic Preus. Jack explained that the evening before the action, board members Milton Carpenter, Robert Hirsch, and St. Louis pastor Gerhard Nitz had paid a courtesy call at the Preus home. Delpha was convinced Wolbrecht must go. As was their custom, he and Delpha got in their car, bought some ice cream, and drove around talking it out. Delpha convinced him, Jack told Wolbrecht.

Delpha persisted after Wolbrecht's survival. She was so disconcerted that Jack even had Roland Wiederaenders try to assure her that Wolbrecht's continued presence was workable. Months later, at the 1971 convention, Wolbrecht's position was abolished. He was presumably eligible for a new, restricted post of administrative officer, but it was clear he was not wanted. He became president of a Lutheran Church in America seminary in Chicago, a career cut short later by illness.

The Preusian rule by surprise was employed exquisitely in the termination of Richard Jungkuntz. He had offended some on the Missouri theological commission by releasing opinions without "adequate" clearance, but at the October 1969 commission meeting, no serious complaints were raised. Everybody who spoke, spoke favorably or in neutral terms, but when the votes were counted, he was out. Bewildered moderates looked at one another in surprised shock. It was star-chamber dealing all the way, they thought. Later, as they reflected, they admitted it should not have been such a big surprise because, after all, back in 1965 Jungkuntz had originally been elected by only a one-vote margin.

Preus had no overt part in this action. But the extent to which conservatives tap-danced around the reasons for the Jungkuntz termination left little doubt that the Preus administration considered Jungkuntz too liberal. The house cleaning was beginning in earnest. Jungkuntz considered an appeal, even drawing up a formal document with the aid of an attorney, but he declined to fight his termination in church courts. Within a year, he became an educational administrator for an American Lutheran Church college in Washington state. Indirectly, Preus had put in a good word for Jungkuntz's application there.

The ambivalence of Preus toward the district presidents was symptomatic of much of his early administration. He burned hot, then turned cool. He wrote them off, then went to the other extreme of promising to integrate them into the upper echelons of his administration. He took great patience in explaining—after the fact—what he was doing. Never taunting or assaulting them, he strove in his way to be club member. But he found this most widely representative assembly of Missouri clerical leaders too unwieldy and much more difficult to deal with than mixed or lay-dominated boards. Preus snorted more than once that the council couldn't agree on the time of day, which, incidentally, was also charged by moderates trying to mobilize the council. Most council actions came out ambiguous or in opposition to Preus. Council leadership was chiefly responsible at the 1971 convention for a compromise that gutted Preus's attempt to make convention resolutions on doctrine binding on all members.

In Missouri's thirty-eight jurisdictional districts, pastors were elected by their regions to the bishoplike office of district president. (Missouri does not use the term *bishop*.) The council of presidents had no standing authority on other than minor matters. The council meets three times a year or when called to special sessions by the synod president or one-third of the members. Nonetheless, one of those minor matters, the routine certification of new pastors, became politically crucial after Seminex was formed. And the district presidents carried moral weight and were helpful for Preus goodwill among clergy. Before the virtual standoff, the Preus-council relationship resembled the Wolbrecht-Preus relationship. Basically a moderate-minded group, the council figured it could tame tiger Preus while Preus figured he could tame it. Efforts were made by the council to sanitize Preus. In the fall of 1969, the council unanimously condemned Otten's *Christian News*—an action Otten regarded as hypocrisy by Preus and the right-wing district presidents. Motivation for this action was to help clean up the Preus image and nudge him to the middle, but it was Preus who was to do most of the taming. Moderate district presidents would seemingly have been no match for Preus even if they had had the autonomy needed to defy him. In presession pep talks among themselves, some district presidents would indicate they were going to give Preus hell for sure this time. They were going to pin him in the corner. They were going to get a commitment from him, but Jack Preus slipped by them, at least until the schismatic showdowns developed after mid-1975.

Meanwhile, Delpha's confrontations with the liberal-moderate authorities at Lutheran North High School might have generated much more heat had they become public knowledge. Somehow this explosive story was never discovered by the St. Louis media. At any rate, the episode served to confirm suspicions the Preuses had for Missouri moderates and the moderates for the Preuses.

Two Preus children, Jack, Jr., and Margaret (Peggy), were enrolled at the school. Early in the fall of 1969, Delpha and two other mothers had been shocked by use of an untraditional translation of the Apostles' Creed in Peggy's religion class taught by part-timer James Fackler, a moderate pastor. The phrase "Jesus descended into hell" had been replaced by "he went to the dead." This raised a whole host of questions in Delpha's mind about theories of afterlife taught at the school.

She pressed Fackler and Art Repp, Jr., religion department head, on a full range of presumed false teachings. She persisted until the following June, but she got no satisfaction from various boards and officials. She unsuccessfully sought to have her children exempted from religion classes. Finally, she withdrew Peggy and Jack, Jr., from the school although Jack later returned and graduated there, apparently with parental approval.

It was a classic case of righteously conservative and fearful mothers meeting equally righteous and arrogant moderates. An anxious, determined Delpha saw only flip religion teachers playing with the simple catechism faith she held and wanted for her children. When she asked Repp whether he believed Mary was a virgin, Delpha was in no mood for "only she knows" as an answer. When she wanted clarifications, she was in no mood for Fackler's "your husband was not elected pope!"

For their part, Repp and company saw only an icy steel heresy-hunter whose absolute self-possession sent shivers down the back. Delpha seemed intent on revamping the school's religion instruction along ultraorthodox lines. She wanted absolute purity. She was out to destroy what was not acceptable by her standards. Justified or not, Repp and company had experienced what George Aus had experienced, and had learned never to underestimate a Preus.

Jack Preus never got directly involved in this affair although he made several overtures and later criticized the moderates. The episode served mainly to drive another wedge between the Preuses and the liberal-moderate establishment—if one were needed. Both parties told horror stories about the boorishness of the other.

The tensions of being married to an increasingly controversial churchman were not easy for Delpha, who is intrinsically shy. The couple had few close friends to help lighten the load of bitter invective that flowed during peak periods of the Missouri war. Delpha remembered a non-Lutheran woman who called after New Orleans to ask her how it felt to be married to such a horrible man. She remembered the petty practical jokes, such as mysteriously arriving subscriptions to such magazines as *Playboy*. She was offended by the injustice of John Tietjen and company returning from New Orleans in an orgy of publicity while her husband, the real victor at New Orleans, had to slink home from the airport unnoticed.

But she reconciled much of this, at least theoretically. The bitterness from Preus Lutheran enemies was understandable, she has said, because the plans of many families had been disrupted by the Preus election and agenda for the church. She understood that would cause a lashing out. The lopsided publicity was understandable too, once one realized moderates planned all that while conservatives quietly avoided publicity.

If Missourians were not ready for Jack Preus, the stuffy, diligent inter-Lutheran establishment in New York was doubly unprepared. Both his style and theological agenda clashed with the ecumenical goals and politesse of the Lutheran Council in the USA and of the leaders of the major Lutheran denominations. No rank isolationist, Preus wanted cooperation on practical matters. He could plunge into council-related social projects as well or better than the more liberal Lutheran presidents— as he did briefly with the 1975 Vietnamese resettlement program run by Lutherans. Often in the position of defending the council to suspicious Missourians, Preus sought to anchor Missouri in it. Moreover, he seemed genuinely to enjoy wielding power in high council assembly.

But Preus did not hold the club commitment to Lutheran unity, and he displayed no burning desire to strengthen the council beyond limited goals. Insiders felt Preus wanted chiefly a noncontroversial, ecumenically gutless council. Preus wanted a clearinghouse where Missouri browsed for needed goods, then went home. He seemed ambivalent or bored with ecumenical goals.

At the first executive meeting he attended, Preus, arriving late, plopped his feet on a tabletop. It was symptomatic of his cavalier approach, particularly irksome to sober, hyperprofes-

sional churchman Robert Marshall of the Lutheran Church in
America. Preus often forgot to bring or read agendas. He
needed rebriefing from one meeting to the next. Overall, he
seemed to be signaling: "I'm taking all this on my own terms,
and not very seriously at that."

What Preus took seriously was the thorough coverage the
council's news bureau gave to the soap-opera-like Missouri war.
Preus felt the bureau's blow-by-blow accounts were a thinly
veiled put-down by the Eastern elite. The Preus administration
eventually eliminated Missouri funding for the news service and
reduced other council funding as troubles intensified in Missouri ranks.

Preus's espousal of conservative principles did less to under-
cut his inter-Lutheran standing than his habitual bluster followed by apparent backtracking. Friendly, good-natured Jack
did not want to be odd man out in New York. He occasionally
promised more than he delivered. He allowed items to pass
without his criticism, then later appeared to be sandbagging
them.

Lutheran ecumenist Preus is richly portrayed by his handling
of the installation ceremony in November 1974 of George Harkins, top council executive. Harkins meticulously cleared with
Preus the arrangements for a religious service to involve Preus,
Marshall, and cousin David Preus. Saying initially there would
be no problems with his full participation, Jack sent a confirmation letter fourteen days before the event with this message: "I
will be there with bells on." But seven days later, he canceled,
mentioning vaguely he was getting flak from right-wingers.
Present at the service in the front pew, he gave a formal greeting
after the service. This from a man who had conducted an
ecumenical service at the Nixon White House did not please
Lutheran ecumenists.

In 1900 there had been more than twenty Lutheran synods
in America. Most were the result of ethnic, language, and pecu-
liar religious traditions from mother countries. But common
understanding of ministry, agreement on most theological is-

sues, and mutual acceptance of forms of church government had resulted in mergers over the years. By 1969 almost all American Lutherans were in the three large denominations: Lutheran Church in America; the Lutheran Church–Missouri Synod, and the American Lutheran Church. There was hope in some quarters that the big three might carry American Lutheranism to what seemed its logical and theological conclusion— organic unity.

For good or ill, the Preus regime has anchored firmly the standoff between conservative Missouri and the two more liberal denominations, Lutheran Church in America and the American Lutheran Church. The great Missouri war has complicated the response of the other two churches. On the one hand, there is even greater pull toward the traditional stance of bending over backward to please conservative Missourians. On the other, there is new thrust to write off Missouri forever. By electing Preus and giving him all he wanted, some say it is clear Missouri has shown the desire to live or die on its own and wants no part of the Lutheran mainstream. With either reaction, the dreams for a more unified, perhaps even united, Lutheranism in America have been shelved indefinitely.

Any appraisal of Jack Preus's style and agenda for his inter-Lutheran dealings must be balanced by several observations. Jack is not the first person to be bored to distraction by the Lutheran Council bureaucracy or to have had trouble reading council reports. Lutheran councilese has put many a non-Missourian to sleep as well.

Second, what is so bad about an ultrapragmatic council, a clearinghouse for services? The fever for organic unity has peaked everywhere as most American Protestant churches move into a stage of seeking unity in diversity rather than a uniformity which abolishes diversity. Not that Preus's Missouri runs any risk of seriously considering either of those options, but to assume the élan of church history moves automatically with all the current objectives of the Lutheran establishment for its council is arrogant. Preus vis-à-vis the council may well stubbornly represent the future, not the past.

Finally, there seems to exist in the power centers of world Lutheranism an unarticulated assumption that when Preus Missourians criticize excesses they perceive in the moderate denominations, that is irresponsible obscurantism, while criticism from the moderate churches to Missouri is responsible brotherly advice. Preus's Missouri cannot be right on anything —and if it is, it's probably for the wrong reason.

Preus may ultimately have much to contribute to Lutheran geopolitics, but a Preus who could not keep his own house in order had little to contribute toward solving old problems or generating new models for the wider Lutheran executives. If one expected to influence the club, one had first to be recognizable as club member. In both personal style and theological agenda, Preus was an outsider. Lutheran potentates found it hard to deal with an Isaiah from the right who seemed to them to be running nude through the current theological marketplace.

The Jack Preus foray into civil religion was as spectacular as it was brief and innocuous. On February 1, 1971, in Washington, Preus announced a massive pan-Christian effort to free or improve the lot of American prisoners of war in North Vietnam. A modern-day "crusade," he called it. Citing names like Norman Vincent Peale and Billy Graham, Preus said he was going to enlist leading American churchmen to accompany him to Hanoi.

Six days later Preus conducted the monthly Nixon religious service in the White House East Room. His sermon on "The Power of Prayer in the Space Age" was more Peale than Preus. He spent several weekends in Washington preparing for the trip. In late March he and three relatively obscure churchmen departed for a three-week journey with hopes of touring POW camps. After valiant efforts failed to open doors to Hanoi, the group returned from their tour in the Far East and European capitols, including a papal audience in Rome.

There followed a Washington press conference (held in an American Legion hall and generally ignored by the media) and a personal report to Nixon. That was the end of it. The effort made more news than history. Preus has not returned to political Washington.

State Department sources recalled that the Preus trip did no harm and probably helped in the wider effort to improve treatment of POW's by generating public pressures on Hanoi. The government was then tolerating and even encouraging freelance diplomacy by amateurs. Preus impressed government officials with his sophisticated eagerness and perception.

Preus took a lot of shots for his POW efforts, particularly slurs that it was gimmickery to take heat off domestic problems in Missouri. Responding to those criticisms in late April 1971, Preus told a reporter: "We've got some people in this church that, if I came out for motherhood, they'd say I'm for the population bomb, or if I came out for apple pie, they'd say I'm against the grape growers in California." No evidence has come to light that Preus entered his POW crusade with anything but genuine motivation to do good. Moreover, an ecumenical mission of the sort envisioned was rather innovative for a midwestern-based churchman.

Yet there were revealing aspects about this episode. Politically, POW crusades were safe, hopeless causes. Anything else said or done about the Vietnamese War was political quicksand. Despite the ecumenical intent, Preus planned and executed his crusade virtually as an independent. Missourians were not consulted and other Lutherans were ignored in the planning—even though Preus was presumably representing them. Preus's special assistant and crusade designer was a conservative propagandist named William Hecht. Missouri pastor turned secular politico, Hecht was associated at the time with the anti-Communist American Security Council. The Hecht connection made it virtually certain no doors would open in Hanoi. Hecht had impressed Preus with his public relations abilities, and Hecht left little doubt during his brief stay around St. Louis headquarters that his chief duty was improving the visibility of his boss. Even some of his friends thought Jack was desperate to latch onto Hecht and traipse off on a "crusade."

Although technically within limits of Missouri rules, Preus's White House service drew some criticism on ground of its "unionistic" flavor. Moderates secretly cheered it because they thought it would get Preus in deep trouble with right-wingers and because they liked the precedent-setting tone. If Preus was preaching at an utterly nonconfessional setting of the Nixon White House, he would have a hard time condemning them for worshiping with other Lutherans. Preus's "crusade" also brought some backhanded praise from several moderate district presidents. Admiring Preus's ability to move in diplomatic circles, several presidents lightheartedly discussed contacting the Nixon White House to urge that Preus be named U.S. ambassador to Norway. It would, they joked among themselves, be a great service to both the country and their church.

Although he has never tried it again on such a scale, the Preus foray into civil religion, like much he did, probably won him a thousand votes for every one lost. The finer points of doctrine tend to fade when the president of one's church is on the front page.

Preus's popularity with Missouri laymen was enhanced by his preaching and communicating abilities. His forté was always the nonsacramental fireside chat, which he laced with zippy yarns, jokes, and punchy similes. ("This meeting's getting nowhere . . . I feel like a bilious porcupine with a hangover.") He felt constrained by formal presentations prepared by his staff. Reading papers was never his style. He sought a chemical reaction with his audience and wanted rapport, but his folksy style produced a few embarrassing moments through the years. In an ecumenical Springfield audience, President Preus once told the joke about the young priest asking the monsignor if it was acceptable to kiss a nun. "As long as you don't get into the habit," was the punch line.

Preus's sermons were marked by simplicity and clarity. He

buttressed his biblical themes with various related biblical passages, which he knew by heart and which he could make come alive with graphic descriptions, but he tended toward an analytical and moral rather than a personal approach to Bible themes. Critics noted that Preus's preaching was consistent with his theology: It reflected man's need to conform to Bible texts, not conforming Bible texts to man's needs.

Despite his built-in handicap with a liberal-leaning secular press, Preus fared well. With rare exceptions, he was gracious and as forthright as could be expected of a man on a tightrope. Syndicated religion columnist Lester Kinsolving sent Preus into a rage more than once, but Kinsolving had done that to even seasoned churchmen. Preus resented the editorializing captions in *Newsweek* dubbing him a "Lutheran Pope." He complained of a few biased newspaper reporters, once comparing them to propagandists in the Hitlerian tradition.

For a controversial churchman, Preus actually was treated rather superficially by the secular and religious press. About the only person with adequate conservative sources to try to criticize Preus fairly was Herman Otten. Preus wavered on just how to handle Otten. He once pointed out the window of his fifteenth-floor headquarters office to the Mississippi River, telling an executive he paid no more attention to Otten than a fish swimming down there in those muddy waters. Other times he railed against Otten for constantly stirring the pot. Martin Mueller, editor of the official *Lutheran Witness-Reporter,* recalled Jack remarking once: "Can't you print all the news so we can put Otten out of business?"

Although to wane later, Preus's sensitivity to criticism and his fortress mentality were in ample supply earlier. He was not a thick-skinned reformer. Much time and energy was spent trying to protect the Preus image from bitter but impotent opponents who spent their time coining nicknames such as "Chairman JAO." Preus seemed tempted to spend more time extracting public apologies than waging true ideological war. The slashing personal invective against Preus from the pen of moderate Wayne Saffen of Chicago consumed time of Missouri's theology commission for months.

The new Missouri president seemed abnormally sensitive to living in a glass house, his every move observed and recorded. As controversial churchman he seemed not to realize his actions constituted semipublic business. He resented any tape recording of which he was unaware. In the fall of 1969, he scolded a moderate Lutheran reporter for taping his remarks at a *public* pastors' conference.

In September 1972, the St. Louis editors of a moderate newsletter were called on the carpet by Preus and his vice-presidents. As the meeting began, Preus abruptly stood up. He glared at moderate layman Leslie Kuhlmann and asked excitedly, "Have you got a tape recorder under there?" A startled and apologetic Kuhlmann brought his hands up from under the table and displayed his fingernail clipper.

In a backhanded acknowledgment that he considered himself in all-out war, Preus had a tendency to maximize information in and minimize information out. He was not adverse to accepting privileged information on moderates supplied by conservative sources. During late 1970 and much of 1971, a secretary of moderate Dean Lueking, pastor of Grace Lutheran Church, River Forest, Illinois, was leaking crucial documents and private correspondence to conservative Waldo Werning. Werning fed them to Preus. The spy system led to embarrassing moments for the bemused Lueking. Moderates who drew up a list of sympathizers one Saturday at Lueking's church later discovered Preus had the list the following Monday. Lueking had to send out a note to moderates warning them that Preus had seen the list whether they wanted him to see it or not. Once also Preus administrators cross-examined moderates with the moderates' own "secret" reports.

When Lueking privately confronted Preus on the leaks, Preus responded that if Lueking were ever Missouri president he'd discover how easily inside information flows in.

Lueking had questioned his staff several times. When the

leaks continued, all were requested to take a lie detector test in early August 1971. When her turn came, a middle-aged secretary declined to submit. She left Lueking's church and wasn't seen there again. The conservative myth is that she told Lueking, in effect, "I'll take a lie detector test if you will."

The extent to which the early Preus administration was as much defense of Preus as enhancement of the causes of Missouri is reflected in the "White Paper" episode. Prepared partly from leaks, anonymous letters, and secret tape recordings, this document was a ringing defense of Preus over against leading moderate enemies. Hoping to fight the underground rumor-war against him with all the moral weight of his office, Preus was eager to publish at least the summary of this "White Paper." He was eventually dissuaded in part because the writer of the report balked against such use.

The document was officially entitled "A Summary of the Actions and Responses Concerning 'A Declaration of Determination.' " The "declaration" referred to was an anti-Preus statement first circulated by the Lueking-Fry moderates in late 1970. The relatively mild summary was approximately thirty pages long, but the supporting "documentation" ran on for more than two hundred pages. On one level, Preus was doing no more than exercising his moral right of self-defense. Moderates were not known for holding back information they had on Preus. More significant is the how and the why of what was done.

Preus had requisitioned a staff member from another headquarters department under the pretext the man was to work on the routine convention workbook. Preus ordered ultrasecrecy during the preparation of the "White Paper." Copies were provided to his vice-presidents and board of directors. Pleased with the document's favorable impact on his high level colleagues, Preus hoped to publish it for the church. The staff member who wrote it consulted an attorney as part of his effort to prevent its publication.

The Yankee church-builder and activist instincts in Jack

Preus were to emerge most noticeably in his lavish support for evangelism, world missions, and social concerns. He was an eager, can-do churchman. He rarely missed an opportunity to urge his colleagues to press on with Kingdom building. He spoke frequently and passionately of what he cherished most— a Missouri aglow with evangelistic and missionary zeal.

Under Preus, the Missouri Synod joined the pan-Christian "Key '73" evangelism program. Concordia Publishing House contributed substantially to this effort through publishing services. Missouri support came despite the obvious "unionistic" overtones of participating with other Christians. Preus supported the Billy Graham Crusade in St. Louis in November 1973.

Preus delighted in the Missouri missionary efforts in twenty foreign countries and traveled to the mission fields every chance he had. His administration had serious troubles with its moderate mission staff in 1974. Six of the headquarters mission staff of eighteen resigned to protest actions of the conservative board headed by the ubiquitous Waldo Werning.

But Preus had worked to prevent this disruption. He later pushed for reforms in the structure of Missouri's mission agency, many of which were adopted in 1975. One change declared the synod president the "chief ecumenical officer" in relation to Lutheran missionary churches.

Pragmatist Preus was never a blind ideologue on practical mission questions. Inter-Lutheran and inter-Christian enterprises were accepted as long as Missouri missioners didn't flaunt untraditional approaches. Preus told missionary executives, in effect, "We'll give you the operating space you need— just don't get us in trouble back home with the right-wingers."

Preus never hedged on civil rights for blacks. He was attuned to concerns of black churchmen. With typical Preus zest, he spent a week living in a Chicago black community as participant in a Lutheran Human Relations Association program designed to immerse white Lutherans in black culture. It was the kind of gesture black Lutheran leaders appreciated and remembered—even if they found it increasingly difficult in later years to tie into the authoritarian Preus regime.

Yet the Preus enthusiasm and leadership in these areas of churchmanship often had an unrealistic air. He sounded like a wartime president promising the nation both guns and butter —when everybody knew it had to be one or the other. The reality at hand was a theological civil war. Preus had declared to the world in early 1972 that Missouri "faces a great crisis of faith and confession" because of alleged false doctrine entrenched at Concordia Seminary and elsewhere in the denomination. After the formation of Seminex, Preus talked of a "constitutional crisis" set off by those district presidents and congregations accepting Seminex graduates in defiance of synod bylaws.

With so many Preus-proclaimed crises going on, the Preus drumbeating for evangelism, world missions, and social ministry sounded surrealistic. An ambassador announcing in one breath that his country's currency is shaky and in the next breath urging stepped-up programs to circulate that currency should hardly be surprised if he has a credibity problem. One cannot consistently declare his house is crumbling and then go go on as if times were normal.

For all his cloud-nine fervor each time he returned from mission fields, Preus revealed an "ugly American" attitude toward foreign nationals. He remarked repeatedly to associates about the astuteness of native Lutheran clergy and leaders—as if he were surprised any talent existed in the Third World. In late 1975 after a three-week tour that included stops in the black African nations, Preus reported his impressions to headquarters executives. He managed to slip in descriptions of black Africans at worship—with their bare bottoms, bugs crawling on their legs, and the like. It wasn't a blatant put-down. It was just a touch of condescension that some Missouri executives came to believe tainted the Preus missionary fervor.

After the Denver convention, the conservative United Planning Council disbanded. A seven-member Continuation Committee was selected to coordinate the political goals and strategy, but rightists were not yet unified. Some wanted to press Preus to void the ruling establishing fellowship with the American Lutheran Church. Alvin Wagner, a member of the Continuation Committee, eventually became part of a splinter group that left the Missouri Synod in 1971. Some synod politicos who had helped elect Preus hoped to pressure him on the fellowship question. There was even talk of an ultimatum to try to get Preus to publicly disown fellowship by Easter of 1970, but most backed off and let Preus carry on his way.

The Continuation Committee activated a fund-raising and publishing arm in late 1970. Called Balance, Inc., the organization's first president was Robert Preus. A one-hundred-thousand-dollar fund drive was launched to prepare for the July 1971 convention in Milwaukee. The fund fell considerably short, producing forty-three thousand dollars.

The conservative high command made a serious tactical error at the Milwaukee convention. They concentrated on issues more than on electing their kind to church boards and commissions. Lists of preferred candidates were circulated, but a definitive list to be followed absolutely was not activated. A vague "vote your conscience" directive was given instead. On several key elections, notably the Concordia Seminary of St. Louis board, conservatives failed to gain control.

That mistake would not be made again. At the 1973 convention, the list of candidates supported by the Continuation Committee was pushed hard and successfully. By 1975 the conservative list was a near-infallible guide to who would be elected. Of some 150 positions in contention, all except one on the list was elected. Even a conservative not on the list but nominated from the floor won on the first ballot. It was an incredible political tour de force. After the pattern was established, moderates suggested sarcastically that the convention adopt the conservative list to save delegates the time and trouble of balloting.

When moderate Melvin Kieschnick of the synod's parish services division complained to Preus of losing some of his best board members after that convention, Preus tried to assuage him with the remark: "I told those fellows they should have let twenty or thirty of the other side win."

After 1971, Balance, Inc., began publishing *Affirm,* a monthly journal eventually with a circulation of one hundred thousand. The organization's income grew from $43,000 the first year to $140,000 in 1975.

Members of this and other conservative groups communicated with Preus after he became president. Sometimes he was challenged. Often conservative leaders wished Preus would keep his mouth shut and get quietly on with the business, but just as with the moderates, it was Preus who stayed on top. As he did with Missouri's majority, Preus convinced the conservatives he knew what he was doing. Occasionally, he had to convince his brother, Robert, who believed in later years that Jack was dallying on discipline and needed to consolidate conservative gains.

Besides Robert, Jack's principal theological advisers were rising conservative star Ralph Bohlmann, who had taken the Jungkuntz post, and college president Paul Zimmerman, the staunch Lutheran-Conservative Preus had first met when Zimmerman was a science teacher at the Little Synod's Bethany College. Zimmerman was special assistant for Preus in 1972. Preus was heard often saying "Zimmerman would never buy that," but Preus largely played his own hunches.

As moderates eventually got politically organized and posed greater threats, Preus's participation in partisan conservative rallies increased. His appearances were double-edged. By appearing, he was indicating support, but frequently what he said was moderating. He could claim he was on the conservative circuit to keep the troops from getting too far out. In September 1975 Preus was top billing at a rally of the Doctrinal Concerns Program at Belleville, Illinois. Requested to cancel because of the partisan nature of the group, Preus promised to tell the hard-liners they shouldn't be vindictive and punitive in their battle with moderates.

Yet this rationale did not stretch far enough to cover all Preus actions. To claim he was really not partisan because hard-line conservative parties upheld the true synodical tradition was to beg the question in a polarized church. Many theological conservatives never aligned themselves with extrasynodical political factions. At the peak of the Seminex crisis in early 1974, Jack Preus took time to inject himself in a conservative attempt to unseat district president Herman Neunaber of Southern Illinois. Neunaber's reelection was being fought by Doctrinal Concerns leaders. On the Sunday before the weekend election, Neunaber emerged from a Lutheran service in Belleville to discover all the cars in the parking lot had conservative flyers on the windshields. Exhibit A of the flyer was a copy of a letter from Preus to Neunaber. Dated the previous Friday, it was a Preus rebuttal of Neunaber's earlier criticism of a Preus report to the church. By Tuesday Neunaber still hadn't received the letter in the mail. He took a witness to confront Preus, who acknowledged he had released the letter to a layman for distribution. Preus brushed off the episode and expressed hope their friendship was still intact. Although Marvin Mueller of Columbia, Illinois, the Doctrinal Concerns chief, would neither confirm or deny, rumor was that Jack Preus had delivered the letter personally on the Saturday evening before its use by Mueller.

John Tietjen has denounced the Preus administration as "morally bankrupt." Others have claimed Preus displayed amoral tendencies. What might safely be said is Preus was rewriting the job description of the Missouri presidency and altering Missouri customs. Customs being the unwritten laws of a society, the moderates were hardly ones to be pointing accusing fingers for breaking unwritten laws. Customs were up for grabs before Preus got to St. Louis. That was why the Missouri war has been so bitter. Missouri was a homogenous family held together more by custom than written laws. When brothers began to break custom, the victims' frustrations were even more intense than had they suffered lawlessness. Victims couldn't bring their self-righteous oppressors to the bar of ecclesiastical justice for breaking custom. There were conservative victims before. Then came the moderate victims.

If Preus was not morally bankrupt, he did stir up the Missouri war and acclerated the erosion of custom. He brought in a whole new set of customs. He pumped more and new kinds of fuel on the fire. If one believed he was true prophet, that was all part of his purifying mission. If one believed he was false king, Preus's aggressive partisanship was evidence to support that opinion.

11

Doing It
the Preus Way

Several months after his 1969 election,
Jack Preus had a long discussion at St. Louis headquarters with
Christian News editor Herman Otten. Outlining his belief that
most Concordia Seminary professors were teaching heresy,
Otten pleaded for heresy trials to begin. With Preus as president, Otten assumed heresy charges would again be taken seriously. The issues would be once-for-all brought into the open,
and a witness to solid Missouri doctrine could be given to the
whole church and the whole world.

Jack Preus agreed there were doctrinal problems at Concordia and elsewhere. Something definitely would be done,
Preus said, but not Otten's way. Did Otten realize the red tape
involved in Missouri heresy trials? That would take two hundred years. He would do it his way, Preus said. The Missouri
president had constitutional authority to oversee doctrine. If a
man knew how to use authority rightly, he could corral the
Concordia crowd. Otten should cool it, Preus advised.

Between Preus's conception and his act stood John Henry
Tietjen. Then an unseasoned forty-one, Tietjen had become
Concordia president in a surprise election only a few months
before the Denver convention. A New York native, Tietjen had
been an Eastern student (Ph.D., Union Theological Seminary),
pastor (New Jersey), and public relations director for the Luth-

eran Council. Although he had taught several summers at Concordia, he had moved more in inter-Lutheran than in Missouri circles since graduation from Concordia in 1953. An ecclesiastical rookie, he had held no synodwide office.

In theological world-view and personality, Tietjen and Preus did not mix. Fastidious, intensely serious, and self-determined, Tietjen clashed with the breezy, quixotic, but equally self-determined Preus. The great Missouri war was to be symbolized in the long Preus-Tietjen confrontation.

It was a face-off with many ironies in the background. Tietjen's postgraduate study was financed by the second of the special education grants initiated in the '50s by Jake Preus's Lutheran Brotherhood Insurance Company. Impressed with Tietjen, Jake once invited him to give a talk on Lutheran ecumenism at a national Brotherhood meeting. Also, the right-wingers' suspicions that Tietjen's appointment had been rushed by liberals in case of a disaster at Denver had added fuel to the campaign for Jack's election.

Richest irony of all was that both Preus and Tietjen in their own ways were outsiders destined to do the dirty political work of the old-line Missourians. Tietjen had spent the first sixteen years of his career outside the political flesh and blood of Missouri. Liberal Eastern Lutheranism was easily as alien to Missouri as was Little Synod sectarianism. No wonder the center collapsed instantly. The two chief antagonists were fighting for ecclesiastical territory neither knew well.

Hurled unprepared into a firestorm, Tietjen had to bear liberal leadership burdens far beyond the walls of Concordia. He fought heroically for his cause, as Preus did for his. But with his back to the wall from the start and his equilibrium left of Missouri center, Tietjen never got his politico-ecclesiastical bearings. He played into Preus's hands. After each Preus hammer-blow, Tietjen's Concordia looked even farther left than it actually was. Each time Preus barked, Tietjen's Concordia looked less Missourian.

Preus realized very early that Tietjen would obstruct the

conservative takeover of Concordia. Tietjen would have to go, Preus told Otten and others. At first the antipathy was impersonal and ideological, but as the sturggle intensified, the Preus-Tietjen clash personalized.

Before the end of 1969 most seeds for the subsequent showdown had been planted. Preus and Tietjen had a private dinner meeting on November 3 at the downtown Missouri Athletic Club. Preus told Tietjen he believed his Denver election was a mandate to clean up Missouri theologically and that the starting point would be Concordia Seminary. It was a clear signal to Tietjen that if Preus didn't get what he wanted he would go around, over, or through Tietjen.

Despite his public remark a few days later that Tietjen would make a "great president," Preus was disturbed about Tietjen's bold effort to hire Dick Jungkuntz. In mid-November Preus made appearances at Concordia—the last of any friendly confabs in the enemy camp. Preus was irked by the grilling the liberal faculty gave him after his opening remarks at a November 18 meeting. He had told them they would have to get back to the theological center. Robert Preus, one of the five conservatives on the fifty-member faculty, recalled that "liberals" then tore shamelessly into brother Jack. Jack was lectured and personally demeaned. The tone was "Defend yourself if you can, you creep." For their part, the professors felt no compunction about probing new president Preus. It was a backhand tribute —because they were treating him as one of the boys. Was he so tender he couldn't take some tough questioning?

Two days later Preus may already have been subconsciously blacking-out Concordia. Scheduled to preach at a morning chapel service, he arrived embarrassingly late. All readings and hymns completed, the liturgist was stalling. Preus arrived, walking hurriedly down a side aisle. In plain view, he shed his coat, tossed it over a front-row seat, slipped into the vesting room, walked to the pulpit, took a deep breath, and preached a brief devotional.

At the December 1969 meeting of the seminary board, Preus

alluded for the first time to his plans. False doctrine was being taught at Concordia. He was considering an investigation. Beginning a pattern that was to hold, Tietjen reacted sharply, defensively, and melodramatically. The Preus suggestion was sickening, frightfully unjust. Preus had spotted heresy even before any facts were known. Preus also began a pattern. He revealed in advance what he was going to do and then disappeared, leaving opponents wondering when and how. It was the Preus way of rattling sabers in hopes the opponents would be moved to bargain. Perhaps naïvely, it was his way of trying to avoid confrontation, not invite it. Although Tietjen alluded to it as the *Mein Kampf* syndrome, Preus's habit of alerting subjects to the coming storm was not unlike other Christian officials issuing warnings with the hope of softening the resistance to coming changes.

Jack Preus has little taste for nose-to-nose confrontation. Left to his own devices, he would have dealth with Concordia "liberals" the way he dealt with his own back at Springfield: remove them quietly and with the least embarrassment to either party; work behind the scenes to get everybody in the right place. The railings of some Missourians aside, the tactic is hardly an ecclesiastical sin crying to heaven for vengeance. It is, in fact, a freedom granted to virtually every other Catholic and Protestant head in the world today. The difference with Preus of Missouri was that his goals and intentions were unknowns. Missouri moderates began, not without reason, to wonder when and where the Preus house cleaning would stop. They began to wonder what Jack Preus *really* wanted.

Concordia Seminary, a pleasant Gothic complex on a seventy-two-acre campus in the wealthy suburb of Clayton, had an ambivalent status in the Missouri Synod. It was older than the synod and had helped spawn it. Over the decades Concordia had enjoyed enormous prestige as an unofficial oracle. Most theological questions were settled by Concordia opinions. But in more recent, troubled times, it became lightning rod attracting the bolts of right-wingers.

Concordia's image was foggy compared to the Springfield seminary. In a professional opinion survey completed in early 1970, only 43 percent of Missouri pastors indicated they "strongly agreed" (marking 1 on a 1 to 5 descending scale) with the statement "Concordia St. Louis is true to sound Lutheran principles." Almost 75 percent "strongly agreed" that the statement applied to the Springfield seminary. Overall, the survey showed no horrendous credibility problems for the St. Louis seminary, however, and Tietjen's Concordia cited the findings as evidence that Preus was acting independently. Still, in a strongly doctrinal church, the survey finding that 57 percent of the clergy could not instinctively rate the top seminary as acceptable should have given pause.

Concordia had a conservative minority on its faculty who had been increasingly shocked, not only by the liberalizing theology, but by the life-style of some faculty members. The first complaint Tietjen had to investigate was raised by an excitable conservative who thought (wrongly) there was wife-swapping going on. Concordia community cocktail and swimming parties were lively but hardly the basis for charges of wife-swapping. It was symptomatic of the deep differences of worldview and style.

Crusty Martin Scharlemann, who had actively sought the Concordia presidency, began unfairly attacking Tietjen, or trying to keep him in synodical bounds, depending on one's viewpoint. Scharlemann had politicked heavily for the Concordia presidency, a fact moderates cited to denounce his authority when he was appointed acting president after the Tietjen suspension. Among other things, Scharlemann seemed shocked that Tietjen wasn't employing rigid discipline to silence student antiwar sentiments and displays. In mid-April 1970, Scharlemann, Ralph Bohlmann, and Richard Klann, three conservative professors who opposed Tietjen's administration, visited Jack Preus at synod headquarters. They complained, in effect, of a Concordia running wild. Scharlemann presented indictments to Preus and requested an official inquiry.

Several days later Preus announced to the seminary board that he would create a special "fact finding" committee to investigate doctrine at Concordia. By late May when he announced it in a newsletter to pastors, Preus had partially changed his mind. He would do the inquiry himself. Preus had buried the brief announcement on page 2 of a six-page newsletter, as if it were routine business.

In reality, the investigation was unprecedented in Missouri history. Right-wing proposals for such investigations had been brushed aside by governing conventions for two decades. Responsibility for processing false doctrine charges was with the seminary presidents and the boards of control, who in troubled times had been moderates. So right-wing complaints hadn't brought the sweeping condemnations and changes desired. Right-wingers had hoped for more than a decade to make a federal case out of Concordia "liberals."

Although within his constitutional rights, Preus was undertaking an inquiry previous conventions had specifically rejected. He had only his private interpretation of Denver as a mandate to clean house. It took brass. Not surprisingly, Preus repeatedly stressed he was responding to complaints from the hoi polloi. He belabored the history of John Behnken and Oliver Harms, who had tried so hard in the past to clear up the doctrinal unrest generated by Concordia. Preus seemed to want to show he was reacting not acting.

The fact that Preus got away with his investigation politically meant it was all downhill for him. If Missouri would allow him to conduct a lock-stock-and-barrel investigation of Concordia without specific authorization and ground rules from a convention, it would allow him virtually anything, anywhere, anytime. It was as if the U.S. president had announced he was going to investigate West Point Military Academy because he had been getting some nasty letters, and when neither Congress nor a majority of Americans had authorized it. Missouri was Preus's to have and to hold as he saw fit. The political war was over without a single serious battle.

Back in his early Springfield days, Preus had marveled privately at Missouri executives' giving orders and the troops' obeying instinctively. Norwegian Lutherans would never fall in line like that! Now President Preus was experiencing just how marvelously this Missouri lock step worked in the crunch.

Following almost on cue the cycle of Preus action–Concordia overreaction, Tietjen had pushed Preus into an even wider investigation than Preus wanted. Preus was after about ten teachers, most in the exegetical or Bible interpretation department. All or none, Tietjen responded. He would throw Preus no sacrificial lambs. The faculty majority was to repay him when he was deposed. One for all and all for one. The same "our president right or wrong" attitude that helped Preus also helped Tietjen get what political foothold he did.

The explosive story finally got into the public media on July 13 when investigative reporter Robert Teuscher of the *St. Louis Globe Democrat* broke it. Before the summer ended, Preus had taken a bath in several national publications. He cited the bad press for reverting again in early September to his fact finding committee. That would look less like *his* inquiry. The five-man panel, which had been supplied with the previous writings of the faculty, began interviews in December and completed most by March 1971. Headed by Paul Zimmerman, the four investigators included only one man considered mildly moderate. Preus explained that if a conservative panel cleared Concordia then the seminary's troubles would be over forever. It was roughly equivalent to telling General Motors to be happy that Ralph Nader was investigating because if he found the company flawless that would be the ultimate seal of approval.

At the first round of interviews, Scharlemann had been allowed to answer questions about colleagues. The faculty majority and the seminary board asked Preus to stop the practice. When they got no satisfaction, the faculty issued in early January a statement soundly criticizing Preus for presumed irregularities in the committee's approach. They agreed to continue with the whole program only "under protest." It was the first of many public statements Preus regarded as personal attacks orchestrated by Tietjen. Months later Preus was still reminding Tietjen he hadn't yet publicly apologized.

At the July 1971 convention, Preus won a commendation for his investigation. Essentially, he was instructed to carry on and present his recommendations to the appropriate boards. It was a symbolic victory, but the key political reality that would determine the outcome of his investigation had not changed: moderates still held a one-vote margin on the seminary board.

Preus would have to mount public pressure on this board to get any action. He turned over the summaries and the sixteen hundred pages of testimony from the fact finding committee. Months later, in February 1972, Missourians got their first clue of how the board was reacting. It was a sharp public relations blow for Preus. The editor of the Lutheran Layman newspaper front-paged a story headlined "False Doctrine Not Evident at Seminary." This story quoted, not a liberal, but a conservative lay member of the seminary board. The extent to which this poked a Preus administration nerve can be judged by the garbled "apology" that appeared in the next edition of the layman paper. The editor, in effect, had to apologize for doing his job well.

The next month Preus issued his "Statement of Scriptural and Confessional Principles." It was a catalog of fundamentalist-leaning condemnations against contemporary liberal interpretations of the Bible. The Preus thrust was toward literal interpretation of all Scripture not obviously poetical, such as the psalms and the Book of Revelation. Preus (rather Ralph Bohlmann, who wrote it) cited more than sixty false views, some touching indirectly on basic Christian doctrines.

Preus said he was offering these as guidelines to help the board evaluate the inquiry findings and to take appropriate action. In a cover letter, Preus added that "our church faces a great crisis: it is a crisis of faith and confession." He then raised a basic premise of his campaign against the seminary: the "domino theory." If the church tolerated speculation about miracles of the Old Testament, then it soon would be facing heresy on such basics as the incarnation and the resurrection. Releasing his "Statement" publicly was putting massive pressure on the board. Also, it was suggesting to the church what the faculty members were teaching. The professors condemned the Preus catalog as "un-Lutheran" and later denied they held many of the condemned views.

The churchwide release of the "Statement" was one of the most clever maneuvers of the Preus administration. The gist of it, churchly wise, was this: Suppose the pope was having difficulties with the theology of the Jesuits. After an investigation, the pope formulated a list of sixty false theses, some of which he knew some of the Jesuits taught. Instead of privately offering the Jesuit superiors the list as internal guidelines, the pope issued the list to the whole church and included a cover letter suggesting how bad things were all around as far as theology was concerned. When Catholics would read the list, many would say to themselves: "My, the Jesuits are worse than we thought. No wonder the pope's after them." Not without reason, the Jesuits to a man would probably have felt the pope had played a dirty trick on them.

Many Missouri moderates saw immediately that this new Preus instrument might become a doctrinal standard spelling trouble for them. Preus protested mightily that no new doctrinal test was intended. These were just internal guidelines he wanted to share with the church, but soon he was hedging. Could he help it if the masses had arisen with one voice begging Missouri to make this their new law? In November, he wrote a Connecticut pastor saying that the matter was out of his hands. Preus noted that when the reformer Melanchthon had written the Augsburg Confession he had no intention it become normative. But, alas, it became so despite the author's intentions. Preus was reacting to Missouri, not acting on Missouri.

The Preus "Statement" and cover letter were also the first public hint of the still secret contents of his inquiry. The fact he used the "domino theory" suggested his investigation had turned up no evidence of universally recognized heresies. That is what he reported in September. There was no evidence of "false doctrine concerning such great doctrines as the Trinity, the deity of Christ, justification by faith or the sacraments of Baptism and the Lord's Supper, etc." But, Preus declared, the committee found "a distressing amount of diversity" in theology around six specific areas which called for "decisive action." Among them were a "false doctrine of the nature of Scripture" eroding its authority, a "permissiveness toward certain false doctrines," and a "conditional acceptance of the Lutheran Confessions." At last, the Missouri rightists had it from the highest office! Their slogan that "liberals are taking away your Bible" had been vindicated after all the years.

Meanwhile, Preus-Tietjen confrontations were continuing unabated. Preus had intervened with the Concordia board to argue against tenures for several faculty members, including shy, Arlis Ehlen, an Old Testament teacher. Ehlen had waffled on the existence of angels and personal devils. He had indicated he interpreted naturalistically parts of the account of the Israelites crossing a miraculously parted Red Sea. An unconvincing witness for himself in various forums, Ehlen eventually slipped by the board with a one-year contract that was later voided by a higher board partisan to Preus.

The Ehlen affair prompted one of the sharpest of many cat fights between Preus and Tietjen. They had agreed before the February 1972 board meeting to work out compromises to reduce tensions, perhaps defuse the confrontation. Tietjen heard Preus agree to about a dozen peace proposals, among them the one-year pact for Ehlen. At the opening board session when Tietjen presented the compromise package, Preus objected to the Ehlen matter and he disagreed on other points. Tietjen exploded in rage and frustration. Turning to mediator Roland Wiederaenders, Tietjen extracted a nod from Wiederaenders that indeed there had been agreement on all points. The session ended in confusion.

Tietjen, Preus, Wiederaenders, and education executive Art
Ahlschwede met later in Tietjen's office. Tietjen snarled at
Preus pointblank. *"Jack, you lied,"* he began. Preus was seeth-
ing, his face growing livid, his eyebrows jumping uncontrolla-
bly. He shot back blistering remarks to Tietjen. He stomped to
the door to leave. Wiederaenders stopped him with a remark
about healing one's anger before the sunset, and about his going
to hell for sure if he died that evening. Preus continued to
unburden himself, gradually cooling under Wiederaenders's
suasions.

At the urging of the district presidents, Wiederaenders tried
to serve as peacemaker for a series of five Preus-Tietjen sessions
later that year, and another series before the New Orleans
convention. Some communication but little empathy, trust, or
forgiveness ever emerged between the two. To Tietjen, Preus
remained a politician manipulating around proper procedures.
To Preus, Tietjen remained stiff-necked, unreasonable protec-
tor of wild-eyed theologians who were disrupting the church.
In early January 1973, Wiederaenders took them to lunch at a
busy restaurant in downtown St. Louis. No sooner had they sat
down and a dispute started. Nearby patrons were staring. An
embarrassed Wiederaenders had to change the subject.

What kind of showdown New Orleans would be depended on
whether the pivotal seminary board would do what Preus so
obviously was suggesting—clean house, or at least make a show
of cleaning house and provide a few token scalps Preus could
parade before the convention. Preus got his answer from this
eleven-man board in mid-February 1973. Zero. Not a single
indictment. Not even slaps on wrists. After all the hubbub, the
board had voted on whether to "commend or correct" each of
the forty-four professors. All were commended. True, five survived by only one-vote margins, two by two-vote margins, but
ten polled no negative votes.

Nothing could have done more to mobilize Preus and company into decisive action for New Orleans. Preus began saying
publicly that "Tietjen must go." Before New Orleans he told

Tietjen the hammer would fall on Concordia. If Tietjen wanted to prevent it, he should begin immediately to fire professors and restore ideological balance to the faculty. Preus wanted Tietjen to know New Orleans didn't have to happen.

If Jack Preus had fallen in a manhole on his way to New Orleans and never been seen again (to use his phrase), could Missouri have lived with Tietjen's Concordia? Probably not for long. Some hard compromising would have been necessary even if calm, moderate-leaning conservatives had been in control. *A Study of Generations* data (1970) had revealed that 40 percent of Missourians believed so strongly the Bible was inerrant that they were willing to say dissenters "are not true to the Christian faith."

After the highly publicized Preus shakedown of Concordia, the percentage would hardly have dropped. Regardless of Preus, something would have had to give somewhere, if not at New Orleans then later. A church in which 40 percent demand unconditionally an inerrant Bible and another 40 percent are leaning that way would sooner or later have called Concordia to task. Had Concordia been sustained somehow in its biblical approach, a substantial exodus of the right would seemingly have been inevitable.

Whether Preus and company challenged Concordia responsibly and fairly was open to question. Whether Preus incited Missouri to the ecclesiastical riot that was New Orleans, whether he indulged in massive theological overkill, whether he forced an issue prematurely, whether he really believed in his heart of hearts that the opinions of the Concordia faculty members were heretical, whether he personally believed it all that crucial that a Big Fish actually swallowed an Old Testament preacher named Jonah, whether he was politician who bent bylaws and flaunted customs, whether he was opportunist—all may be open to question.

But these questions were ultimately marginal to the underlying fact of life in Missouri: Concordia Seminary was too far left, and its president was giving no signals of doing anything about

that. The question was open whether Tietjen would have negotiated with another man. There were some signs he might have
done so, but there were other signs he was fighting an all-out
ideological war. Our way of interpreting the Bible is the *only*
Lutheran way, and you cannot ask me to compromise that
without asking me to give up my Lutheranism, he seemed to be
saying. Tietjen's Concordia had been asked to negotiate a little.
It refused. Now it would be asked to surrender all.

12

"Gospel" Preachers Versus "Bible" Teachers

One Monday morning in early spring 1956, Alton Frank Wedel, then thirty-four and a typically energetic and theologically smug Missouri Synod pastor, was driving along River Des Peres Boulevard in south St. Louis on his way to Concordia Seminary. Wedel had spent a year settling in at his third career parish assignment, Salem Lutheran Church. Now he was signed up for a thirteen-week course entitled "The Place of Holy Scripture in Lutheran Theology" taught by (the late) Paul Bretscher, long a respected theology professor at Concordia.

Wedel, married and father of three, was a lifelong Missourian. He was the son of an Eau Claire, Wisconsin, Lutheran pastor and a product of the Missouri educational and clerical system. After graduation from the synod's Concordia College in Milwaukee, Alton Wedel attended Concordia Seminary in St. Louis, graduating in 1945. He served for a year as missionary in Saskatchewan, Canada, before taking his first parish call at Trinity Lutheran Church in Bessemer, Michigan. Beginning in 1950, he served for five years at Zion Lutheran Church in Poplar Bluff, Missouri, then he moved on to his St. Louis parish.

As he drove toward the Concordia campus for his first Monday morning class, young pastor Wedel had mixed feelings. He eagerly anticipated getting a refresher course and linking with the Concordia community again after eleven years in the active ministry, yet he wondered what he could get from such an obvious course as this. Maybe his selection had been a mistake. He knew the place of the Bible in Lutheran theology just as every Missourian did: The Bible was a miraculously designed catalog of self-evident truths which, when put in a column and totaled, produced that robust Lutheran catechism of the Christian faith. Bretscher's course would be boring rehash.

To his surprise, Pastor Wedel found that he was wrong. Those thirteen successive Mondays under Bretscher brought anything but a rehash of what Wedel later came to believe was the rigid, dogmatic biblicism he had been taught a decade earlier at Concordia. Bretscher's mind-opening exploration of the Bible as wellspring and witness for a Christ-centered gospel was a turning point in Wedel's theological vision and his ministry. He was never again to view the Bible in the traditional Missouri way. Avoiding "legalism" was to become an integral part of his daily ministry. He had experienced a revelation which would determine where he would stand when the great Missouri war peaked two decades later.

Wedel, who went on to become a prominent Minneapolis pastor, never forgot the concluding lecture of the course. For two hours, Bretscher had theologized eloquently on what was for him—and from then on for Wedel—the key biblical passage revealing the fundamental purpose of Scripture. Bretscher cited the account in Luke 24 where the risen but unrecognized Christ walked along the road to Emmaus with two disciples. The two were anxious, confused, and on the edge of despair because their hopes in the just-crucified Christ had been shattered. "Then, starting with Moses and going through all the prophets, he explained to them the passages throughout the scriptures that were about himself" (Luke 24:27). Later, as the risen Christ blessed and broke bread with them, he was recognized. The two disciples remarked: "Did not our hearts burn within us as he talked to us on the road and explained the scriptures to us?" (Luke 24:32).

Here was the Bible in action. Here was the paradigm for approaching and interpreting the Bible. Here was what the Bible was *for:* to elicit faith in Jesus Christ, in his promise, and in the hope of personal and cosmic salvation. As Wedel heard Bretscher, his own heart burned within at this new revelation of the key role of the Bible in Lutheran ministry.

What the risen Christ had done was liberate the two disciples from dependence on their literal view of Scriptures. Doubtless, these two men knew all their Scriptures well. They may even have had much of their writings memorized. But far from freeing them to see Christ and the significance of his life and death, their one-dimensional knowledge of Scriptures limited them. The "evidence" of their Scriptures had not helped them make the leap of faith.

But when the risen Christ related the Scriptures to himself, he empowered the two disciples to see first and foremost the meaning of Scriptures. The letter had left them anxious, confused, and prone to despair. Now the spirit had marvelously freed and empowered them. The message of the Emmaus account was the supremacy of the gospel preached over the Bible taught, the gospel proclaimed over the Bible recited. What mattered was the Christ-centered significance of the Bible, that is, the gospel. All else was secondary.

Recounting his experience more than twenty years later, Wedel said: "I came to see that all Scripture was related primarily to acceptance of Christ, not to acceptance of Lutheran dogmas about Christ or about the Bible itself. We are baptized into Christ, not baptized into the Bible. I see the Bible as a Book which brings the one doctrine of Christ to be preached and proclaimed, not a catalog of doctrines to be defended and guarded."

Wedel experienced firsthand another dimension of the changing Missouri Synod when, beginning in 1958, he became part of the synod's social services board and thus was tied into joint Lutheran ministries then beginning to flourish. He mingled with Lutherans of other denominations in mission and ministry and discovered that they were "just as pure—or impure—as Missourians." These colleagues were not "liberals" unworthy of trust. They were Lutheran co-workers whose theology might not be exactly the same as his but whose "hearts burned every bit as warmly for the gospel as the hearts of Missourians." Well before he became pastor of Mount Olive Lutheran Church in Minneapolis in 1962, Alton Wedel had made the psychological and theological break from the old "triumphalist" Missouri. Inter-Lutheran ventures, and ultimately some form of Lutheran ecclesiastical unity, had become an integral part of Wedel's Missouri identity and ministry. His ecclesiastical radar included Missouri but was not limited by it.

With variations to fit particulars, Alton Wedel's evolution as a Missouri "moderate" could be retold in hundreds of cases of Missourians in his generation and the later generation. His story is not atypical, and it is significant for several reasons. It reveals why moderates see themselves as integral Missourians and why they resent so bitterly the implication that they are theological interlopers who can and should be silenced or deposed. It shows that the theological and ecclesiastical views Wedel came to were sparked by other Missourians. Wedel was a creature of Missouri—granted, a changing Missouri, but Missouri nonetheless, not some alien "liberal" environment. His personal evolution was a spinoff of what was happening in the Missouri Synod of his time. Wedel did not see himself as a loner swimming against the Missouri current but as a team member swimming with plenty of company in midstream.

Also, Alton Wedel was a career pastor who felt he was never far removed from the Missouri laity. He never occupied an ivory tower. He did not become a moderate despite his parish responsibilities but because of them. True, Wedel's Mount Olive Lutheran congregation in Minneapolis was not typical Missourian in some ways. It was a large polyglot congregation with a full socioeconomic mix in a Lutheran city in Minnesota, the state with the highest population of Lutherans in the country. Moreover, the pastor for forty-two years prior to Wedel was Theo Schroedel, a "moderate" before his time. Schroedel was one of the notorious "forty-four" who had signed their synodwide protest in 1945 against "narrow legalism" in the old Missouri. Nonetheless, Wedel's evolution as a moderate, like hundreds of others in Missouri, came in the workaday parish context rather than in some elitist atmosphere.

The liberalizing of the Missouri Synod was for Wedel a natural and unorchestrated phenomenon. It was a spontaneous development, no more staged or programmed than the phenonomen of Pope John XXIII in the Catholic church of that same era. Had it been staged by anxious, political-minded moderates, there would have been a compulsion to tie up all the loose ends precisely to prevent something like the Preus party takeover in 1969. The suggestion that the Preus conservative party is doing in reverse what a moderate party did a few years earlier distorts the spontaneous, gift-of-the-spirit character of "Missouri's flowering under Oliver Harms," Wedel believes.

Pastor Wedel acknowledges there was agony enough for some Missouri conservatives during the '60s. Reminded that the worst form of punishment for a true believer is to ignore him, Wedel insisted that Missouri moderates never ignored, feared, or belittled conservative colleagues. "There was hope we could pull these brothers and sisters along, just as others had pulled us," he recalled. Some might easily have interpreted moderates' responses to fearful conservatives as arrogant, Wedel conceded. But he added, "When we laughed at what seemed like the hysterical fears of conservatives, this was not so much laughing at them as laughing at ourselves in them—because we had been there ourselves once."

Whatever case may be made against the way moderates came into and used their brief ascendancy in Missouri, the charge cannot be sustained that moderates surprised, shocked, or intentionally deceived their colleagues, Wedel said. Within the limits of Missouri's traditional censorship policies, moderates communicated as much and as responsibly as they could, he contended. The notion is nonsensical, he said, that hapless conservative pastors through no fault of their own woke up one day to discover "heretics" and "Bible doubters" were teaching at Concordia Seminary. Even a casual reader of the *Concordia Theological Monthly,* the seminary's scholarly journal that went to many pastors, could have kept abreast of the new hermeneutic emerging at Concordia.

Like many moderates outside the St. Louis area, Wedel never knew much about Jack Preus and has never had a personal consultation with him. He never developed intense feelings about Preus, but what he saw of the Preus administration from a distance was enough to make him sharply critical. Preus seemed quintessential polarizer. He tended at every turn to divide Missourians between loyal "Bible believers" and traitorous "Bible doubters." Then, operating as if Missouri was some privately owned business conglomerate, Preus set out to clean the roster of the undesirable employees. To Wedel, Preus seemed to exploit a legalistic model of the church readily understood by lay persons whose secular lives revolved around management-labor environments.

Charges that Missouri moderates hold "false doctrine" because of their nonliteral interpretation of some biblical sections are "ridiculous," Wedel says. But even if those charges were given a certain legitimacy, and even if every Missourian admitted that two irreconcilable views of the Bible were involved, the next responsible step would be to move to a slow unpoliticalized consensus on the nature of the Lutheran church. What are its ideals? What are its limits? How much authority may it exercise solely on the basis of majority votes and tradition? Because majorities have power, should they use it to resolve specific, disputed questions?

That the Preus regime seemingly feared it could not withstand the light of full, free, and unhurried consensus-seeking on the nature of the church and its authority is an indictment of that regime, Wedel believes.

For Pastor Everett Grese, as for a majority of Missouri clergy and laity, there never was a liberalization of the Missouri Synod which so captivated Alton Wedel. No new hermeneutic had taken root except in the minds of a few professors. There was no new theory that the "gospel" could somehow be isolated from the Bible. There was no new ecumenical imperative which gave any Missourian a right to expect, much less to demand, the freedom to live out a pan-Lutheran identity while drawing his sustenance from Missouri. As Missouri's great war unfolded, there may have been a need to talk more about the nature of the church and its exercise of authority, Pastor Grese would admit. But the moderates with their rash and haughty resistance to any compromise were as much the cause of the act-first, maybe-talk-later pattern as anything Jack Preus ever did.

Pastor Grese is theologically, culturally, and emotionally a Missourian. Wedel claims to be the same, but for every Wedel, there are three Greses. What Pastor Grese saw from his vantage point and how he reacted to the pre- and post-Preus developments in Missouri exemplifies what many Missourians saw and felt.

Everett Gustav Grese, father of eleven, was born in 1917 in Collinsville, Illinois. From his parochial school days on through all his active ministry of more than thirty-four years, Grese never spent so much as an hour in a non-Missouri educational institution. He attended high school and junior college at the synod's St. Paul's College in Concordia, Missouri. He studied at Concordia Seminary in St. Louis, graduating in 1942. Unlike Wedel, Grese was never to return there for any update courses which might have given him firsthand exposure to the liberalized Concordia of the late '50s and '60s.

After several years at a North Little Rock, Arkansas, church, Grese became pastor at Immanuel Lutheran Church in Memphis, where he served from 1945 to 1961. The next six years he pastored at First Lutheran Church in Chattanooga. From 1967 to mid-1974, Grese served in a Memphis office as executive secretary of the synod's Mid-South District. He was an all-purpose agent and liaison with synod headquarters for about

188 | Preus of Missouri

one hundred congregations in Arkansas, Tennessee, and southern Kentucky. He moved to the St. Louis area in 1974 as pastor of Concordia Lutheran Church in Maplewood where his parishioners included some Seminex professors and their families. As was the case with most Missouri "conservatives," Pastor Grese was never a member of any organized conservative party. He knew, and knows, little about Jack Preus. He never worked to unseat Oliver Harms, whom he admired and respected. Grese was as surprised as any Missourian when Jack Preus was elected president in 1969. But unlike Wedel, Grese was neither surprised nor shocked when Preus later interpreted his election as a mandate to settle doctrinal unrest and when Preus initiated his investigation of Concordia Seminary.

What Pastor Grese had experienced of the liberalized Concordia Seminary conditioned him to see Preus's intervention as a right and a necessary duty. The problem of the left-leaning professors and their graduates was an old one, and long delayed in solutions more because of professional courtesy between fellow pastors than because it wasn't a serious problem. For fifteen years prior to the New Orleans convention, there had prevailed a hope that private, unpublicized persuasion would deter the Concordia professors. Even after New Orleans, Grese was one who hoped for quiet compromises.

One of the first disturbing signals Grese encountered personally was in the late '50s when he talked with two Concordia seminarians from his Immanuel Lutheran congregation in Memphis. What those two described to him did not seem to be the "confessional" Concordia he knew. Rather, it seemed like the big union Protestant seminaries which offered a theological grab bag. What was finally and firmly *the* Missouri position on all questions was no longer being stressed. Traditional Missouri doctrines were left to fend for themselves in the students' minds. It seemed Concordia seminarians were being educated as Christian theologians with vague and open-ended goals rather than trained to think like Missouri pastors whose function was to preach and teach the Bible. Grese noticed with alarm that the two seminarians had apparently never cracked a single book by Franz Pieper.

For a time in the early '60s, Grese had been an officer in the synod's old Western District which had jurisdiction in the St. Louis area. Then as later, he never sided with Herman Otten in Otten's frontal attacks on the seminary, but the corporate defensiveness of the seminary in the Otten episodes nonetheless left lingering doubts for Grese. He also saw from a distance what he and many others in the district regarded as a classic case of elitist arrogance by a leading Concordia theologian. The late Arthur Carl Piepkorn, brilliant and independent-minded scholar in the Scharlemann vein, once filled in for an extended period at a Lutheran Church in America congregation in south St. Louis. To workaday pastors in the district, this was blatant "unionism." Additionally, it seemed to be undercutting their pastoral discipline because some members of that congregation were former Missourians chastised for belonging to Masonic lodges. Missouri's great Dr. Piepkorn was ministering in a non-Missouri church to ex-Missourians, all a few steps from synod's world headquarters! Complaints to Concordia, Grese recalled, were greeted with what amounted to "how dare you narrow-minded plebians question us!" Ultimately, the complaints seemed to be virtually ignored. Concordia was above its Missouri environment, it seemed.

Grese sat in on more than three pastoral conferences during that era in which Concordia professors—including Norm Habel with his trial balloon on the symbolic interpretation of the Adam and Eve account—outlined their new hermeneutic. Grese does not recall a single soul in the Mid-South District ever buying into any of it. Wedel's Missouri spontaneously igniting with progressive ideas was neither spontaneous nor igniting as far as Grese could see. If Concordia would be Missouri's corporate Pope John XXIII, it would have to be lighting a lot more fire elsewhere than it did down Grese's way.

As district executive, Grese cooperated with agents and pastors of the two other Lutheran denominations. Joint Lutheran programs were especially important for him because Lutherans were relatively isolated and constituted only a tiny minority in his mid south Bible-belt area. Grese recalls being deeply impressed with many Lutherans in other denominations considered "liberal." He was tempted, he says, to practice "selective fellowship," a form of limited, individual intercommunion never officially accepted by the Missouri Synod. But unlike Wedel, Grese never came near crossing the Missouri frontier into some sort of pan-Lutheran Shangri-La. Seven years after Missouri approved fellowship with the American Lutheran Church, Pastor Everett Grese remained "uncomfortable" about that relationship. He clings to the old Missouri notion that full intercommunion is possible only when two churches indeed "believe and teach the same things." The fact that the American Lutheran Church ordains women is evidence enough for him that the two churches do not really believe and teach the same on doctrinal questions.

As to scriptural matters, Grese believes he can match Wedel any day of the week when it comes to devotion to the gospel preached, to Christ proclaimed. However, Grese believes the power of the gospel is somehow in the words of the Bible. The gospel is in the words of the Bible, as any pastor knows. It is the power of the Word that comforts when the pastor reads the Bible to that sick or dying soul. The theologian's theory *about* that Word gives no comfort then.

Grese summarizes his attitude toward Scripture this way: "I believe Scripture is the Word of God. I have never accepted the notion that Scripture only contains the Word of God." The Bible does not and cannot contain contradictions, only things that seem contradictory because of one's limited human vision or limited faith. Theoretically, God could have inspired any kind of document to report his salvation history, but because he inspired this Bible, one must assume that its words as written are what God wanted said. One must assume God did not intend to play games with his words. He intended to communicate the basic meanings denoted by the words. More than that, perhaps, but at least that. Otherwise for Grese, God would appear to have created a self-negating instrument, an unreliable tool. Would God give the Christian church a rubber crutch to go hobbling its way down through the ages? "No," is Pastor Grese's answer. "If you can't be sure of all Scripture, you can't be sure of any of it." To fly gloriously to Wedel's "gospel" heights, one must first walk simply through Grese's plain Bible.

But literalist he is not, Grese says. Some parts of Scripture, as revealed by the text itself or by the wider context, are specialized literature. The psalms and the Song of Solomon are obviously poetry, but when the Bible speaks definitively of individuals, times, dates, places, and events, it ought to be given simple credence. The Bible scholars, who, at any rate, can never prove all their elaborate revamping of the Bible, should not be given the benefit of the doubt over against the clear words of the Bible.

Lutherans who do not see the Scripture his way are not necessarily heretics for Grese. Very likely, if he spent a day with Wedel, Grese would not consider his moderate colleague a preacher of false doctrine. Grese clearly has accepted the judgment that John Tietjen is not a heretic. Nor would a conservative Missourian like Grese give any indication he believes moderates are particularly dangerous in *some* ministries. But moderate ideologues teaching at synod seminaries, colleges, and Sunday schools is a different matter for Grese. "It is eventually an either-or situation. If I'm going to teach in a church institution, I have to accept the limitations that church obviously demands for its teachers."

The New Orleans condemnation of Concordia professors was "a little sharp," Grese admits. Had he been in a position to influence it, he would have softened that condemnation considerably, he hints. Generally, the ethical questions surrounding the treatment of Missouri moderates and the cases of aggressiveness of some Preus sympathizers on synod boards appear to be the only dimensions of the great Missouri war about which Grese has any nagging doubts. There was never any question of accepting the general theological world-view of moderates, or specifically their biblical interpretative schemes, he says. But how Missouri dealt with its aching sons and daughters who held those unwanted views is no source of pride for Grese. He points no accusing fingers. He professes not to know how the wave of ecclesiastical fratricide and/or suicide could have been avoided; yet the stigma is there—a vague feeling of corporate inadequacy, if not personal guilt.

That is why, Grese believes, the moderate camp is not filled with Missourians who are deeply committed to the moderates' ideology. That is clear from the fact that they have yet to draw up any theological manifesto or even attempted to do so. Much commitment flows from sympathy for colleagues who, if not ruthlessly wronged, were deeply humiliated.

And, yes, there may be one other aspect of the great Missouri struggle about which Grese indicates less than typical old Missouri certainty. Who prevails in the long run? On the one hand, Grese speculates vaguely about the pendulum of Christian history swinging back toward the basics, in the Missouri Synod as elsewhere. Missouri doctrines will hold, and hold indefinitely. Pastor Grese cannot bring himself to think otherwise. Missouri, as religion sociologists Charles Glock and Rodney Stark suggested in the mid-'60s, is "impervious" to liberalization and secularization.

On the other hand, good Pastor Grese has a very specific and personal reality pointing in the other direction. William, one of his sons and a graduate of Tietjen's Concordia, is a moderate. So is one son-in-law. Not political, upfront moderates, perhaps, but moderate nonetheless. And while Everett Grese sits at home in St. Louis and talks confidently of the pendulum moving again to his rhythm, young William Grese is at the (non-Lutheran) Claremont, California, School of Theology digging out the relationships between the New Testament and the writings of Plutarch. How much longer, indeed, will there be three Everett Greses for every one Alton Wedel?

13

Preus at the Brink

"Robert Preus is willing to be the last surviving member of the Missouri Synod, but Jack is not," goes a flip observation of Preus-watchers. While hardly fair to Robert, it captures the difference between theologian Robert and politician Jack. Jack wants a pure *and* big Missouri.

Certainly Jack Preus knows better than anyone that he will have a deplorable place in American Lutheran history if he turns Missouri into a Little Norwegian Synod with a German accent. After his stunning victories at New Orleans, he began to face problems with that potential. Feeling new vigor, aggressive conservatives threatened to take a runaway revolution to every corner of Missouri, particularly after the 1975 convention. Feeling new desperation, moderates began steeling themselves for open rebellion and schism. Just when Jack Preus seemed most in control of Missouri's destiny, he was seemingly losing it.

Ironically, his dubious posture of reacting to Missouri rather than acting on Missouri was at last becoming true. Preus's psychological need had become Missouri's ecclesiastical reality. After New Orleans he was reacting to the plunder of conservative raiding parties, which in turn set off the open rebellion and schismatic maneuverings of moderates. If Preus had helped put moderates on the plank, he now found them running to the edge, threatening to jump overboard and to take as many hands as they could with them.

Some moderates and their sympathizers had decided Missouri could survive Jack Preus—however ugly and costly that might be. An underground movement could be kept alive and eventually resurrected. History, presumably, was on their side rather than on Preus's side. But most moderates seemed to have no long-term strategy for relating to the Preus occupation, much less for recapturing and making Missouri safe once again for their brand of pluralistic Lutheran theology.

Beginning at Concordia Seminary, moderates rebelled in such politically inept ways it suggested an ecclesiastical death wish or, better perhaps, an unconscious desire to be born into a new church. Concordia professors had somehow decided that they could enter the plains of Armageddon without losing a single soldier. Tietjen had shown before New Orleans that he preferred sacrificing all of Concordia rather than losing a single professor. After New Orleans, moderates showed they preferred sacrificing their stake in Missouri rather than losing John Tietjen.

Missouri moderates proved in the end that they personalized the ideological struggle more than Preus did. Their personal vision of truth, their personal freedom, and their personal Lutheranism were more important to them than Missouri as politico-ecclesiastical prize. They proved more interested in damning Preus than in neutralizing him or accommodating themselves to his inevitable if temporary control. Taking a cue from Tietjen, they seemed more interested in moralizing than in politicalizing.

Missouri moderates should have taken their survival lessons from those badly outnumbered conservatives in Presbyterian, Methodist, Episcopal, and other denominations, where liberals, not known for their gentleness, had been ruling for two or more decades. Instead, Missouri moderates assumed they could win in both the short and long runs—or at least neutralize the conservative party—simply by forcing the issues. "Exposing"

Preus would be enough. Moderates could fight Preus in the press, in the wider Lutheran and mainline Protestant communities, in their own limited Missouri fan clubs. But when it came to fighting and bleeding in the only forum that counted, the dark belly of Missouri, many turned ecclesiastical pacificists and come-outers. Preus showed, perhaps perversely, that he loved Missouri more than the moderates did. At least he prized it enough to want to control it regardless of the great personal and corporate cost.

In early 1974, Missouri's best and brightest gave Preus the theological nerve center of their church. They walked away from Concordia Seminary. They abandoned the fortress despite their apparent strength to fight on and perhaps win a long guerrilla war. On the basis of the general theological world-view of Missouri moderates, the assumption would be that their highest churchly goal was to bring Missouri into the Lutheran mainstream, to coax back the remnant that was Missouri when Missouri's isolationism no longer seemed relevant. Thus, wouldn't the higher ethic have called Missouri moderates first and foremost to survival within Missouri so that goal could eventually be achieved?

Moderates would doubtless respond that Preus ruthlessly forced on them three equally distasteful choices: (1) Abandon Missouri; (2) fight the slow-burning underground battle; (3) conform to his theological totalitarianism. First psychologically, then physically, abandoning Missouri was viewed as the only Christian option. Perhaps it was. When the crunch came, moderates saw themselves as Lutherans first, Missouri Lutherans second. However sound theologically, it was a shaky platform for waging a long-term ecclesiastical war.

When Preus began his investigation of doctrinal views held and taught at Concordia Seminary shortly after he became president, Tietjen declared that Concordia "welcomed" the opportunity to show the whole church how "Lutheran" the seminary community really was. It was a telltale signal that Tietjen moderates were going to set their struggle with Preus in a prophetic and ideological, rather than an ecclesiastical, key. How genuinely "Lutheran" they were in terms of mainstream Lutheranism was ecclesiastically marginal, if not totally irrelevant. Rank-and-file Missourians supporting Concordia to the tune of one million dollars a year did not want to hear how Lutheran Concordia was but how *Missourian* Concordia was. Preus understood that. Tietjen's Concordia apparently did not.

The moderates' pattern of looking toward the wider Lutheran community had been set within months of Preus's election. Several executives began quitting in moral outrage at this earthy "Norwegian carpetbagger." When dismissed, Jungkuntz sought solace at Concordia and soon after left the battlefront entirely rather than fight Preus down to the last footnote of canon law.

This is not to condemn moderates and justify Preus. Freedom in the gospel is at the essence of Lutheranism. There were pressing ethical questions about personal and family psychological health. Trying to work with a colleague who seriously believes the King James Version of the Bible is the only "inerrant" version, for example, is no easy or fruitful fate. Some moderates feared that the longer they fought a church war on Preus's terms, the greater the risk they would end up like the enemy. Nor is this to suggest that Preus can win in the long run. Occupation armies ultimately breed virulent resistance.

Yet it must not be recorded in American church history that Jack Preus and the conservative activists who supported him won control of Missouri by their prowess alone. They won much of Missouri by sheer default.

Moderates admit as much with such laments as "if we'd only known then what we know now" and the like. Jungkuntz has been reminded more than once by his moderate colleagues that he might have struck a significant blow against the Preus juggernaut if he had put up more resistance. The hindsight speculation is interesting. Preus might indeed have been successfully diverted from Concordia Seminary, which was vulnerable, had Jungkuntz and others forced Preus to fight attention-grabbing and paralyzing canon law battles before the theological issues surrounding Concordia, and favorable to manipulation by Preus, had jelled synodwide. Preus was not invulnerable early on. In October 1969, he was still learning where the john was at St. Louis headquarters, and, as we have seen, he was not at the peak of personal security in the job. A celebrated quasi-heresy trial with an articulate Jungkuntz on the stand and network television cameras grinding could have immobilized Jack Preus for years or forced him into a synodwide showdown before he was capable of handling it creatively. Instead, not only did Jungkuntz fail to divert Preus from Concordia, the deposed synod theologian made Concordia even more of a Preus target by going to the seminary where his teaching contract created yet another "Concordia problem" Preus had to deal with.

One reason Missouri moderates never developed a sound, long-range politics of survival was their seemingly infinite capacity to be shocked and surprised by Preus. How they could continue to be shocked after New Orleans, or how they could think that most Missourians would eventually be shocked into rejecting the Preus party, is difficult for an outsider to understand. Yet maybe a case can be made. Moderates had had no experience with colleagues determined to get them out. They were up against Preus conservatives who were bent on removing them, without the procedures moderates might have expected.

Moreover, the convention committee, with the help of conservative board members from the seminary, had tacked onto Tietjen's false doctrine charges a series of executive irregularities that allegedly amounted to "administrative malfeasance." The board majority had cleared Tietjen of these charges prior to New Orleans. Under the charge of usurping powers rightfully belonging only to the full board, Tietjen was censured for ordering the "unbugeted" seven-thousand-dollar professional opinion survey without authorization and other nit-picking items that could have been dredged up against many Missouri executives. It was not uncommon for Missouri executives to buy something and figure out later where the money would come from.

Synod headquarters had in the early Preus years lost eight hundred thousand dollars on a white elephant building adjacent to the old Lutheran headquarters. The Missouri Synod never got a full documented report on how that happened—much less any word of malfeasance! There were no malfeasance claims when a professional audit turned up evidence of black-marketing of synod funds, dual bookkeeping, and slush-funding in the Brazil district administration.

This stampede to get Tietjen before the fall term collapsed embarrassingly in late August 1973 for the newly-elected board of control at Concordia. Under crusading chairman E. J. Otto of Quincy, Illinois, the hardest of the hard-nosed traditionalists and a colleague with Jack Preus on the pre-Denver "Balance" effort, the board had telescoped too many of the constitutional protections for the accused Tietjen. He had been suspended, but for fear of being legally vulnerable, the board had to back off. Tietjen was suspended and, in effect, reinstated all in one weekend.

Ironically, the only perfectly logical proposals being made after New Orleans were by Otto and the ultraorthodox. They were calling for shutting down Concordia. Indeed, if an overwhelming majority of professors held and taught heretical views, Missouri constituents had every right to demand the seminary not open until the mess was sorted out.

Missourians at New Orleans had said too much and not enough simultaneously. The theology of the professors had been lumped together and judged heretical, but no individuals other than Tietjen were specifically accused. It was as if a company's stockholders had accused their board of directors of embezzlement but didn't know or didn't want to name which individual members were guilty. Presumably the truly guilty were supposed to resign under the cloud or sit around indefinitely and wait for the summons from the sheriff. But strangely, the stockholders were all supposed to go home and let the board carry on as if nothing had happened.

This Alice-in-Wonderland flavor dogged the administration of pragmatist Jack Preus. Missouri had just used the most awesome concept in its lexicon—false doctrine. It had applied the concept to the men training more than 60 percent of its new pastors. Now surely this was serious business. Or was it? It must not have been very serious after all if Concordia doors opened that fall. Presumably the Preus administration cannot go on indefinitely using serious and sacred concepts of conservative Missourians without their insisting on the logical follow-ups.

As if to demonstrate that the longer Tietjen stayed the harder it would be for all the rest of the Concordia community, the board went on that fall to enact new mandatory retirement age limits to squeeze out several older professors, including former seminary president Alfred Fuerbringer. Curriculum changes were ordered. Tough new screening procedures were introduced for all seminary courses.

But no formal heresy charges were filed against any of the forty-five professors in the months after New Orleans. Obviously, Preus still wanted to do it his way, not Otten's way. The plan was to depose Tietjen first, or get him to resign. Preus sent feelers to several faculty leaders trying to get them to discuss privately the options that might be opened up if Tietjen would resign. His overtures were rejected. The faculty insisted that the future of the seminary and Tietjen's future were linked. "If they would only stop forming that phalanx around Tietjen," Preus lamented to his go-betweens.

Meanwhile moderates in Missouri had realized after New Orleans the necessity of an umbrella political organization for survival and perhaps, ultimately, a lifeboat to escape Preus's Missouri. Evangelical Lutherans in Mission (ELIM) was formed at a Chicago assembly in August 1973. ELIM grew impressively in three years to more than twelve thousand dues-paying members and a budget of about $1.5 million. Its weekly newspaper *Missouri in Perspective* eventually had a national circulation of more than one hundred forty thousand. With this moderate muckraker and Otten's *Christian News,* Missourians in mid-1975 could easily have been the best-informed church constituents in the history of Western Christianity. There were few official secrets in Missouri. It was a strange claim indeed when Tietjen and others kept repeating that Missourians just didn't know what was going on in their church.

Despite their official organization, however, moderates still did not seem to be forcing rough political decisions on themselves. Perhaps they felt that giving Tietjen orders on how to fight the battle for Concordia was a cure as bad as the Preus disease. Perhaps they would have fought it the same way. At any rate, the liberal-moderate caucus fell into the pattern of following its far-left wing and trying to justify and build on that wing's political liabilities. For Missouri moderates to have to made their last stand for Seminex, which wasn't even in Missouri, meant that they were romantically adrift even before they could gear for a respectable battle.

Efforts were made by synod Director of Public Relations, Victor Bryant, beginning in late 1973 to negotiate a compromise to avert the seminary showdown. With Preus's blessing, Bryant approached the seminary's Public Relations man Larry Neeb with feelers on arranging a graceful exit for Tietjen. The stampede against the seminary could be halted if Tietjen would resign and take a parish assignment through a moderate district president. The heresy charges would be dropped, in effect, because Tietjen would then be under the jurisdiction of a moderate. Tietjen later denounced the proposal as a "deal" symptomatic of the "moral bankruptcy" of the Preus administration and Preus himself.

Arranging gracious exits for troublesome clerics is one of the oldest practices in the Christian church. Preus was hardly displaying immorality by participating in Bryant's proposal. Bryant issued a highly personalized press release confessing to the world that if he sinned it was sin of a desperate man trying to

ave a church he loved. He went on to dub Tietjen as "the
ighth public relations wonder of the world" for Tietjen's abil-
y to paint black all things Preus touched and color white all
is own actions.

Yet Tietjen had made his point. Preus was dealing politically
vith heresy charges. Sacred concepts were being used as tools
nd bargaining points. Tietjen the archheretic could not be
olerated at Concordia Seminary but could be made pastor in
irtually any parish of his choosing! At the very least, it was not
)tten's way. Moreover, if Jack Preus was so secure about these
:inds of dealings with Tietjen, he could have arranged for a
•ipartisan and mutually agreeable synod commission wherein
he options facing Tietjen and Concordia were openly nego-
iated. Preus later apologized in a predominantly moderate
egion of Missouri for his part in the Bryant proposal. The
ipology was aimed more at the fact that he had meddled in
omething he presumably had no control over than for what he
iad proposed. Preus was consistent in one way in this matter.
-le had never said that Tietjen had to go because Tietjen was
ı heretic. Tietjen had to go because he was blocking the con-
ervative revival and control Preus wanted at Concordia and
hroughout the Missouri Synod. Beyond that, Preus admitted
ınce that he had no desire "to hound Dr. Tietjen out of the
ynod."

The inevitable suspension of John Tietjen came January 20,
1974. The next day students voted to strike until the board
dentified the heretical teachers supposedly being harbored by
Γietjen. The professors, to some extent radicalized by their own
itudents, followed the next day. They declared they would not
·eturn to teaching until heresy trials were initiated against them
ır they were in the process of being cleared. They directed their
ırotest to Preus. Martin Scharlemann, who had been named
ıcting president of Concordia, was denounced as a shameless
:urncoat. Scharlemann bravely brushed aside their blunt rejec-
:ion and took the offensive. Rebellions aren't negotiated, they
ıre crushed, he declared.

Preus responded to the synod in a January 28 "Message to the Church." Publishing two of his earlier letters to the faculty and other caustic items, Preus was definitely not turning the other cheek. If Tietjen's Concordia was attempting to provoke the gut-fighter in Jack Preus, they were not unsuccessful. At his sarcastic best, Preus opened one response by thanking the faculty for its letter "which arrived ten minutes before a reporter called to ask for my comments." He accused the professors of staging "theatricals" for the media and "devising ways to trick people." He demanded that they beg the church's mercy for their arrogance and self-righteousness and for having "tried to change the theology of the church without telling the church."

The most controversial section was an appendix from an unspecified number of unnamed conservative students who charged they had been "harrassed and bullied" by the moderate professors. Traditionalist students were ridiculed and given lower grades. Chapel services were used to villify Preus. Scharlemann had been called "obscene names" by a moderate professor—in chapel, no less. The students suggested that they were so terrified they couldn't release their names. Doubtless, they were. Any outspoken conservative at the post-New Orleans Concordia would have been something comparable to a Jew caught in an Arab command post.

Nonetheless, Preus was challenged on the truth of many allegations by several conservative students who weren't on strike. The truth or falsity of the allegations, however, faded in significance before the searing fact of a head of a major Christian church using in a churchwide report sensational material from unnamed sources. This was total war indeed. The "White Paper" syndrome was alive and well at Preus headquarters. Interestingly, Preus for years had not missed an opportunity to blame a provocative secular press for washing poor Missouri's dirty linen.

A war of nerves began. Preus struck a paternalistic pose. When the boys calmed down, they would come back to their senses and their classrooms. But the striking professors were making plans for alternative teaching arrangements off-campus. When it was clear these were not idle threats, chairman Otto's board was mobilized. Their real or imagined deadline was Tuesday, February 19, the day the professors had indicated they would begin alternative teaching. Ostensibly, conservative hard-liners on the board took this deadline as an ultimatum that the professors were, in effect, going to institutionalize their strike. They were going to teach the students, but on a free-lance basis and apart from any board supervision. Rebellion indeed, and begging for firm response.

But a rumor persists that a small cabal of key conservatives had hoped to spring a surprise on the rebelling Concordia professors. The alleged plan was to go down to the wire with the posture of negotiation and then confront the professors with an ultimatum too tough to swallow. In other words, the idea was to hang the professors with their own rope. Jack Preus acknowledged later only that sometime between January 20 and February 17 the question had changed in the conservative war council from "how to get them back" to "do we want them back." Missouri grapevine has it that a leading traditionalist close to Preus said of the events to follow: "We weren't sure we could pull it off, but we did."

Fresh from a synod board of directors peace-seeking forum the day before, vice-president Edwin Weber, Preus's personal envoy on the seminary board, pulled a document from his pocket at a Concordia board session Sunday, February 17. The document was couched in legalese; so it was presumably drawn up with the help of a corporate attorney. It ordered the professors back to work by Tuesday morning under threat of dismissal and eviction from their seminary housing. Written compliance was to be submitted by noon Monday. Shocked moderates on the board begged the conservative majority to desist, but they were not to be swayed. The action was taken by a 6–5 vote.

This, incidentally, was not atypical of the "peace-making" efforts of the Preus administration during those days. The board of directors' peace-seeking committee had broken off on

Saturday with a request that all parties consider various alternatives for attempting a settlement, alternatives which had just been discussed for two days. No alternative discussed even remotely resembled the blunt legal one Weber presented some twenty-four hours later.

The ultimatum was stuffed into the mail slots of the Concordia professors or under their office doors. Some did not know about it until 8 A.M. Monday. Alfred Fuerbringer, awaiting surgery in a hospital room, had the ultimatum read to him by a clerk over the telephone an hour before the noon deadline.

Moderate professors and staff members, some with their wives, met in an emotional assembly midmorning Monday. No, they would not return under such terms. Yes, they would go into exile together and invite the students to follow them. At high noon, they sang "The Church's One Foundation," which had become their equivalent of the civil-righters' "We Shall Overcome."

Some of these men at Denver had urged moderate bureaucrats sick at the Preus election to hang in and fight to the end. Now that the Concordia cheerleaders were deeply into the fray, they had declared an ecclesiastical "end" when there was no such end. What had ended, and drastically, was their tactic of a strike, but certainly not all the ecclesiastical ways and means to continue to resist Preus from within synodical structures. Surely, they were not so shocked by the ultimatum that they couldn't devise another tactic short of self-exile, which put them adrift in an ecclesiastical no-man's-land.

Many Concordia professors had urged their colleagues to be brave, cunning, and long-suffering in the struggle against Preus. Now the boosters were being brave but hardly very cunning or long-suffering. The Preus syndrome of "reacting" because he had no choice had infected his opponents' thinking. They were going into exile because they had no choice! They were helpless victims. And maybe they were. If one is victimized, he begins thinking like a victim, then begins acting like a victim. No doubt also, there was a certain political miscalculation involved n the self-exile move. There was hope that it might somehow force the Missouri Synod into an emergency summit meeting in which the Preus party would not be calling the shots. If Missouri wouldn't come begging the professors to come back, at least Missourians would have to negotiate under pressure to keep their major seminary going. Surely, the synod didn't expect Concordia Seminary to survive without them, the self-exiled professors seemed to believe.

The next day the students assembled to "vote" on whether to join the professors in exile. Student leaders had already helped plan the media display for the walk-off. Although the momentum was probably too strong to stop, a talented orator might have blunted it. A cooling-off period might have been manipulated. Ironically, the church's most persuasive orator, Jack Preus, was scurrying around his downtown headquarters trying to find a lieutenant to present to the students the arguments against any walkout. Preus was not up to the challenge, or, more likely, he had been advised his appearance would be counterproductive. He urged canon lawyer Herb Mueller to go, who urged education executive Art Ahlschwede to go. But no Preus official spoke that day in the Concordia gym although a sheet warning students of the consequences was circulated. About four hundred students roared their approval of self-exile after what was largely a pro forma discussion of a predetermined conclusion.

Concordia in exodus was melodrama fitting sacramental-minded Lutherans and media-conscious activists. White crosses for all the fired professors were planted in the seminary quadrangle. The statue of Martin Luther was draped in black. The main entrance was boarded with plywood sprayed with the word "EXILED." These scenes were captured in news service photos and television film clips used around the world. There was prayer and song. Then there was a procession to a nearby park where liberal Protestants symbolically greeted the victims and welcomed them into the religious wild blue yonder.

From an ecclesiastical viewpoint, a seemingly perplexed

Scharlemann, the old military chaplain with a keen sense of institutional realities, uttered the most incisive judgment. It was madness, he said.

In an authoritarian church, a strike had been political folly. A self-exiled, rebel seminary was political wrist-slashing. It had little chance to prove its point—namely Preus and his party were "morally corrupt." Instead, all it proved for many Missourians was the exact point Preus had been trying to make for years. Tietjen's Concordia would do literally anything to avoid confronting the "doctrinal" issues.

Jack Preus was on a news film on the CBS "Evening News" with Walter Cronkite the next evening. To be sure, the brief story was the cutsey "kicker" at the end of the program and yet another opportunity for the Eastern elite to chuckle at the oddities of organized religion in the heartland. But Preus, at this milestone of public exposure, did not miss the opportunity to play his eternal theme of aggressee rather than aggressor. This board we have here, well, it probably went too far. These professors we have, well, they definitely went too far. But statesman Jack Preus and wise Mother Missouri would pick up the pieces.

Seminex posed headaches for Preus because, at least for several years and maybe longer, its students could secure pastoral jobs with sympathetic district presidents and congregations. Eventually, it would provide the showdown where Jack Preus proved that he could be Missouri's purifying angel.

Yet there were signals that the self-exile of Concordia moderates took an enormous psychological and moral burden off Jack Preus the man. Here indeed was proof that, not he, but his opponents were irresponsible and fanatical. Not without some basis, Preus had an assuaged conscience. They, not he, would have to be recorded in Lutheran history as taking the first tangible schismatic step.

Preus was strangely relaxed. He began apologizing publicly for any of his sins that might have contributed to the debacle. The word may even be stronger. He seemed to *celebrate* his uman imperfections, his humanity. "I have more faults than leas on a dog," he sang in an October newspaper interview. He vas speaking gracious words and talking a moderate tone wher-ver he traveled. There were overtures to the exiled professors vho wanted to return. He did not make a federal case to try to purge the exiles from the synod's welfare and pension plans.

"Peacemaker" Preus could not and did not relent on the pedrock issue of tolerating "uncertified" Seminex graduates. This certification had been upgraded to bylaw status largely at he pushing of moderates. Now they were caught by it, and Preus felt if he held the line Seminex could be defused. His administration began to set the stage for disciplining moderate district presidents who were ordaining Seminex students. Preus also kept up his verbal attacks on ELIM, which was financing Seminex. Yet Preus stayed flexible, largely because he had the upper hand. He showed willingness to accommodate Seminex professors on the details for their return. They did not have to grovel, just nod in passing. If Seminex professors or students would do so much as a courtsey in his direction, that would seemingly have been enough to get them back—minus Tietjen, of course.

A gracious Preus went along with a council of district presidents' proposal for a bipartisan "theological convocation" in April 1975. Designed with the latest elite models for group processes that had helped groups ranging from fractured Protestants to troubled business firms, more than one hundred Missouri theologians and district presidents met for a full week at Concordia Seminary. The assembly would not have legislative powers, of course, but maybe it could have a moral impact. The convocation proved Missourians could still sit down together, but it proved little else. When a hard-line convention unfolded three months later, it seemed almost cynical that it was even convened—much less billed as a major step for reconcilation.

Many leading conservatives boycotted the closing communion service, so convinced they had become that moderates were intolerable. By contrast, Jack Preus communed with moderates, and he couldn't praise the work of the convocation enough. It was a truly magnanimous Jack Preus presiding at that theological convocation. Here was the churchly statesman Preus could have been if only the moderates had given him the space he wanted! But Preus was making neither news nor history that April. The assembly was one of those safe, hopeless causes, like his POW ventures—nothing to lose, everything to gain in terms of public relations.

About the only fact related to the theological convocation that was significant was where it convened—on the campus of old Concordia Seminary. Despite the thinly disguised hopes of many Seminex exiles, loyalist Concordia survived without the elite. A handful of teachers and students manned the patched-up institution. Concordia started the 1974 fall term with a fourth of the Seminex enrollment. But they went on eventually to impressive rebuilding under a blank-check backing of the ruling Preus party and the direction of Ralph Bohlmann who had become president of the seminary. Initially, survival was at the annual cost of thirty-four thousand dollars per student—doubtless one of several McGuiness-style records in American religious history the Missouri war produced.

Meanwhile, and no less impressive in its own way as the survival of old Concordia, Seminex was planted and bloomed. Missouri moderates were supporting it as if there were no ecclesiastical tomorrow. Privately, some were saying Seminex was a political disaster of monumental proportions, but there was no breaking ranks. No serious efforts came to light within the moderate-liberal camp to nudge the left wing back, no suggestions that Seminex cut losses and negotiate some return. At a late August rally in Chicago, ELIM moderates were still meekly accepting the political agenda set by the Seminex expatriates, but there was at least some indication that many of them did not like that agenda. There were signals that many moderates felt the Seminex syndrome amounted to declaring an end too hastily and giving Preus spoils he never earned.

After his suspension, Tietjen had announced that he would

not submit to a heresy trial under the Preus administration. It would have been rigged, he said. At the Chicago rally, ELIM officers bent over backward to make Tietjen a hero. They floated a resolution to support him in that decision. What looked like a slight majority rejected the resolution in a show of hands. The ELIM elite quickly backed off taking any official action after that straw vote had indicated criticism of white-knight Tietjen.

Independent-minded George Loose of Florida, who had been chairman of the seminary board during the Preus onslaught before New Orleans, told the assembly, "We shouldn't make it easy for anybody to kick us out. If we go out, let's be sure it's out the front door—kicking and screaming."

Tietjen was found guilty by Otto's board in October 1974. That set off another round of moderate moralizing and a boost in income. ELIM strategy was to play up its martyrs until—until what? Soon the martyrs of the moderate movement had to produce something, either the seeds of change in the old church or seeds for a new church, but it seemed to be doing neither.

Then, in an ironic turn, the very Missouri system Tietjen had damned cranked out a decision in his favor. In June 1975, a peace-starved but theologically conservative pastor named Oscar Gerken of Cape Girardeau, Missouri, who had been saddled with ruling whether Tietjen was to be defrocked from the Missouri ministry on the basis of the board's heresy conviction, declared that Tietjen was no heretic. True, Gerken's analysis of Tietjen's theological views about the Bible was not the kind of thorough work to earn a graduate degree with. It was bending over backward to try to close a theological chasm. Nonetheless, here was a relatively unpoliticized, workaday Missouri pastor declaring John Tietjen acceptable to teach Missouri's sons and daughters catechism! Through Gerken, mysterious Missouri had shown once again how desperately it wanted to be one, or at least not to be fractured hopelessly in two.

Gerken's ruling was moral justification the moderates latched onto quickly. It was a most embarrassing development for the Preus party although not specifically for Preus, who, it should be remembered, never claimed Tietjen was a heretic. But it was intrinsically embarrassing also to Tietjen and the moderates because it revealed that their posture of ecclesiastical pacifism might have been politically premature. A middle, however tenuous, was out there somewhere to appeal to. The moderate's theological approach to the Bible might not be considered doctrinal anathema after all to rank-and-file Missourians. Preus's ideological base was thinner than it seemed. The political props to keep the Preus regime moving would have to be shored up.

Just as they had suffered embarrassment prior to New Orleans when all the Preus-accused professors at Concordia had been cleared, so here the Preus party suffered another embarrassment with the Gerken ruling, which came only days before the 1975 synod convention in Anaheim, California. As at New Orleans, Preus and company would not be deterred by this blow but rather mobilized by it. Anaheim would be New Orleans II. Preus would again have to mount the podium and bring all his skills with him.

President Preus was at the peak of his career during the 1975 convention. His appointed committees had all barrels loaded for him. Proposals included authorization for him to fire all moderate district presidents who continued ordaining Seminex graduates; abolishing the so-called English District, a nongeographical unit and haven for aggressive moderates, and ousting from the church all ELIM leaders whose activities were "divisive."

High drama came over the proposal to fire the moderate district presidents. Eight of them previously had threatened to continue support of Seminex regardless of convention action. Essentially, they argued the time-honored Missouri tradition leaning toward congregational autonomy. If congregations wanted Seminex graduates, the district presidents would honor the requests. In the highly politicized Missouri Synod of 1975, however, some of the eight district presidents were doing more than simply honoring requests. Some were promoting Seminex graduates. Preus argued that Missouri, or any other church, could not long tolerate officers who refused to obey the rules and operated by their own lights.

When at midweek, the Anaheim convention declined to dissolve the English District (as Preus had predicted), Preus leaned on English District president Harold Hecht to respond in kind on the Seminex ordination question. After delivering a folksy recount of the issues, Preus turned ceremoniously to the district presidents' gallery: "Pastor Hecht, are you going to walk with us or are you going to insist on your own way?" Boos from moderates interrupted his remarks but gave way to applause from the conservative convention majority. A rattled Preus continued. When he finished, he threw open his hands in a gesture of finality. After a long prayer lead by a delegate, Preus was asked if he had more remarks. He dabbed at his eyes to dry the tears. ". . . I'm sorry, I get a little emotional at times." Not that Preus's tears aren't genuine. He has a sentimental streak.

President Preus used similar two-to-tango pleas the next day to argue for ouster of ELIM leaders. From the podium, he scolded moderates for planning a demonstration after the expected vote against them. "Must we constantly be faced with this threat that if you don't get your rights, you'll go to the patio?" The ouster proposal was a "desperate move on the part of an harrassed church," Preus lamented. What was a church body to do? "Please help us," Preus concluded.

Both resolutions passed by roughly the 57–43 percentage holding firm among Missouri convention delegates since New Orleans two years earlier.

Unlike New Orleans, which had decreed too much too vaguely, Anaheim had decreed too much too specifically. Preus was ordered to fire any nonconformist district president sixty days before the district conventions began in early spring of 1976. His first deadline was in late December. It was not ideal legislation for Preus the maneuverer. He had shown a preference for more maneuvering room in the past. How Preus allowed himself to be pinned down to such specifics was an unexplained element in the Anaheim convention. At any rate, Preus seemed to believe that he would never have to pull the trigger. The district presidents would resign or give him the courtsey he needed to avoid axing them.

ELIM leaders and the eight district presidents assembled in Chicago several weeks after the Anaheim convention. They declared they were ready to resist Preus indefinitely and that they might even lead an exodus from Missouri if any district president were fired. Deposing a duly elected district president would be the decisive act spelling the end of the Missouri Synod as they had known it, they hinted.

Preus began sniffing the air. As he was to say later, the post-Anaheim future seemed to belong to the party making peace. After the ELIM assembly, several worried board of directors' members, including steady, peace-seeker Harry Barr, an industrialist from Fort Smith, Arkansas, and moderate vice-president of synod August Bernthal of Florida, met with Preus in a day-long session in Minneapolis. Preus seemed convinced of the seriousness of schismatic threat from the left.

In August, Preus issued a churchwide letter claiming he found himself "moving more into the middle" between the two extremes than at any time in his career. He urged conservative agents to avoid punitive and vindictive actions, moderates to stop talk of schism. Without covering up deep divisions on theology, couldn't Missourians give it one more yeoman's try? Couldn't Missouri return to its old habit of being one? As was typical of Preus proclamations, there were no substantial concessions, but the words disturbed conservatives nonetheless

Herman Otten immediately published an impeccably logical editorial arguing that Preus's record was one of a "first-class extremist" for an inerrant Bible and against moderation. Preus ought to be proud of that, not put up some pose of neutrality which nobody would believe for a moment. "No, President Preus, there is no middle. The Synod is extremist. The conservative majority is extremist. ELIMites all are extremists. Only freaks can claim the middle."

Heat from the right was intense. Letters as harsh as any Preus had received over the years from moderates poured in from conservatives. Telephone callers, some handled in the evenings by Delpha at the Preus apartment, questioned Preus's integrity. Why was he waffling when total victory was in sight? Why was he compromising biblical doctrine for ecclesiastical convenience?

President Preus "clarified" his "middle of the road" statements in another letter two months later. Of course, he was not talking about compromising doctrine. He was talking about a style of churchmanship which sought only to deal fairly with opponents. Conservatives should not fear for the doctrinal ship of state. They should, in effect, let Preus take care of Missouri's political and diplomatic affairs.

Clearly, Jack Preus was not rolling back any of the watershed acts which had brought Missouri to a showdown, but he was trying to prevent independent-minded conservatives from starting more brush fires than his administration could handle at any one time. Preus was sitting on crusading conservatives, many of whom got him elected in 1969. Cantankerous Waldo Werning of the synod's troubled board for missions had been dumped by the Preus administration at Anaheim. Preus later squeezed Werning out of the running for a headquarters job in the stewardship department. Preus had leaned heavily on aggressive conservative board members at Concordia College in St. Paul, where moderate president Harvey Stegemoeller eventually resigned.

Preus tried to rein in the board at the predominantly moderate Concordia College in Bronxville, New York. In late September 1975 he made a presidential foray to warn against extremism. Issuing pragmatic guidelines, he declared, in effect, that Missouri out East was by nature more liberal and that that ought to be recognized and accepted, within limits of course. Under the leadership of conservative Merlin Meyer, the board ignored Preus's "Eastern tolerance" policy. Meyer set up new rules to interrogate prospective faculty for doctrinal purity.

When moderate president Robert Schnabel resigned the following April, Jack Preus, politician, went to work. Chairman Meyer was the problem, he said. Meyer resigned his chairmanship after a face-to-face confrontation with Preus. Missouri's die-hard conservatives had always been meek in the crunch against Preus. Few ever broke ranks although by fall 1975 there was some talk that conservatives were becoming dissillusioned with Preus's political dealing.

The genuineness of the Preus trial-ballooning for political compromise came with his first four decisions on the dissenting moderate district presidents. Obviously wavering on the late December decision to oust Herman Neunaber of Southern Illinois, Preus went literally down to the last hour of the deadline before declining to oust. He used the technicality that Neunaber had only tolerated ordination of Seminex graduates rather than ordaining them himself. Some conservatives were in an uproar again, suggesting that Preus was defying a clear order of the synod convention.

His agreement to let Neunaber off the hook included a plea that Southern Illinois Lutherans, at their convention in late February 1976, instruct their district president to obey synod bylaws. Preus and Neunaber then took their respective cases to the grass roots in a series of seven local meetings.

Southern Illinois was bellwether territory, full of earnest, heartland Missourians. A mixture of rural and urban congregations within rumor-range of St. Louis headquarters, it was one of the more politicized and polarized in the synod. It seemed about evenly divided along ideological lines.

The short, scrappy Neunaber had long been partisan for moderate causes. He had maintained a solid base of support among both clergy and lay, but he had a solid bank of opponents as well. Although most of his constituents were open and cordial in their disagreements, some had communicated bitter, anonymous messages. In the heat after Anaheim, a plainclothes policeman was once planted for a Neunaber public appearance. In genuine concern, apparently, a conservative party leader had alerted Neunaber that tempers might flare out of control.

Neunaber later got a baby chameleon in the mail—presumably someone's statement about Neunaber's synodical disloyalty.

But only calm, patient churchfolk assembled for the joint Preus-Neunaber presentations at the seven grass-roots meetings. Preus on the hustings was his usual likable, folksy, plain-speaking self. After Neunaber had delivered a Bible-allegorizing defense of the Seminex protest, Preus consciously took the low road. Order was the essence of church survival. One didn't need to quote the Bible when the issue was chaos. What if the church board at First Lutheran decided for conscience reasons to cut off a pastor's paycheck? Conscience-mongering moderates would be the first ones to complain about that! A district president had to obey the rules. He didn't have to agree with the rules. Nothing could ever be solved if lawlessness prevailed.

How persuasive had Jack Preus been in the trenches? Several weeks later, the Southern Illinois convention delegates voted unequivocal support for Neunaber's stand on the Seminex placement question. But when moderates tried to push forward with a resolution to recognize Seminex as a legitimate Missouri operation, they were rebuffed. As often happens at Missouri grass roots, neither side won a clear victory. Nonetheless, Preus went on to interpret the convention as highly favorable to his cause. Psychologically and practically, it showed the people were still looking for solutions within Missouri. They would tolerate a dissenting district president and even encourage him personally, but they would not follow him down any primrose path that led out of the synod.

Yet for Jack Preus, populist church politician, these grass-roots meetings were surely deeply disappointing. He had thrown himself heart and soul, with all his personal charm and presidential prestige, into seven townhall meetings with a simple request of Missourians in the pew. Please instruct your district president to obey church bylaws. He did not get his minimal symbolic request.

When there were no committees he could appoint, no ultimatums he could wave; when the opposition had an equal advantage; when it was a face to face confrontation; when Jack Preus had to convince the people they should tell their district president to nod in the direction of synod headquarters—he had failed. Making big news at the top had been easier than making simple history at the bottom.

If he had waltzed to explain his Neunaber decision, Preus was jitterbugging soon afterward when he let three other moderate district presidents off the hook. In what seemed the heaviest strain he had ever put on the interpretation of any ecclesiastical reality, Preus declared the convention ruling had been implemented with respect to the three district presidents. Actually, none had apparently given him any written or oral compliance to conform. All had Seminex ordinations on tap in their districts at the time Preus made this move. Perhaps some hedged in a way Preus could see a penlight at the end of the tunnel, but the implication was all too clear. No Missourian could have had any doubts. Preus did not want to act. Preus at the brink wanted a big, unfractured Missouri Synod more than he wanted a pure, or even an orderly, Missouri Synod.

Compromiser Preus went several more steps. He repeated loudly an earlier offer that if even one of the eight district presidents showed signs of conforming, he would let all them off the hook. He proposed that they agree to a moratorium on ordaining Seminex graduates. Let the bygones alone. Even that would be enough of an olive twig to take to the next convention without dismissing any of them in the meantime.

But Preus kept the final barrel loaded. He could go no farther than this, he hinted in a message to the church. The four remaining district presidents would have to conform. The four said they would not conform—at least not until the congregations of their districts instructed them to stop ordaining Seminex graduates or until Preus agreed to roll back Missouri to its pre-New Orleans environment.

The four defiant district presidents ostensibly represented the ecclesiastical frontiers that heartland Missourians had never recognized as fully integrated into their denomination. Three were on the Eastern Seaboard: Rudolph Ressmeyer of New York City, head of the Atlantic District; Herman Frincke of Buffalo, New York, head of the Eastern District, and Robert Riedel of Springfield, Massachusetts, president of the New England District. The fourth was Harold Hecht of Detroit, head of the English District, so named because it was the first unit in Missouri to regularly use English rather than the German language. As suggested earlier, the English District was a liberal-leaning jurisdiction and roughly comparable to the Jesuit Order in the Catholic church. Some conservative Missourians thus found it easy to picture these district presidents and their constituents as marginal to the "real Missouri." Wasn't it appropriate that these experimenters and hangers-on out East become the focus of schismatic showdown? Hadn't they always been more "American Lutheran" than "old Lutheran" anyway?

In fact, the schismatic confrontation with these four district presidents pointed up just how deeply Missourians out East, or anywhere for that matter, were rooted in old Missouri. It revealed just how much Missouri had remained an extended religious family with few strangers anywhere in the ranks.

The four district presidents were Missourian head to toe. All were of German ancestry. Ressmeyer was related to Franz Pieper, the great Missouri father. All four were graduates of Concordia Seminary in St. Louis. All had been pastors who worked their way up to the office of district president. Herman Frincke, the oldest, had entered the Missouri pastoral ministry before Jack Preus was out of high school. Harold Hecht, the youngest, had been in Missouri ministry a decade before Preus came into the synod from the Little Norwegians.

All the dissenting district presidents considered themselves integral and loyal Missourians. They were not innovators, "liberals," radical newcomers. That they might be "rebels," much less schismatics, in their own church was inconceivable to them. They found their plight unbelievable. Yet there they stood, ready to be deposed with the blessing of their church by an ambitious Norwegian Lutheran latecomer who, except for the vagaries of fate, might never even have had an adult career in the Missouri Synod.

The other four had similar old Missouri credentials. Besides Herman Neunaber, they were Elim Jaech of Portland, Oregon, head of the Northeast District; Paul Jacobs of Belmont, California, president of California-Nevada District, and Waldemar Meyer of Denver, district president of Colorado. The eight were clinging together as old Missouri teammates. They were far from heroes. Like traditionally bland Missouri leaders, they were more products than shapers of their church environment. The eight promised to hold out against the Preus administration as long as they continued to reflect the wishes of their Missouri constituents. They would be products of the old Missouri rather than shapers of a new Missouri.

But if Preus pushed too hard, they warned, they might be "forced" to lead an exodus. Even then, they would not be so much leaders as followers of the Missourians who elected them. They were as reluctant in their own way as Preus in his to acknowledge they were actors. They insisted they were only reacting to Preus. They could not see that in the Preus-Tietjen Armageddon such distinctions between offense and defense were pointless.

Later in 1976, most of the eight dissenting district presidents were to end their struggle from within Preus's Missouri and offer their leadership in the formation of a new church. These included Ressmeyer, Neunaber, Hecht and Riedel. Riedel took the additional step, in resigning his district presidency, to renounce even his personal membership in the Missouri Synod. "I had hoped," he said, "that by working from within, the synod might yet reverse its plunge into heterorthodoxy and once again become the evangelical synod it was. But that hope is now gone."

Jack Preus seemed to make his watershed decision on the hunch it would be no watershed decision at all. There would be no major exodus from the Missouri Synod by moderates. Preus may have known his enemy district presidents better than they knew themselves. He knew that precisely because they were old Missourians to the core it would be difficult for them to shepherd any irrevocable split. The ties were too strong. Despite their bluff, they would always look back to Missouri. If they didn't, it wouldn't matter because few would follow them.

In an interview shortly before he made his decision, Preus showed he had carefully assessed the political strengths of the dissenters in their regions. Symbolic loyalty to them was strong, but not nearly as strong as loyalty to the synod. Preus seemed heartened by the fact that even in the Atlantic District there had been a close vote at a special spring convocation on a proposal to suspend further ordination of Seminex graduates. The proposal was defeated, yet Preus felt it showed even many East Coast Missourians still harked back to St. Louis. It was a safe bet that moderates couldn't or wouldn't pull off a major schism.

The Lutheran Church–Missouri Synod in March 1976 was strangely and quietly busy. The ELIM machinery was being geared for exodus. Preus administration attorneys were busy checking corporate law in the eight rebel districts. Treasurer Milton Carpenter was establishing lines of credit in various cities to protect against a run on the districts' church extension fund—Missouri's savings and loan operation handled in each district but underwritten by the national church.

All this hardly was the routine business of an "orthodox, united, and growing" denomination, the three goals Preus had declared several years earlier for his Missouri, but then, neither was Preus's Missouri in any real trouble, it seemed. Despite all the brinkmanship, Missouri was marvelously intact. It had survived when other bodies might have long since crumbled under the pressures. Frail, earthen vessel that it may have been, Missouri still hadn't been shattered. Soon (perhaps by Christmas?) Missouri would move beyond the temporary stalemate toward those cherished Preus goals of orthodoxy, unity, and growth.

Ironies abounded in the phenomenon of Jack Preus at the

ecclesiastical brink. He had started his Missouri presidency talking about the supremacy of the Bible. Now he was talking about the supremacy of bylaws. The Preus revolution was supposed to bring theological honesty and purity to Missouri, but it had produced mostly equivocation and strife. Preus had orchestrated airtight rules for theologizing in his denomination, but now he seemingly would tolerate district presidents who not only rejected the official theology but defied elemental canon law besides. At Denver, moderates had begged him not to mount an ideological purge. Now they were all but begging him to purge in order to give them political fuel for an exodus from Missouri.

But there were consistencies also. Preus had never waivered on what he was doing—only how he was going to do it and the deadlines for doing it. Preus had never given conscious signals in seven years on the job that he wanted to split the Missouri Synod. He wanted to control it. He wanted to shape it. If there seemed to be inconsistencies now, it was only because Preus wanted to avoid an "unnecessary" split and minimize Missouri's losses from any splintering.

On April 2, 1976, Jack Preus announced at a press conference in St. Louis that he was firing the four district presidents. He was a bit edgy, but he seemed deeper down to be a calm man. This was an unpleasant day for his Missouri, he said. He had wanted more than anyone to avoid this day. He noted that the minute the ouster order was authorized the previous summer he had said he didn't want to implement it. He had tried his best. "But it became impossible not to do this," he said.

To the end, Jack Preus was the coy churchman. He was compelled to react to forces beyond his control. The remark richly summarized his career and his personality.

14

Preus Triumphant?

Jack Preus was buoyant in late July 1976. He was in Boston to give a routine presidential greeting from the Lutheran Church–Missouri Synod to the Lutheran Church in America convention. His high spirits stemmed from the rousing welcome he had received a few days earlier at the Lutheran Laymen's League convention in St. Paul, Minnesota. The message he had for the eagerly receptive league was not new. He had been suggesting as much since at least the summer of 1970. The Missouri Synod struggle was ending. The crisis had passed. Orthodoxy, peace, and prosperity were just around the corner. As to the moderate dissenters who just couldn't agree with the church, well, they should be given a fond good-bye if they wanted to leave but welcomed back if they decided to return to Missouri. The league lapped it up.

Now Preus was in Boston to tell liberal Lutherans his good news. Their response was hardly enthusiastic, but a plucky Preus gave them his crisp victory statement anyway. "I know you will be pleased to hear that the controversy in the Lutheran Church–Missouri Synod is drawing to a close," he began.

"Missouri had an identity problem. As she entered the second century of her existence, there were some within the structure who attempted to alter the Synod's historical confessional position and witness to the world. What has now been proven to be a small minority who sought to change Missouri's doctrinal stance is presently engaging in an effort to form a new church body separate from Missouri."

But, Preus told his audience, those trying to bleed Missouri wouldn't have much success. Why less than ten of the synod's sixty-two hundred congregations have decided to leave! Many more congregations had already rejected proposals to join the new church. Above all, in the heart of Missouri territory, the Midwest, "very few attempts to restructure are even being considered. Missouri has overwhelmingly . . . decided that she is going to remain Missouri."

Preus went on to chide the liberal Lutheran denomination for its criticism two years earlier of the Preus theological platform —a platform the Lutheran Church in America had suggested was needlessly divisive because it tacked onto Lutheran identity alien doctrinal requirements about an inerrant Bible. Preus countered that what his Missouri does exalts God's Word. Rather than fracturing God's people, Missouri "strengthens the unity of God's people." Missouri had been "tested in the fires of affliction and had emerged triumphant over the forces that had the effect of muffling her voice in Christendom and throughout the world." Missouri could once again confidently invite "bewildered and confused" outsiders into her ranks. Come join us, Preus concluded.

Jack Preus's Missouri had made history. The pattern of American Protestant history in the twentieth century had been inverted. Instead of battered and beaten Protestant conservatives leaving denominations controlled by liberals, battered and beaten "liberals" were leaving Missouri. Once on that wide and winding highway of liberalism, no major Protestant body had ever been returned to the straight and narrow, not, that is, until Preus's Missouri Synod. And what more appropriate place than a liberal Lutheran convention for Preus to parade his achievement, to gloat ever so judiciously, and perhaps even to convince a few Lutherans in another denomination that his Missouri now represented a significant and imposing force for the future.

If a Preus-watcher that July 1976 could have believed Preus, and let the imagination run, he might have envisioned epochal triumphs ahead. At age fifty-six, Preus had ten, maybe fifteen years of physical vigor in him. So in 1990, as head of some mighty pan-Lutheran or panevangelical Protestant federation, Preus could well be parading his epochal achievements in, say, Rome or Geneva—Jack Preus gloating, as it were, in the religious capitols of the world on the eve of his retirement as consummate ecclesiastical geopolitician of the right.

Preus had suggested more than once that he had no such pretensions. He didn't want to become a conservative standard-bearer beyond Missouri. He was soul and body a Missouri Lutheran. But, one might recall, Preus hadn't wanted to be Missouri's president prior to Denver, prior to the divine call. So maybe Missouri was indeed Preus's place to plant his feet so as to move the Christian world. One wondered, for example, if it was mere coincidence that a few weeks after Preus's Boston speech, Herman Otten of *Christian News* issued "A Call for Realignment" of American Lutherans into one federation of Preus-style conservatives and another camp of "liberal" Lutherans.

In October 1976, when he addressed the national convention of the American Lutheran Church in Washington, Preus hinted again that such a major realignment of Lutheranism might be on his mind. He chided Missouri moderates for planning to form their own church body, suggesting instead that they join the existing American Lutheran Church or the Lutheran Church in America. In turn, conservative pastors and congregations in those denominations "who would feel more comfortable with Missouri might contact our officials" to discuss joining the Missouri Synod, he said.

Returning from the clouds, a Preus-watcher realized several basic questions needed attention. First, would Preus survive as an effective power in Missouri? Then, if Preus did survive and closed out his presidential career by 1985 (which seemed likely), would he have a lasting influence in American Lutheran and Protestant Christian history?

Despite Preus's brave front at the Boston and Washington conventions, uncertainties abounded in late 1976 in Missouri. The left wing of the moderates was now firmly committed to a break from Missouri. That move was clustering around a new Association of Evangelical Lutheran Churches, a key part of which was a new English Synod formed by breakaway moderates from the perennially progressive English District. Admittedly, the new association resembled a board of directors in search of a company. Less than 3 percent of Missouri congregations were showing much interest by the time the association assembled for its constituting convention in December, and not all those were necessarily renouncing their membership in Missouri. Still, it was a beginning and might prove to become much more of a drain on Missouri than Jack Preus calculated.

Many moderates would remain in Missouri. They would not be committed to Preus's platform. Many would be convinced that Preus himself was a reckless adventurer to be feared but not respected. These men would be scattered up and down the ranks, from dozens of district presidents and hundreds of clergy to thousands of parochial school teachers and lay leaders. Although he might have subdued their ecclesiastical bodies, he had not won their hearts and minds for himself or his program. Likely, he would never do so even if he was Missouri president until he was eighty-five years old. Survival despite Preus would be their long-term goal.

Whether this minority would or could exercise any political pressure to try to influence Missouri in the immediate future was uncertain at best. But even as Preus was making his Boston victory speech, word was circulating that unaligned, middle-of-the-road district presidents were planning to run a candidate in the next synod presidential election in mid-1977. This was significant, not because such a candidate with a compromise platform had a ghost of a chance to succeed, but because it revealed that hopes for reversing Missouri's turn to the right remained alive and that Preus's version of an "orthodox, united, and growing" Missouri might be a long time in coming. An era of passive resistance tougher to deal with than Tietjen-style confrontation might await triumphant president Preus.

In some ways, the more moderates that left, the easier it would be for Preus. He could concentrate fully on consolidation and rebuilding. Uptight conservatives might relax for the first time in fifteen years and give Preus elbow room. In other ways, a Missouri suddenly without moderate dissenters might prove a political disaster for Preus. There would be no "liberal" wing to blame. All the scapegoats would be missing. Preus would no longer have handy any excuses to give to steely eyed Missourians for why he wasn't establishing the Missouri they wanted.

Before, he could always tell ardent conservatives that he had to steer the middle course to keep the ship afloat. He had to compromise here and stall there till the synod was ripe. Well now it would be ripe, and Preus would have to get on with it: break fellowship with the American Lutheran Church; cut Missouri out of the Lutheran Council in the USA; revoke women's voting rights in the churches; ferret out and expel all charismatics; tighten censorship; demand all pastors and teachers sign doctrinal loyalty oaths; rewrite the constitution to weed out that pesky provision about congregational autonomy; and so on until Preus's beloved Missouri resembled Preus's discarded Little Norwegian Synod.

This is the tiger-by-the-tail theory that has tamer Preus devoured by the right-wingers in Missouri's conservative party. Several moderate strategists, in fact, were suggesting that no break from Missouri be initiated until after the 1977 convention in Dallas. By then, it was said, Preus might even be dumped for an unimaginative conservative ideologue whose purification would make Preus's look like child's play. Then it would be clear to all fence-sitters what was happening to the Missouri Synod. Then they would realign quickly and leave the synod by droves. Or they would see conservatives at one another's throats and so badly weakened politically that staying in to pick up Missouri's pieces would become an option.

Since Preus's election in 1969, moderates have repeatedly based their hopes on the narrowest of margins. They underestimated Preus's cunning and tenacity. They underestimated how much public embarrassment and ecclesiastical gore served up by the clergy most Missourians would endure or ignore so long as they felt their treasured doctrine was at stake and being preserved. Moderates secretly banking on Preus to lose control to the right-wingers are doubtless going to be disappointed again, an experience with which they should by now be quite capable of coping. So Preus has to turn on runaway right-wingers and gets into a Seminex-style showdown with them! So what, one could foresee Mr. or Mrs. Missourian of 1980 saying. He's doing his job just like he did in the earlier days with the "liberals."

Yet Preus's future as Missouri's president could not be judged absolutely secure. He had irritated conservatives with the inconsistencies in his handling of the dissident district presidents. He fired four of them when he obviously should have fired all eight. Preus had "meandered" dangerously, his old conservative friends from *Affirm* magazine had told him in an editorial. Shaking his head solemnly, Robert Preus told a reporter in early 1976 that his brother was pushing it too far and was dangerously close to loosing the support of many once friendly Missourians. The grapevine as early as the fall of 1975 had it that many of the same conservatives who put Jack Preus in the running in 1969 were considering a new man for 1977. *That* man would be consistent not only in doctrine but in enforcement of doctrine as well.

Jack Preus was not unaware of the moves in that direction. The signals he sent to scotch the rumblings were characteristically confident. He let it out he would stand again for election. He let it be known he considered himself the strongest candidate and a virtual shoo-in for reelection in 1977.

Of all Missourians, surely Preus knew there might be a time when his conservative old-line Missouri backers would want to pat him on the back and tell him to move on and out. He had served well, they would say, but now a man whose name had a primordial Missourian ring—say a Barth or a Maier—was needed to do the consolidating. It was only good churchmanship to replace the controversial wartime general once the war was over.

Surely Preus knew he ran the risk of winding up the eager outsider rejected after he had been used to do the dirty work of the insiders. He knew the last joke might be on him, that old-line German Missourians, whether they be right or left, might want to run their own show again after experimenting with a Norwegian Lutheran curiosity, that for all his pains to become Missouri blue blood—*the* Missouri blue blood—he might be frustrated in the end. Here was the stuff of personal tragedy, or vengeance of sorts on Missouri's avenger.

Jack Preus had been ever sensitive to his ethnic newcomer and adopted-son status when he was fighting moderates with archetypical Missourian names like Fuerbringer and Kretzmann. *They* were not going to drive him out, cut him short, belittle him and his Lutheran vision. That same spunk would now well up in Jack Preus if the conservative elders tried to prevent him from tasting the final glory of being, and being recognized and immortalized, as true Missourian. He would not be cheated.

More than half his adult life, Preus had searched for a Lutheran church he could be proud of and comfortable in personally, theologically, and ecclesiastically. He had arranged his life —perhaps unconsciously, perhaps not—so he could influence dramatically, if not control absolutely, such a church. Even more, there are hints that he wanted to *be* that church incarnate.

Preus might have learned eventually to be proud of the Evangelical Norwegian Lutheran Church of his forefathers and the church of his seminary and early ministerial days, but he could not influence it. He could have controlled eventually the Little Norwegian Synod of his young adult days, but he could not have been as proud of it. Marvelously, he had found Missouri, and Missouri had found him. It was a union of fate. It was the will of God. His election was the divine call. What God has bound, no mortal shall loose.

No, blue-blooded Missouri conservatives would not "dump" Jack Preus. If they did, it would be over his grave, or more likely their graves. If Missouri moderates and conservatives alike can underestimate the desire and ability of Jack Preus to have and to hold the church of his dreams, this biographer cannot. Preus may yet be unseated and subtly rejected by the ever unpredictable Missouri Synod, but he will not submit to that without a struggle. If he is dumped, it will not come without the deep, soul-shattering hurt of a churchman who wanted passionately to belong.

Assuming Preus survived in Missouri, what kind of place in American Lutheran and Protestant Christian history would he hold? Opinions now as later would be radically different. Views would range from the harshest conceivable judgment that Preus did the wrong thing in the wrong way for the wrong reasons, to the laudatory assessment that he did the right thing in the right way for the right reasons.

There would be variables in these two formulas, of course. Some conservative Lutherans and evangelical Protestants might say that Preus's goals and motives were exemplary but he acted too quickly with unsavory means. Some liberal Lutherans and Christians in the mainline Protestant denominations might concede that Preus had clean motives and used morally appropriate churchmanship but that his objective was misguided, even demonic.

For theologians and pastors in perhaps two-thirds of the world's Christian communities today, Preus's doctrine of an "inerrant" Bible is as indefensible theologically as it is unnecessary ecclesiastically. For many of them, Preus is at best a curiosity and at worst a travesty of Christian leadership. Upholding vital and relevant doctrine is challenge enough. Enforcing questionable and extraneous doctrine is dangerous folly.

Much of the Christian world would see the Preus program the way Missouri critic Warren G. Rubel did in an article in the April 1976 issue of *Cresset* magazine:

> Mix together a reactionary political movement with a hermetically sealed interpretative scheme. Add the psychological need to alleviate religious doubt by finding certainty in beliefs in presuppositions about a (Biblical) text. Make the untestable belief in presuppositions about interpretation a doctrine which must be believed. Place the ensuing conflict in a rigid but fragile institutional scene. Pathos and polemic will not only result. They will be the accompanying signs of that cruelest form of religious piety we associate with a church gone awry: to make other human beings victims of oppression in the name of truth ("Pathos and Polemic in Missouri: Tacit Dimensions," p. 32).

Many would see Preus's theological agenda as a desperate and ill-conceived venture: enforcing bad or marginal doctrines to try to protect genuine doctrine; doing the theological equivalent of deputizing the warm bodies nearest the sheriff when they aren't qualified and aren't necessary; making holy what is not because it stands near the holy; deifying the angels one can see because they are presumed to be one's only link to the God one cannot see. Where does it all lead? To more bad doctrine to fence in the other bad doctrine to fence in the other bad doctrine. Meanwhile, there is no assurance that the community one sought to protect in the first place has moved any closer to absorbing the realities of salvation promised in the genuine doctrine, and much less any assurance that community is effectively communicating the genuine doctrine to others.

The case against Preus's antagonistic political ways and means comes out something like this: Rank party politics is self-destructive for churches when irreconcilable doctrinal views are involved. If irreducible doctrinal gaps exist, then a "moral" churchman cannot exploit those gaps for partisan gains. He cannot pretend, as Preus seemed to do from the beginning, that a little maneuvering here and a little psychological pressure there will solve the problem. An ethical churchman could only preside over a peaceful and dignified separation of the parties rather than trying to soothe the faithful with talk that peace was possible if only the right party held the power. Church politics is the art of the possible, but if, as Preus contended, no compromise was possible on the doctrine of an inerrant Bible, then how could Preus have acted ethically by engaging in any politics, much less partisan politics?

Herman Otten felt this moral ambiguity in Preus's political agendas because Otten saw the issues as uncompromisable. John Tietjen had said Preus's leadership was "morally bankrupt." The alleged immorality was based on the fact that Preus presumably was using a nonissue to gain political power. That reflected Tietjen's judgment on the theological case for an inerrant Bible and the need to enforce it. But following the earlier line of argumentation, Tietjen might have made more of a case against Preus if Tietjen had admitted the issues were irreducible.

Preus was all the more vulnerable to charges of "immoral" leadership, it is said by critics, because he was playing rough politics in a supposedly politically naïve denomination. He swept into a religious community where "evangelical" consensus was the tradition, not raw power, demagoguery, fear mongering, and ecclesiastical "dirty tricks."

Speculation about what makes Jack run—his motives—has been a mixed bag in Missouri and in Lutheran circles generally. Suggestions that he is compulsively power-hungry have been heard. These exercises in pop psychoanalysis have invariably come out with Preus acting primarily for extraneous, ego-fulfilling reasons.

One composite profile comes out like this: Preus is an obsessive achiever and dominator because he is trying ultimately to prove to himself that he is a better man than his father, Jake. Jake, this speculation goes, created a vague but indelible ideal of power, influence, and independence that Jack is desperately trying to realize.

Stated negatively, Jack is getting back at the ghost of crusty, superfather Jake by rising to the top of the Lutheran church heap Jake despised for its self-importance and pettiness. Jack is going to show his father-image that being a Lutheran potentate *matters* in this world, that precisely as a (Jake-despised) Lutheran church politician, Jack can make more history than Jake ever did as a two-term governor of Minnesota. Every time Jack goes from glory to glory in Missouri, he scores another point against Jake. But to make this psychological point against Jake, all that is needed is the appearance of epoch-making theological victories, not the reality of significant achievement.

That is why, this speculation goes, Preus never wanted or expected to convert Missouri's dissenters and certainly not to drive them out. He simply wanted them to conform publicly. He never wanted or demanded that they actually *believe* in an inerrant Bible or any of the rest of it. Preus just wanted them to keep their mouths shut and let him have his day in the sun.

Perhaps it was a telling sign when—in the Southern Illinois showdown described earlier—Preus begged Herman Neunaber, in so many words: You don't have to believe what you're doing is right when you agree not to ordain any more Seminex graduates, but just make this public show of conformity so I can get on with running my Missouri. During the confrontations over ordination of Seminex graduates, some dissenting district presidents recall Preus coming very, very close to telling them that what he didn't know wouldn't necessarily hurt him or Missouri. Was Preus dealing in images of authority, games of power, or the real thing?

Jack Preus's reputation at the conservative Lutheran and evangelical Protestant pole is understandably quite different. He is a hero of sorts. He unquestionably has done the right thing in the right way with acceptable motives. What the conservative Missouri majority thinks of Preus is clear. He has ben reelected once. He has been upheld at every key juncture despite the poor public image he had helped create for Missouri and despite a vigilant moderate press which, since 1973, has done an adequate job of dogging Preus and informing Missouri of his actions. It is difficult to buy the remarks of Tietjen and others that most Missourians simply don't *know* Preus or what he is doing. True, they may not know where he is taking them, but they know what he has done and enough of how he has done it to make up their minds. They know and have accepted and praised—at least, it would seem, for the rest of this generation.

How Preus rates with many in the independent evangelical Protestant community can be assumed to be accurately reflected by Harold Lindsell, the editor of *Christianity Today* magazine and long-time apologist for the American evangelical theological tradition.

In a recent book, *The Battle for the Bible* (Grand Rapids, Mich.: Zondervan Publishing House, 1976), Lindsell makes Preus a centerpiece in what Lindsell regards as the epochal struggle to save Christianity by saving the doctrine of biblical inerrancy. For Lindsell, as for Preus, biblical inerrancy is the one gatekeeper doctrine that establishes all the cardinal doctrines of Christianity. For Lindsell, it is "the only sure guarantee that these other doctrines are true." It is so important, for example, that one cannot call oneself an "evangelical" Protestant Christian without holding personally and upholding ecclesiastically an inerrant Bible.

In his reflections on the Missouri struggle, Lindsell hedges a bit on the right methods-right motivations case for Preus by pointing out that "no ecclesiastical battle has ever been waged in full accord with the teaching of Jesus." But having said that, Lindsell generally endorses Preus's political methods: "If liberal advocates are willing to fight against historical orthodoxy, why should not evangelicals in turn fight against the incursion of liberalism? Why is it not correct, indeed essential, for men like J. A. O. Preus to fight with all his might against those who do not believe the commitment of the Lutheran Church–Missouri Synod in favor of an inerrant Scripture?" (p. 207). Doctrinal ends justify ecclesiastical means, even to what Lindsell admits is the "hard and difficult" means of expelling nonconformists.

Conservatives argue that a church as a sovereign entity has a right to its corporate opinion and a right to its corporate self-defense. In the case of an inerrant Bible, those two rights converge, conservatives believe. Thus, what is so "immoral" or even unusual about a churchman who uses political means to coax a denomination to come to a corporate opinion and enforce it? "How do you change a democratic church without some politics?" Preus once asked.

Perhaps the Missouri moderates' case against "immoral" church politician Preus ultimately is weak. If he had followed their ethereal argumentation about what a churchman could or could not do in the Missouri situation, he would have been virtually paralyzed. Maybe what moderates are saying is that Preus did the unexpected. He surprised them in ways they presumably would not have surprised their opponents had they been in the president's seat, but doing something to someone else that he wouldn't do to you doesn't make it "immoral."

Yet there is a sense in which breach of custom, which Preus engaged in and encouraged, is at least a form of amorality. And in some communities and relationships, how one does something carries more ethical charge than what one does. Slighting one's wife or husband when she or he wasn't expecting it is not "immoral." But it may be an act of amorality loaded with more potential hurt and destructive impact than an immoral act that may have been partly anticipated. This is why outsiders should not fall into the trap of dismissing the cries of the Tietjen moderates as whining and moralistic posturing. Their cries are soul-deep, the wails of one-time partners treated unexpectedly like rabble rousers by their former colleagues.

Lindsell's justification for "fighting" conservative churchmen like Preus presumably does not extend to obvious violations of the Christian moral code. For those, Preus is on his own. The most serious charge against Preus is that of Tietjen who said that Preus engaged in deception. If Preus did, surely he would not have been the first Lutheran churchman who ever deceived. Maybe these weren't lies so much as politician's license with language which Tietjen just wasn't tuned into. Perhaps also Preus has made his private peace on these matters and has included them in a general way in his several and vague public confessions to the church of his faults.

Still, if eyewitness accounts of several private Tietjen-Preus confrontations are accurate, Preus made little point of denying Tietjen's accusations. Preus mainly challenged Tietjen's audacity to accuse him of lying. How dare you. Are you so perfect? The king intimidating the prophet. The prophet and his words of wrath and judgment often have a way of standing for centuries while the king and his words are lost. As of now, the words of Tietjen stand: "Jack, you lied."

As we have seen, a generation of Missouri moderates committed their share of amoral acts by genuinely shocking Missouri conservatives who had certain doctrinal expectations. They too had been partners who felt tricked and treated like dirt. Preus repaid the moderates in kind by acts which genuinely shocked Missouri moderates who had certain ecclesiastical expectations. Preus partisans would no doubt argue that the amoral acts of the moderates, the fact that the moderates once fooled them, is not the reason they fight so hard. It is not vengeance. Sure, they would say, it hurt when they realized how "liberal" their brothers and sisters had become, how unexpected it all was, but that shock passed. The issue became what the moderates' amorality involved: a threat to the Bible. *If* they had committed amoral acts against the moderates, it was for the sake of the church's soul and not for the convenience and security of some Missouri professors, pastors, and bureaucrats!

Preus had outlined his case for an inerrant Bible and why it is so crucial in "It Is Written," a polemical pamphlet published in 1971 by Missouri's Concordia Publishing House. "It seems unbelievable," Preus wrote, "that there should be controversy in the Christian Church regarding the doctrine of Scripture. For when all is said and done, there would be no Christian religion, no Christian church, no knowledge whatsoever about Christ without the Scripture."

"Ultimately," he concluded, "the loss of the Scripture will destroy the church, nothing else. That godless men take it from us in the name of a political ideology is terrifying; but that theologians and pastors should deprive the church of the Scripture by destructive criticism is even more unspeakable." Does Jack Preus really believe that? It would appear that he does. Preus may well be the world's last medieval Lutheran who takes with fatalistic seriousness all the implications of the Reformation principle of "Scripture alone" for the Protestant church. It has been pointed out that Preus is pushing one Reformation principle to the point of absurdity and rank contradiction to other key principles. He turns gospel into law, authority into power, commitment into conformity, faith by justification alone into faith by assent to dogma alone, believing the gospel into "seeing" the Bible, and so on. Perhaps it is safe to follow what is doubtless the conventional "mainstream" Christian wisdom on Preus's Missouri: It is or will soon become an impossible sectarian nightmare. If that proves true, then the nightmare will be judgment enough on Preus and his conservative Missouri party.

But no person or party ever intends to realize a nightmare. What is intended is the dream, the vision. Preus has said or written little about his dreams of the ideal Lutheran or Protestant church, but perhaps a few reflections on one category of Reformation dreams not dissimilar to Preus's are relevant.

As envisioned by some early Reformers, "Scripture alone" was supposed to be a functional principle of church unity and authority. It was to be more than a check to balance the excesses of the Roman Catholic tradition. It was to be more than a private escape clause for individual Christians or groups dissenting from erring church law and councils. "Scripture alone" implied that the Bible should and could be normative for the church universal. Loosely speaking, some Reformers believed a Protestant "Catholic" church was not only possible but pref-

erable. They believed a benign "papacy of the Bible" could
generate a vigorous, visible, universal, and unified Protestant
church.

That vision was abandoned because biblical norms that bind
proved elusive for the body ecclesiastic, and ultimately no
norms at all. Their papacy of the Bible, their biblical common
law was a dismal failure from an ecclesiastical point of view. So
the Reformers more or less abandoned the "Scripture alone"
principle for church polity and reduced it to the escape clause
status. "Scripture alone" became a method of telling *me* how
to be saved, but the vision that it could tell *us* how to be saved
was lost. The Bible was for soteriology not ecclesiology. Talk
of the "invisible" church increased. The church would have to
be redefined or held together some other way.

If we give Preus the benefit of the doubt and put his dream
in that lost Reformation genre, is it really so impossible and so
sectarian? In fact, it may be so. By having to resort to political
props and power, Preus's dream has already started the transi-
tion into nightmare, but the intention remains. Is it so sectarian
to want and expect binding, universal norms for a Protestant
church and to want them to flow out of the most logical of all
sources—the Bible? It would be foolish to underestimate the
staying power of that dream. Preus has an indirect grip on an
archetypical Protestant vision of a pax bibliana, of a Christian
empire self-regulated by biblical laws, of a kind of biblical natural law to which all non-Roman Christians could relate. Protestantism cannot finally dismiss Preus's or Missouri's dream
without cutting symbolically one link to its past.

And what are the options if that vision is lost and buried once
for all in the non-Roman Christian world? After a century of
scholarship which has tended to make the Bible even more a
private devotional tool than a fount of ecclesiastically binding
norms, the sources of Protestant polity have pretty much dried
up. It is hardly surprising that the more shaky becomes the
basis for extracting clear doctrines from the Bible alone, the
more the classical Protestant churches look back toward Rome

or at least toward Roman ecclesiastical traditions.

Obviously, higher biblical criticism does not directly grease the skids for a Protestant slide back to Rome, but higher biblical criticism leads inevitably to downgrading Scripture and upgrading the apostolic Christian community (and the succeeding Christian community) in which the Bible was generated and canonized. Each year, the Bible becomes less divine, less a miracle. The Bible did not create the church; the church created the Bible. Christ is God's only absolute gift to the church and the world. His other gifts are relative and are inspired and inerrant only in a metaphorical sense.

The Bible will not err in leading to Christ but only insofar as it was a special definitive act of the inspired Christian community, which community cannot deceive itself so badly that Christ's witness and salvation are frustrated. Enter the notion of negative infallibility, of historically conditioned reliability rather than timeless infallibility. The Bible was the church's gift to itself. Granted, it was a special gift, a kind of centennial landmark, against which all future self-gifts of doctrine must be weighed. But the Bible is hardly an Ark of the Covenant which cannot be probed without the prober being struck dead and the entire Christian community falling into apostasy and oblivion.

Christian scholars know so much more today about the origin and development of the Bible that the church ought to consider convening an ecumenical council to recanonize the Bible. What an excellent opportunity, incidentally, to weed out some of those troublesome "cultural" hang-ups of St. Paul!

Obviously, few Christians in any denomination are at this point, but who can deny that the direction is there and that enforcing an inerrant Bible from now on will be more a church-wrecking than a church-building premise. An epoch is ending. It is unlikely that Jacob Aall Ottesen Preus of the Missouri Synod will do much in the long run to stop it, but he is not going to be ushered away without putting up a good fight.

Index

242 | Index